Many in the body of Christ are struggling against the schemes of darkness with no real understanding or strategy of how to overcome demonic attacks and oppression. God has anointed David Komolafe with insight, wisdom and keys to equip believers with kingdom strategies ensuring success and victory. If you desire to be a victorious overcomer soaring in destiny this book is a must read.

—REBECCA GREENWOOD
PRESIDENT, CHRISTIAN HARVEST INTERNATIONAL
COLORADO SPRINGS, COLORADO, USA
AUTHOR, *AUTHORITY TO TREAD*

Dr. Chamliss and I are blessed to be in relationship with such an awesome man of God. It is truly an honor to be asked to endorse his latest book. *Mightily Oppressed but Mightily Delivered* is written with scriptural authority. The directness about the topic of spiritual warfare and outlined scriptures make it balanced, instructional; easy to read, follow and apply.

Mightily Oppressed but Mightily Delivered identifies challenges but strategically directs us through the Word so we can be victorious in any battle. We encourage all pastors and our Partners to make a kingdom investment and, "buy the book."

—DR. BRENDA C. MILLER AND DR. W.C. CHAMLISS III
BODY BUILDERS TELEVISION NETWORK
ELKTON, FLORIDA, USA

Many are mightily oppressed in our world today from all forms of oppression. Through the power of the Word of God, and the inspiration of the Holy Spirit, Pastor David Komolafe, one of God's great intercessors and prophet, has proven that we have been mightily delivered from demonic, financial, mental and all forms of oppression. You have been mightily delivered.

—PASTOR GABRIEL RONALD DIKU
SENIOR PASTOR, TRUE VINE INTERNATIONAL CHURCH
BRUSSELS, BELGIUM

MIGHTILY OPPRESSED
BUT
MIGHTILY DELIVERED

MIGHTILY OPPRESSED

BUT

MIGHTILY DELIVERED

DAVID KOMOLAFE

CREATION
HOUSE

MIGHTILY OPPRESSED BUT MIGHTILY DELIVERED by David Komolafe
Published by Creation House
A Charisma Media Company
600 Rinehart Road
Lake Mary, Florida 32746
www.charismamedia.com

Unless otherwise noted, all Scripture quotations are from the New King James Version of the Bible. Copyright © 1979, 1980, 1982 by Thomas Nelson, Inc., publishers. Used by permission.

Scripture quotations marked AMP are from the Amplified Bible. Old Testament copyright © 1965, 1987 by the Zondervan Corporation. The Amplified New Testament copyright © 1954, 1958, 1987 by the Lockman Foundation. Used by permission.

Scripture quotations marked ASV are from the American Standard Bible. Copyright © 1960, 1962, 1968, 1971, 1972, 1973, 1975, by the Lockman Foundation. Used by permission.

Scripture quotations marked ESV are from the Holy Bible, English Standard Version, copyright © 2001 by Crossway Bibles, a division of Good News Publisher. Used by permission.

Scripture quotations marked HCSB are from the Holman Christian Standard Bible © Copyright © 2003, 2002, 2000, 1999 by Holman Bible Publishers. Used by permission. All rights reserved.

Scripture quotations marked KJV are from the King James Version of the Bible.

Scripture quotations marked THE MESSAGE are from *The Message: The Bible in Contemporary English*, copyright © 1993, 1994, 1995, 1996, 2000, 2001, 2002. Used by permission of NavPress Publishing Group.

Design Director: Bill Johnson
Cover design by Nathan Morgan

Visit the author's website: www.davidkomolafe.com

Library of Congress Cataloging-in-Publication Data: 2011936192
International Standard Book Number: 978-1-61638-668-9
E-book International Standard Book Number: 978-1-61638-669-6

While the author has made every effort to provide accurate telephone numbers and Internet addresses at the time of publication, neither the publisher nor the author assumes any responsibility for errors or for changes that occur after publication.

First edition

11 12 13 14 15 — 9 8 7 6 5 4 3 2 1
Printed in Canada

DEDICATION

This book is dedicated to the body of Christ, that we might "war a good warfare" (1 Tim. 1:18, KJV) and walk in victory through the finished work of our Messiah and King—Jesus Christ the Lord!

ACKNOWLEDGMENTS

H E WHO COMES from above is above all…He who comes from heaven is above all" (John 3:31, NAS). Truly, Jesus Christ is *above all*! He ransomed my precious soul from the grip of iniquity, rescued me from death, and redeemed me from destruction. What a great grace! I acknowledge Him above all else. He fills me with the Holy Spirit—my Comforter, Guide, and Counselor—through whom all wisdom abounds to write this book.

This book is not just head knowledge, but also personal life experiences and how I overcame through divine enablement and grace. I am, therefore, thankful to God for my dearest mother for bringing me up in the way of the Lord. To God be the glory for my brothers and sisters for their prayer support.

It is also a great honor to be the Lead Pastor of Above All Christian Gathering. My heart is always full of joy for this blessed Holy Spirit-filled congregation. I appreciate their encouragement and prayer support. I pray God Almighty to bless each and every one of them. I also pray for God's unfailing grace to abound as we multiply in favor and miracles. Special thanks to my administrative staff for working with me in completing this book. I pray very special blessings on the ordained pastors, evangelists, and deacons of Above All Christian Gathering.

I will forever be grateful to God for the blessing for a good virtuous wife, Mercy, and my prophetic children, Esther, Grace, and Shalom. I rejoice always in God for the privilege to be a husband and a father to the glory of His name.

I am thankful to God for ministries who are networking with me. God Almighty shall keep you strong for glorious exploits in His kingdom.

CONTENTS

FOREWORD

I GIVE GLORY TO God for the message and the successful completion of this book. I have known the author of this book for over a decade. He is a spiritual son and a co-laborer in the Lord's vineyard. As a full-time minister of the gospel with emphasis on deliverance and spiritual warfare for over thirty years, I can truly identify with the writings of Pastor Komolafe.

In this day and age that we live in, not much is being said about the kingdom of darkness and its effects on our lives, especially within the body of Christ. Rather, we tend to play down the attacks, strongholds, strategies, lies, and deceits of the enemy in our lives and yet we see our lives going nowhere in a hurry. Due to ignorance or a lackadaisical attitude, we have allowed ourselves to be boxed in and tied down in bondage, allowing the enemy to tamper with our destinies, causing us to live a life of mediocrity, shame, and reproach. God's original plans and intents for our lives are now illusions that we long for but cannot attain.

Thank God for His abundant mercy in touching the hearts of His children such as Pastor Komolafe to put down in writing the truths about the kingdom of darkness and how we as God's elect can rise above the wiles and deceits of the devil and live victoriously on a daily basis. I have lived on either side of the fence at different times in my life; in other words, I was once literally serving the kingdom of darkness having been born into a family of fetish priests and voodoo worshipers. Being the son of a renowned fetish warlord of his time, trained to take over for him as his successor, I had seen firsthand how the kingdom of darkness operates. I have also witnessed firsthand the power and mercy of God that rescued and delivered me from darkness. I was then given the mantle to take this message of deliverance, freedom and liberty from the powers of darkness through Christ Jesus to the whole world.

Through his personal testimonies, everyday life experiences and divine guidance, Pastor Komolafe exposes the root cause of most of the problems we face in life. Things that we might take for granted as coincidence or discard as "one of those things" actually have very deep spiritual foundations and implications which if left unchecked or not handled properly will hunt and hound us for the rest of our lives. Once these hidden vices have been exposed, he then reveals how we can get our permanent breakthrough and maintain our deliverance by listing some powerful prayer points and topics which we can use on a daily basis.

Pastor Komolafe is well read and educated and widely traveled, and this reflects in his writings. One of the things I love most about this book is the real-life examples and illustrations that Pastor Komolafe uses to get his point across. He also takes the time to explain various concepts and terminologies using appropriate imagery, so that the reader is not left confused or in doubt about what he is saying. Anyone reading this book can actually relate to the contents because it cuts across all kinds of barriers—age, gender, race, culture, and so on. No matter what part of the globe you come from, this book is bound to have a profound positive impact on your life.

In a nutshell, I would say this book is a "Do It Yourself" book on spiritual warfare and deliverance and it is a *must* for every believer to read and own.

—Rev. James A. Solomon
Jesus People's Revival Ministries
Norcross, Georgia

PREFACE

DARKNESS IS GETTING dense, but it cannot overpower the light of God in us. Hell is at a deadly rage recruiting souls but shall not prevail. The oppressed and the afflicted are crying for help, but their voices could not be heard. So I strongly believe that there is a power clash at the gates of lives. But, when two powers clash, the lesser has to bow. And truly at His name, Jesus, every knee bows and every tongue confesses His supremacy and Lordship. (See Phil. 2:9–11.)

I liken the spiritual atmosphere of this age to this wonderful passage of the Holy Scripture:

> Now it happened, the day after, that He went into a city called Nain; and many of His disciples went with Him, and a large crowd. And when He came near the gate of the city, behold, a dead man was being carried out, the only son of his mother; and she was a widow. And a large crowd from the city was with her. When the Lord saw her, He had compassion on her and said to her, "Do not weep." Then He came and touched the open coffin, and those who carried him stood still. And He said, "Young man, I say to you, arise." So he who was dead sat up and began to speak. And He presented him to his mother. Then fear came upon all, and they glorified God, saying, "A great prophet has risen up among us"; and, "God has visited His people." And this report about Him went throughout all Judea and all the surrounding region.
>
> —LUKE 7:11–17

A great multitude of people followed Jesus as He was going into the city. There came another crowd coming out, and both clashed at the gate of the city. Jesus had just performed diverse miracles and healing, so there was great shout of joy and praise around Him as they were going into the city. The other crowd coming out of the city was carrying out a dead man, "the only son of his mother, and she was a widow"

(Luke 7:12, KJV). This was a gathering of mourners, wailers, and those who were lamenting, clashing at the gate of the city with the assembly of joyful people. Jesus had compassion on the widow, and said unto her, "Weep not" (Luke 7:13, KJV). All that Jesus needed to do was to touch the open coffin, "and those that bare him stood still" (Luke 7:14, KJV). His touch forbade further proceeding. I can imagine what the crowd would do. His touch stagnated the evil procession. He then commanded him that was dead to arise. He came alive and sat up in the open coffin. He sat upon those who were carrying him for burial. May we also heed to the voice of our Master Jesus and subdue those who want to bury us with our destiny.

This is a type of what many people are going through today: a widow—one who has lost her husband. Haven't we lost touch with our Maker, who is our Husband (Isa. 54:5)? This widow lost her only son. God so loved the world that He gave His only begotten Son (John 3:16). Haven't we lost contact and our relationship with Jesus—God's only begotten Son? This attracts mourners, wailers, and those who lament, not to sympathize with us, but to shame and reproach us. Therefore, there is a great clash at the gates of our lives. Would we permit Jesus to have His way? His compassion will awaken us to restore us to His will. Those who have been bearing us on their shoulders to make us go under and be forever forgotten must stand still at the touch of Jesus, our Redeemer. They shall proceed no further.

If we surrender the battles at our gate to Him, He will restore us to life. And the company of wailers, mourners, and those who lament shall forever be silenced. "The evil will bow before the good, And the wicked at the gates of the righteous" (Prov. 14:19, NAS). The oppressed can be mightily delivered.

This book is in two parts. The first part unfolds strategies to kingdom warfare, which covers a wide area of spiritual warfare. As a prophetic intercessor for over three decades, I have seen many believers engage in wrong battles by choosing wrong enemies, and lacking knowledge on how to break free from foundational issues and walking in the liberty in which Christ has made us free. We would also learn how to establish our authority in Christ in marketplace warfare and territorial spiritual warfare, which determine whether we break down or break through in life. The second part is kingdom prophetic prayers releasing creative words and issuing divine decrees to turn reproaches to glory; shame to honor; failure to success, and defeat to victory. As you pray believing, though mightily oppressed, you shall be mightily delivered.

INTRODUCTION

The beauty of Israel is slain upon thy high places: how are the mighty fallen! How are the mighty fallen in the midst of the battle! O Jonathan, thou wast slain in thine high places. How are the mighty fallen, and the weapons of war perished!

—2 SAMUEL 1:19, 25, 27, KJV

THIS WAS THE prophetic lamentation of David after he heard of the death of Saul and Jonathan. The mighty fell in "high places" (v. 19); "in the midst of the battle" (v. 25) and their "weapons of war perished!" (v. 27). The mighty are fallen from their place of strength and dominion. This gives the spoilers the confidence to attack us from every direction (1 Sam. 13:17–18). Oh! For a people who will arise in the strength of God to dispossess the adversary of our souls and regain lost ground; for those who will quench the fire of adversity and proclaim jubilee to free the oppressed. As we arise to our place of dominion, we can paralyze the fist of the wicked and fortify our defenses.

The spiritual state of this generation could be likened to the declaration of the prophet Isaiah, "For the bed is shorter than that a man can stretch himself on it; and the covering narrower than that he can wrap himself in it" (Isa. 28:20, ASV).

The bed should be for rest while the blanket is for comfort. But when the bed is short and the blanket is narrow, we would be exposed to harsh weather and multiple stripes. No wonder we are not comforted in our sorrow and confusion; it is because we have despised the Holy Spirit— our Comforter and Counselor. The rage of invaders has wearied our souls, and we are losing grip on our glorious heritage. Nonetheless, the counsel of God for us, the "church," abides forever. Even in the midst of torments and affliction, God's people can walk triumphantly over every foe. "Though I walk in the midst of trouble, You will revive me; You will stretch out Your hand against the wrath of my enemies, And Your right hand will save me" (Ps. 138:7, NAS).

Therefore, understanding different levels of attacks and the right strategies to victory should be the essential ingredient for success, because he who steals your bed is wicked, but not as he who steals your sleep. He who steals your food is wicked, but he who steals your appetite is more wicked. One who destroys your certificate is bad, but one who destroys your destiny is worse. I can recall an incident in my college days when we were preparing for our final examination. The use of a computer was not popular then, so we did a lot of writing. In this particular examination—analytical chemistry—we had three big notebooks to study. My friend lost two of his notebooks, and textbooks were too expensive to buy; even the few copies available in the library were borrowed. My friend wept bitterly because of fear of failing the exam, having only one notebook out of three to read. It was so unfortunate that no one was ready to lend out theirs, because we kept referring to them and studying back and forth. After much weeping, he resolved to study the only available notebook. Fortunately for him, three quarters of the questions came from the only notebook he studied. After the exam, he found his two missing notebooks by the entrance of the exam hall. Obviously, somebody had stolen them. He picked them up and was thankful that they were stolen because he would have devoted his time studying what would not have been part of the exam questions. When the results came out he scored an A. He did well in the area he did not study. Though the notebooks were stolen, his residual knowledge helped him. His books were stolen but not his brain. We wrestle with a worse enemy—one who steals both books and the brain. He contends with what is written about us. His mandate is to "steal," "kill," and "destroy" (John 10:10, KJV).

> **As we arise to our place of dominion, we can paralyze the fist of the wicked and fortify our defenses.**

In pursuit of our life's ambitions, we are often confronted with oppositions. People's opinions and actions may disagree with us. So the way to success is not always smooth. Lots of issues are demanding our attention to the point that we are almost being pulled to pieces. Apostle Paul witnessed many such oppositions, yet he finished his course and won the race. I will share about his several bitter experiences and how God rescued him.

> For Sadducees say that there is no resurrection—and no angel or spirit; but the Pharisees confess both. Then there arose a loud outcry. And the scribes of the Pharisees' party arose and protested, saying, "We find no evil in this man; but if a spirit or an angel has spoken to him, let us not fight against God." Now when there arose a great dissension, the commander, fearing lest Paul might be pulled to pieces by them, commanded the soldiers to go down and take him by force from among them, and bring him into the barracks.
> —ACTS 23:8–10

There were conflicting authorities over Paul—the Sadducees and the Pharisees. Both were in disagreement with one another, until it became so strong and broke into chaos. Apostle Paul was in the midst of this, about to be "pulled to pieces." The intervention of the chief captain (the commander), rescued Paul from their midst. In like manner, we are also surrounded by conflicting authorities, each trying to pull us to their side. Our flesh with its lust is pulling us to unrighteous living, so is the kingdom of darkness desperately raging at us that we might lose focus on God. Our worldly pursuit is also demanding our attention and energy. We are torn amidst multiple demands, but our Chief Captain (the Commander), Jesus Christ, is watching over us. He is aware of our struggling and is willing to rescue us. He will "command the soldiers to go down and take" us "by force from among them" (Acts 23:10). I love the description of our rescue—"by force." This shows that the rescuing operation permits no options. God will do whatever it takes to deliver His people, even to the point of giving His only begotten Son. Paul was to be pulled in pieces but was delivered by force.

The angelic rescue teams are still at work to deliver, break the prison gates, shatter the chains, and set free the captives. After apostle Paul was rescued, he was put in the barracks (Acts 23:10) where access generally is strictly supervised. When God rescues, He defends us with His presence, where there is fullness of joy (Ps. 16:11). We need not fear the encompassing forces all around us; rather we should look up to our Commander, Lord Jesus Christ, who paid the price for our redemption. He will surely deliver and become our Refuge. There is, therefore, hope for the oppressed. Though mightily oppressed, they shall be mightily delivered.

Part One
KINGDOM WARFARE

Chapter 1

THE FOUNDATION

YOUR FOUNDATION WILL determine how far you will rise." This was the voice I heard as I passed by a construction site in downtown Toronto where the foundation of a high rise building was under construction. I then stood for a moment and watched. I discovered that large-scale construction is a feat of multitasking. How well fortified the foundation is will determine the structure upon it. Building on a weak foundation could cause the structure to collapse, so also is a life built on a weak and faulty foundation.

It is understandable that the "Spirit of God has made me, and the breath of the Almighty gives me life" (Job 33:4, NAS), and He formed us as we were planted in our mother's womb. Hence the process of growth began. While some could not survive the womb, many survived and were trusted to life. So the womb to most people became our first home in contact with the earth. It is a place where something is generated, formed, or produced. Therefore, the very seed and egg that formed us, the circumstances surrounding the time in the womb until birth, constitute our foundation.

Taking time to mediate on the voice I heard at the construction site in downtown Toronto, I found more troubling questions in the Word of God: "If the foundations are destroyed, What can the righteous do?" (Ps. 11:3, NAS). Truly if the foundations are destroyed, much more effort will be required to build, repair, and restore. And for effective work, unless the repairs start from the foundation, not much will be accomplished. I have heard people say, "My life is ruined" and "I'm shattered," and they try to fix it but to no avail. It is easier to repair a part of the building than the foundation. It takes an expert to redesign and carefully map out the strategies of reconstructing the foundation.

I read a socking revelation from the Word of God about Ephraim, which means "double fruitfulness."[1] "As for Ephraim, their glory shall fly away like a bird, from the birth, and from the womb, and from the conception" (Hosea 9:11, KJV). This verse pictures the dispersion of Ephraim among nations. The departing of the glory was in three stages: the birth, the womb, and the conception. "The" denotes particularity, specified persons or things. How then can Ephraim (double fruitfulness) become fruitful or increase if the glory is taken away from birth, the womb, and conception? I even considered the manner of arrangement of this verse on how the glory flies away: "the birth," "the womb," and "the conception." It is reversed because the conception comes first, then the womb, and later the birth; but when glory flies away, life order is reversed and things turn upside down. These three—the conception, the womb, and the birth—provide the platform at which life will operate, thus setting the pattern or direction to lead a life. People's lives can be altered from the womb or at birth depending on the circumstances they are subjected to, favorable or unfavorable.

I will consider what happened between Mary and Elizabeth. "Now Mary arose in those days and went into the hill country with haste, to a city of Judah, and entered the house of Zacharias and greeted Elizabeth. And it happened, when Elizabeth heard the greeting of Mary that the babe leaped in her womb; and Elizabeth was filled with the Holy Spirit. Then she spoke out with a loud voice and said,

> Blessed are you among women, and blessed is the fruit of your womb! But why is this granted to me, that the mother of my Lord should come to me? For indeed, as soon as the voice of your greeting sounded in my ears, the babe leaped in my womb for joy.
>
> —LUKE 1: 42–44

Just hearing Mary's salutation, the baby in Elizabeth's womb leaped for joy and she was filled with the Holy Spirit. It is so unfortunate that many mothers are unaware of the worth and the uniqueness of the baby in the womb. It is important to know that there is the natural world so also the spiritual, and they are both real. Naiveness does not change the existence. The spiritual affects the natural to a great extent. From Elizabeth's experience, we can deduce that voices can affect the baby in the womb positively or negatively. Either the voice of the mother or other voices can be comforting or damaging to a child. Elizabeth, who was carrying John the Baptist at that time, was filled with the Holy Spirit. It is also possible to be filled with any other spirit apart from the Spirit of God, which may wrestle to shift the child's destiny for good or evil. "The wicked are estranged from the womb; They go astray as soon as they are born, speaking lies" (Ps. 58:3). Whatever spirit that takes hold of a child from conception until birth controls the child except there is divine intervention.

Nakedness, crying, and blood: these are the situations surrounding our birth. We are all born naked—prince, princess, and slave. The moment a child comes out of the birth canal, due to sudden discomfort and change of environment different from the womb, the child cries out. And evidently there is no birth, whichever way it comes, without blood. So every child's birth involves nakedness, crying, and blood. As soon as a child is born, the midwife cleans up the body; the baby is then well wrapped and covered. One who is naked seeks for protection or cover; while crying could be an emotional reaction over situations that affect us, hence the need for comfort and attention. Regarding blood, "For the life of the flesh is in the blood" (Lev. 17:11, KJV). As natural as these could be, there are spiritual implications: we are all born helpless and in need of protection and care, so everyone is crying and seeking for help and encouragement; but when it is not found, it could lead to life-threatening issues. Nakedness, crying, and blood are foundational issues confronting all mankind. Being naked shows our vulnerability, and so we express our grief and pain by crying.

The good news is that our Lord and Savior Jesus Christ conquered nakedness, crying, and blood on the cross. They "parted his garments, casting lots" (Matt. 27:35, KJV); being naked confronted the cross. There was darkness over all the land for the space of three hours, and He "cried out with a loud voice, saying, 'Eli, Eli, lama sabachthani?' that is to say, 'My God my God, why have You forsaken me?'" (Matt. 27:46). He cried unto Him that was able to save Him. He shed His blood through the crown of thorns on His head, nails on His hands and feet, and through the piercing of His side with a spear. "But one of the soldiers pierced His side with a spear, and immediately blood and water came out" (John 19:34). He died, was buried, and He rose again, thus conquering nakedness, crying, and blood. Because of these, we also can receive help, comfort, and protection.

The King Who Knew Not Joseph

Joseph was a pampered child, loved by his father. He was protected and well taken care of by his father to the point of honoring him with a beautiful garment above his brothers. This stirred up envy and he was hated by his brothers. They put him in a pit and later sold him out to slavery. He ended up in Egypt and was well favored even as a slave, until he was imprisoned by his master. From prison his gifts brought him to fame, and he became a leader in a strange land. This exalted position enabled him to rescue his family from famine. His family migrated and settled in Egypt, so also did their descendants. Joseph made Egypt great and was honored. After his death, the children of Israel still prospered in the land of Egypt. Even though Joseph was dead, his works still abounded in the land. But another king arose after Joseph's death who must have been familiar with Joseph's exploits as his works were evident in the land; however, the king was terrified by the unceasing fruitfulness of the children of Israel. "But the children of Israel were fruitful and increased abundantly, multiplied and grew exceedingly mighty; and the land was filled with them. Now there arose a new king over Egypt, who did not know Joseph" (Exod. 1:7–8). The children of Israel became too dangerous to keep, and they were too important to lose. So Pharaoh proposed a solution to harness them by enslaving them.

Implications

Just like Joseph, many people have enjoyed the comfort and encouragement of their parents: well loved and favored. As people grow under the authority and provision of parents and guardians, they soon discover that the outside world is not the same. Not many people will tolerate us as our parents will do. Going through the different stages of life—schooling, career, and marriage—the authority figures differ, and they may not give us the treatment we are used to. There could be people who may not care about our background or upbringing and may not be interested in our achievements, but only relate to us as they wish. These are the king, ruler, and authority who knew not "Joseph."

Many people are frustrated because they are treated differently from the way to which they were accustomed. Even though you are an adult, you may be under a different authority not familiar with who you were. It is good to know that your husband is not your father, neither your wife your mother. Your school teacher is different from your brother or sister. Your boss in the office may not be the same as your father or mother. So, they will treat you differently. However good they are, there will still be differences which we are not used to. I love the words "a new king" (Exod. 1:8, KJV): authority not the same as what was previously known or done, and unfamiliar with family background and experiences. What is accepted within your family may not be good enough at school or work. We come under different authorities depending on what we are involved in, and each of these authorities may not operate the same way. I attended a Missionary Secondary School. In the boarding house, every student had a chore. Mine was to clean the toilets along with other students, so it was a group of five students. Two out of the group complained everyday because they were not used to it. One was the son of the Chief Justice of the State and the other, the son of the Inspector General of Police. While it did not matter to me because I did the same at home, it did mean a lot to them because they were not brought up that way—people did it for them. Their complaints did not persuade our supervisor to exempt them from their chores. They had come under a different authority that was bent to see them do what they were to do, although he was aware of whose son they were.

Failure to understand this has led to troubled relationships, rebellion to authority, misunderstanding, and strife. When the king "which knew not Joseph" came to reign, he despised history and turned his wrath on the prosperity of God's people. He made life bitter for them and subjected them to hard bondage. "And they made their lives bitter with hard bondage—in mortar, in brick, and in all manner of service in the field. All their service in which they made them serve was with rigor" (Exod. 1:14). The good news is that as the people cried out to God, He raised up a deliverer for them. Whatever oppression anyone may be going through, however difficult, Jesus Christ is our Great Deliverer. Victory is sure, if we trust Him. His authority is above all. He knows all our toiling and pains. More importantly, He cares for every detail of our lives.

Kill Not the Gifts

Gifts are great and are profitable when put to use. King Solomon was blessed with the gifts of wisdom and knowledge. In exercising these gifts, there came a major test. I have read this test from my youth, even acted it in a drama, but now it provides some deep insight.

> Now two women who were harlots came to the king, and stood before him. And one woman said, "O my lord, this woman and I dwell in the same house; and I gave birth while she was in the house. Then it happened, the third day after I had given birth, that this woman also gave birth. And we were together; no one was with us in the house, except the two of us in the house. And this woman's son died in the night, because she lay on him. So she arose in the middle of the night and took my son from my side, while your maidservant slept, and laid him in her bosom, and laid her dead child in my bosom. And when I rose in the morning to nurse my son, there he was, dead. But when I had examined him in the morning, indeed, he was not my son whom I had borne." Then the other woman said, "No! But the living one is my son, and the dead one is your son." And the first woman said, "No! But the dead one is your son, and the living one is my son." Thus they spoke before the king. And the king said, "The one says, 'This is my son, who lives, and your son is the dead one'; and the other says, 'No! But your son is the dead one, and my son is the living one.'" Then the king said, "Bring me a sword." So they brought a sword before the king. And the king said, "Divide the living child in two, and give half to one, and half to the other." Then the woman whose son was living spoke to the king, for she yearned with compassion for her son; and she said, "O my lord, give her the living child, and by no means kill him!" But the other said, "Let him be neither mine nor yours, but divide him." So the king answered and said, "Give the first woman the living child, and by no means kill him; she is his mother." And all Israel heard of the judgment which the king had rendered; and they feared the king, for they saw that the wisdom of God was in him to administer justice.
>
> —1 KINGS 3:16–28

The story began with two women that were harlots—giving up themselves to iniquity and being slaves to sin. In like manner, so many things are sharing us with God—our Maker. So this is a type of a sinner. They both had things in common: they were both women (v. 16), both were harlots (v. 16), both stood before the king (v. 16), and they both dwelled in the same house (v. 17). They both had a child but three days apart. One rolled over her baby until he died. I wonder how deep her sleep was as to suffocate her baby! The mother who is supposed to protect her child became an instrument of death. So also are many people today. They have been suppressed and suffocated by life's pressures. What many are supposed to derive joy from has turned around to become a burden—a crushing load. I figure that in this situation, even if the baby had been crying out because of the mother's weight on him, she was so deeply asleep she could not hear the cry. Does this not resonate with us also? Nobody seems to care or consider our cry for help and comfort. This is so because they are deeply asleep with dead consciences, although they seem to be around us.

"And she arose at midnight, and took my son from beside me, while thine handmaid slept, and laid it in her bosom, and laid her dead child in my bosom" (1 Kings 3:20, KJV). The exchange of babies took place at midnight. This is a dark hour; the transition time period from one day to the next. It could mean a quiet and lonely period to many people. The powers of the night take over when we are asleep, causing us to lose consciousness of our immediate environment and become insensitive. I cannot imagine the nature of sleep that one's child will be taken away from the bosom and replaced with a dead child, at the bosom, and still be asleep until the morning! In our bosom lies our gifts, we can either develop and use them to profit our lives or suppress them and allow others to take them out of reach. May we never lose sensitivity to the point that life will be taken from us. I pray that what gives joy and peace will not be exchanged for sadness and confusion. They both dwell in the same house—just like we are sharing the world with others. While many suppress and destroy their gifts, others are asleep until they are traded with the inferior. The one whose child was exchanged with the dead child could not get back her child until the intervention of the king. In like manner, so many people try getting back what they have lost or misplaced, but to no avail. Fighting and struggling between each other could not help the matter. So do we struggle with one another and no one is willing to submit. Many people go through life with suppressed gifts until they kill what would have profited them.

The king's verdict brought justice over the matter. I, therefore, recommend to any person whose joy, peace, and blessings have been taken away, to bring the case to the Almighty God—the Judge, whose judgment is always right. The sword of His judgment will penetrate "to the dividing line of the breath of life (soul) and [the immortal] spirit, and of joints and marrow [of the deepest part of our nature], exposing and sifting and analyzing and judging the very thoughts and purposes of the heart" (Heb. 4:12, AMP). The king's order was, "divide the living child in two and give half to the one, and half to the other" (1 Kings 3:25). Carrying out this order would mean the death of the child, having both children dead. One of the women was happy about the verdict while the other was not: "Let him be neither mine nor yours, but divide him" (v. 26). She wanted the baby dead like her own. This is the sad thing in the world today: "If I don't get it, nobody else will"; "I will try to be successful, but if I don't, nobody else will"; or "Either I will be in control or nobody else will." The other woman was willing to see her child live, thinking that if she gave it to her, even if she didn't have him, she knew that her child would be alive.

"Her bowels yearned upon her son" (v. 26, KJV)—deep pity, sympathy, tenderness, and compassion. Something in her moved to save her child. She would not let go or see her child die. This is the true spirit of someone who is determined not to see the will of the wicked prevail. This is the attitude of one whose heart reaches out for her blessings. She entreated the king for mercy. She was deeply stirred not to see her baby die. If we also must retain our blessings, our hearts should reach out to the King of glory who is able to save to the uttermost. Even though out of carelessness her child was exchanged, yet she would identify her own child. "And when I rose in the morning" (v. 21). However, long and dark the night may be, light comes in the morning. The pains of the night shall soon give to the joy of the morning. Darkness shall never prevail against light. She arose in the morning because the darkness was gone and every evil associated with it. The light unveiled the truth. She rejected the dead baby and repossessed her living blessing. I earnestly pray that everyone reading this book will arise into light to reject the evil cast into our bosom. I pray for an awakening of our spirit to identify the blessings due to us and never be weary in taking back what belongs to us.

"So the king answered and said, 'Give the first woman the living child, and by no means kill him; she is his mother'" (v. 27). The king in his splendor uttered an irrevocable decree that mandated her to recover her baby. I cannot image the torture the baby was subjected to and the crying: the denial of early morning feeding and the agony of the mother who was unable to reach out to her crying baby. So also are we when we lose our gifts—frustration sets in. We can seek help and restoration. Oh, that a people will arise who will cry out to the King of kings and Lord of lords to "fearlessly and confidently and boldly draw near to the throne of grace (the throne of God's unmerited favor to us sinners), that we may receive mercy [for our failures] and find grace to help in good time for every need [appropriate help and well-timed help, coming just when we need it]" (Heb. 4:16, AMP).

"And all Israel heard of the judgment which the king had rendered; and they feared the king, for they saw that the wisdom of God was in him to administer justice" (1 Kings 3:28). When God vindicates us, all the people shall hear and fear Him. This in turn shall magnify us and restore us to honor, while the enemy will be ashamed. Those who can't retain their own blessings or gifts, but make a mess of it, often envy those who apply theirs and are profited. May we be awakened in the spirit to guard jealously what belongs to us. She got back her blessings alive and not dead. I pray our blessings are alive and not dead through the power of His resurrection. My counsel to the readers of this book is never suppress your gifts, neither should you slumber and be insensitive to the cry of your gifts awaiting manifestation, nor be careless to allow your gifts be taken away from your bosom, because within you lies the power to achieve success in life. Thank God that this woman was able to identify her child. I ask you, would you be able to identify what you have lost when found? The void and sense of emptiness we are bearing daily could be an indication of a missing gift. Identifying our points of strength and fulfillment, and pursing them could bring joy again.

My Destiny, My Personality, and My Speech

My concern is not to set up arguments about destiny—a predetermined course of events—nor to consider whether it is inevitable and unchangeable, rather to establish how God's eternal purpose can be fulfilled. I can take encouragement from a man who engaged in a noble fight, finished the race, and kept the faith. A person such as apostle Paul can be said to have fulfilled his destiny.

> I have fought the good fight, I have finished the race, I have kept the faith. Finally, there is laid up for me the crown of righteousness, which the Lord, the righteous Judge, will give to me on that Day, and not to me only but also to all who have loved His appearing.
> —2 TIMOTHY 4:7–8

I love his approach to life and pursuit of goals. It was said of him: "'For his letters,' they say, 'are weighty and powerful, but his bodily presence is weak, and his speech contemptible.' Let such a person consider this, that what we are in word by letters when we are absent, such we will also be in deed when we are present" (2 Cor. 10:10–11). Referring to apostle Paul, people considered the difference in his "letters," "bodily presence," and "his speech." Letters denote a written communication directed to another. Bodily presence may refer to his personality, while speech is the vocalized form of human communication. These may be the three viewpoints on how we are judged: letter (what is written about us [destiny]), personality, and how we communicate our destiny and personality.

Jesus came in the volume of the book written of Him: "Then I said, 'Behold, I come; In the scroll of the book it is written of me'" (Ps. 40:7). He manifested to fulfill what was written of Him. He maintained a right personality and speech to align Himself with what was written of Him. When a letter is written and addressed to someone, the communication is not complete until the letter is delivered. If there is a failure in delivery, the purpose is defeated. Therefore, how we express our thoughts and goals will determine fulfillment. This was said about apostle Paul: "For they say, His letters are weighty and impressive and forceful and telling, but his personality and bodily presence are weak, and his speech and delivery are utterly contemptible (of no account)" (2 Cor. 10:10, AMP). So as good as the letter may be, there should be a right personality and speech to make it effective. Even though what was written about apostle Paul was well spoken of, they condemned his personality and speech. He put the record straight by saying, "Let such people realize that what we say by letters when we are absent, [we put] also into deeds when we are present" (2 Cor. 10:11, AMP). In essence, our personality should match up with what is written of us, so also should our speech.

> Building an inward and outward personality will speak so much about you.

Personality is the combination of qualities that identifies a person; it is the sum of the distinctive traits that give a person individuality. It is sad to say that iniquity at its deepest level in humanity has reshaped and reformed our true identity. However, we are to reflect God's image and likeness. Whichever way we express our thoughts, feelings, or perceptions, right words should be put to it. I have seen gifted and well-talented people falling short of their vision, never accomplishing their goals. They seem to lack the behavior, temperament, moral standard, emotion, and words to match up with their gifts. Frustration sets in when goals are not attained and vision not well communicated. Greatness, therefore, should be coupled with right personality and speech. I counsel you to allow your personality and communication to match up with your goals and vision. Building an inward and outward personality will speak so much about you. This will determine who will be attracted to you and who will cooperate with your vision.

Chapter 2

FREEDOM FROM CURSES

TRUE FREEDOM FROM curses begins by considering what the Bible likens curses to be. "Like a flitting sparrow, like a flying swallow, So a curse without cause shall not alight" (Prov. 26:2). It is of great interest to liken curses to the operation of these two birds: "flitting sparrow" and "flying swallow." I researched both birds in relation to curses. Understanding how both birds function may unveil the mysteries of curses. A flitting sparrow moves rapidly and nimbly. This reflects quick motion and agility of curses as darts. Sparrows are chiefly seed-eaters, indicating curses war against our harvest: nothing to sow and nothing to reap. Sparrows have powerful beaks for striking and tearing down.[1] Similarly, curses can strike and tear down anything that could profit us. They have a reputation of being undesirable birds; in like manner curses are undesirable by many people, yet persisting. Sparrows are extremely prolific, so also are curses. Once they are in effect, they keep yielding and producing. A curse in one area of life may soon spread to other areas, just like the curse of poverty may affect marriage, children, and health.

How about swallows? They are extremely graceful in flight, making abrupt changes in speed and direction.[2] So are curses—they are swift and unexpected sudden attacks. They eat insects and catch them at mid-air, so are curses with surprising offensive action. Their nests are vigorously defended during breeding season. This may explain why curses are hard to break and easy to multiply. Regarding migration, if they are successful in one location during breeding, even if they have migrated from the place, they return to the same nest site. This may be the reason why curses reappear and are unwilling to cease in people's lives.

> When an unclean spirit goes out of a man, he goes through dry places, seeking rest, and finds none. Then he says, 'I will return to my house from which I came.' And when he comes, he finds it empty, swept, and put in order. Then he goes and takes with him seven other spirits more

wicked than himself, and they enter and dwell there; and the last state of that man is worse than the first. So shall it also be with this wicked generation.

—MATTHEW 12:43–45

Swallows can journey much farther than would be necessary to find good food and good weather; distance is not a barrier. So much so with curses whether near or afar: their effects can be felt. Swallows can go elsewhere when the resources become scarce or harsh weather arrives, but they can tolerate cold temperatures if food is plentiful. I am aroused in my spirit as I come to this understanding that when curses are subjected to harsh weather and conditions, they flee and never look back. What a revelation! So, when the Word of God is rooted in me and I deepen my walk with God, it becomes too hot for curses to abide in me. Knowing that if food is plenty, they can endure harsh conditions, I, therefore, refuse to feed curses. Sin is a food providing strength for curses. Repentance and forsaking of sin can deny continuity of curses. Swallows return rapidly to nest sites when lost and flying over an unfamiliar land mass. Also, the first time breeders generally select a nesting site close to where they were born and raised. No wonder curses are hard to break. When we feel it is gone and have a sense of relief, the bad occurrences show up. Curses love their host so much and always seek to come back. They do enough damage that even when broken and cast out, someone may spend the rest of his or her life repairing the damage.

> **Curses war against our harvest: nothing to sow and nothing to reap.**

It took God to come in the flesh, pay the price, and break the curse. Jesus became a curse for us that He might free us from curses.

Christ has redeemed us from the curse of the law, having become a curse for us (for it is written, 'Cursed is everyone who hangs on a tree'), that the blessing of Abraham might come upon the Gentiles in Christ Jesus, that we might receive the promise of the Spirit through faith.

—GALATIANS 3:13–14

May I also ask you, "How easy is it to catch a bird?" It takes careful-ness and strategy because of their sensitive nature. But thank God for His unfailing power to arrest and destroy the bondage of curses.

How Do Curses Work?

Curses are words put together to torment and inflict with problems. People curse through their thoughts, imaginations, actions, or words. These can stir up lots of troubles if not prayerfully handled. Lots of people take negative words for granted. We might have been so used to it, as our parents used that to correct and discipline us. It no longer matters as we hear such words everyday, but the damaging results have shaped our lives to the point of breaking down. Negative words are harmful: they can devalue, defame, and destroy us. It is so unfortunate that our memo-ries retain the bad more than the good, the pains more than pleasures, and tragedies more than joyful celebrations. "Then Job answered and said: 'How long will you torment my soul, And break me in pieces with words?'" (Job 19:1–2). So, words are strong enough to break people in pieces; they have penetrating effects to stick to our souls and break our spirits since our souls are the seat of emotions, feelings, and intelligence. Bad words can cause emotional damage, hurt our feelings, and affect our reasoning. In contrast, good and pleasant words can strengthen our emotions, rekindle our passion, and make us feel loved and appreciated.

Job considered curses as "torment" to the soul. It is a great torment when curses are in operation and you don't even know how to be free from them. Curses stubbornly hold their victims because they are deceitful in nature and manifest in diverse ways. Why we feel them so badly could be because they can appear like sword-devouring flames, nets, traps, cords, worms, or stinging insects. When curses are placed on people, things, or places, the effect can be the laying of a trap to impede progress. It can mean such a person has entered into nets and cages. This can prevent good things from happening before they ever show up. It can appear as a cord wherein people are tied and tortured. My years of pastoral experience, counseling, and praying for people have deepened my understanding of some spiritual matters. Sometimes when I min-ister to people, I see in the eyes of the spirit, people tied down to altars, though physically free. I have seen cases of people being devoured by worms and beaten by stinging insects. Just like the psalmist said, "They surrounded me like bees; They were quenched like a fire of thorns; For in the name of the LORD I will destroy them" (Ps. 118:12). Oftentimes I pray against what is revealed; the Holy Spirit wants me break the curse behind it through the name of Jesus.

I had to counsel a man several years ago who was well read but had no job, not even as a volunteer. The Spirit of the Lord led me to ask him to bring all his certificates as we set the next appointment. When he came back, he handed over the certificates to me. Immediately, I felt itching on my hands. I dropped them and picked them up; again I felt things moving and causing itching on my hand. I asked him to hold the certificates with me. I asked if he felt anything, and he said he felt nothing, so I prayed. As I prayed, the Holy Spirit opened my eyes to see soldiers of ant-like devouring invaders. I asked for the Holy Spirit fire to consume them. So, these ants had been attacking anyone who wanted to help. A curse had been placed on the certificates manifesting as invading ants. When curses are broken and destroyed, the cords tying down blessings are broken asunder. Chains and fetters of iron are shattered. More importantly, people are released from bondage to freedom. To the glory of God, within two weeks he got a wonderful job. Many years have past, and he has climbed several positions, being favored and dignified.

When curses are in effect, people will struggle with inadequacy and lack in what would have prospered them; having but not having enough— always coming up short and persistently unfortunate. It is the desire of everyone to have in plenty and be comfortable with great fortune, because curses make people to be without what is necessary. It is easier to see the problems in others than your own. Usually when we see people in problems, we complain and wonder why they cannot do something to get out of it, even if we point to the possible solution or encourage them out of it. It is like their reasoning is suspended and cannot function. They are lacking knowledge, wisdom, and understanding; however, they may function well in other areas. The effect of curses may also hinder favor and prevent true help. Helpers get frustrated easily and give up or are even attacked. For instance, a brother needed help and someone was sincerely willing to help him, so

> **Curses that are difficult to remove might have been made through invocating elemental forces.**

an appointment was set up. On the set day, he got to his office and was told that the man was sick and had been admitted to the hospital. It took a long time for the man to recover. The help could not be rendered again. Much prayer is needed to protect our helpers so that they can be kept strong until they fulfill the help.

Curses are like a continual stroke, an unceasing blow of rage. People don't smite one another for a joke, especially when they are angry, bitter, or at enmity. It is to inflict damage or destruction. I would like to go a little deeper from my years of ministering deliverance to people. Curses that are difficult to remove might have been made through invocating elemental forces—earth, fire, water, air, sky, sun, moon, and stars. Take, for instance, the earth as I consider the following Bible passages:

> So now you are cursed from the earth, which has opened its mouth to receive your brother's blood from your hand. When you till the ground, it shall no longer yield its strength to you. A fugitive and a vagabond you shall be on the earth.
>
> —GENESIS 4:11–12

> Then to Adam He said, "Because you have heeded the voice of your wife, and have eaten from the tree of which I commanded you, saying, 'You shall not eat of it': "Cursed is the ground for your sake; In toil you shall eat of it All the days of your life. Both thorns and thistles it shall bring forth for you, And you shall eat the herb of the field. In the sweat of your face you shall eat bread Till you return to the ground, For out of it you were taken; For dust you are, And to dust you shall return."
>
> —GENESIS 3:17–19

> Is this man Coniah a despised, broken idol—A vessel in which is no pleasure? Why are they cast out, he and his descendants, And cast into a land which they do not know? O earth, earth, earth, Hear the word of the LORD! Thus says the LORD: "Write this man down as childless, A man who shall not prosper in his days; For none of his descendants shall prosper, Sitting on the throne of David, And ruling anymore in Judah."
>
> —JEREMIAH 22:28–30

How about the sun, the moon, and the stars? This is why God rebuked the astrologers, stargazers, and prognosticators.

Stand now with your enchantments And the multitude of your sorceries, In which you have labored from your youth—Perhaps you will be able to profit, Perhaps you will prevail. You are wearied in the multitude of your counsels; Let now the astrologers, the stargazers, And the monthly prognosticators Stand up and save you From what shall come upon you. Behold, they shall be as stubble, The fire shall burn them; They shall not deliver themselves From the power of the flame; It shall not be a coal to be warmed by, Nor a fire to sit before!

—ISAIAH 47:12–14

People swear with their lives, the earth, or anything possible. Unknown to them, these could be a living witness to effect their declaration. The adverse effect of curses through elemental forces has locked a lot of people inside out—locked from within with no strength to attain success, hence operating as mere men. Those who trust God Almighty as their shield and defense, He will preserve from curses that shall be of no effect on them. The strange fire kindled by curses shall not hurt them, neither shall they be drowned by their mighty waves, nor be smitten by the moon, the stars, and the sun. "The sun shall not strike you by day, Nor the moon by night" (Ps. 121:6).

When curses are not effectively broken, they can turn joyful times to mourning. I have watched people who labored to overcome trials and then achieved success. They prevailed while others went down in failure. However, tragedy struck at the time of success, so they became indifferent when success came because of the fear of recurrent tragedy. A friend of mine recently won multiple awards in his career. I called and visited him with my family. We bought gifts to offer him, but when we arrived at his house, he put on an expression of sadness. Even though lots of people were happy for him, he wasn't. His wife was happy but fearful. I asked if anything had gone wrong. The wife said, "Anytime good things come our way, tragedy appears." Although they were victorious, they were also mourning. They were confused in the midst of happiness wondering what tragedy would follow. "So the victory that day was turned into mourning for all the people. For the people heard it said that day, 'The king is grieved for his son'" (2 Sam. 19:2).

Types of Curses

Curses come in different ways, but whichever way they come, they have damaging effects.

Time release curses

When people get into trouble, their greatest time of distress might not be when the act was committed but afterwards. So many people fight their greatest battle not when in a problem but when trying to get out of a problem. The man that was born blind and healed by Jesus in the Gospel of John, chapter 9, had his greatest opposition not when he was blind, but after he had received his sight. He was opposed by his neighbors and the Pharisees. Problems rooted in curses may not manifest immediately when the curse is released but may take some time before manifestation. When an individual is cursed, he or she may not take it so seriously because nothing seems to happen immediately, although some may manifest almost immediately. One of the major effects of curses is that it has a long lasting destructive consequence on people. The time of manifestation may affect areas you least expected.

> **A time release curse is a curse that seems hidden and harmless, which may have no effect as at the time issued but may be activated when good things are appearing.**

> Now there was a famine in the days of David for three years, year after year; and David inquired of the LORD. And the LORD answered, "It is because of Saul and his bloodthirsty house, because he killed the Gibeonites." So the king called the Gibeonites and spoke to them. Now the Gibeonites were not of the children of Israel, but of the remnant of the Amorites; the children of Israel had sworn protection to them, but Saul had sought to kill them in his zeal for the children of Israel and Judah. Therefore David said to the Gibeonites, "What shall I do for you? And with what shall I make atonement, that you may bless the inheritance of the LORD?" And the Gibeonites said to him, "We will have no silver or gold from Saul or from his house, nor shall you kill any man in Israel for us." So he said, "Whatever you say, I will do for you." Then they answered the king, "As for the man who consumed us

and plotted against us, that we should be destroyed from remaining in any of the territories of Israel, let seven men of his descendants be delivered to us, and we will hang them before the LORD in Gibeah of Saul, whom the LORD chose."

—2 SAMUEL 21:1–6

At this time in history, the kingdom had just been restored to King David. He had just survived a conspiracy by his son, Absalom. His special cabinet minister, Ahithophel, whose counsel was like inquiring from an oracle, had just turned against him. "Now there was a famine" (v. 1). The famine lasted three years. At first King David thought it was a natural disaster, until the third year when he inquired from the Lord. "It is because of Saul and his bloodthirsty house, because he killed the Gibeonites" (v. 1). Saul, who committed this offense, had died. Saul sowed the seed while David reaped the harvest. My concern is, why didn't the disaster happen in the days of Saul who committed the offense? The problem even began from the days of Joshua:

So Joshua made peace with them, and made a covenant with them to let them live; and the rulers of the congregation swore to them...But the children of Israel did not attack them, because the rulers of the congregation had sworn to them by the LORD God of Israel. And all the congregation complained against the rulers. Then all the rulers said to all the congregation, "We have sworn to them by the LORD God of Israel; now therefore, we may not touch them."

—JOSHUA 9:15, 18–19

But Saul in his zeal transgressed against the oath and broke the covenants. The consequences were bound to happen. He sowed the seed, but the consequence never matured until the time of David. A time release curse is a curse that seems hidden and harmless, which may have no effect as at the time issued but may be activated when good things are appearing. It takes effect when least expected, making it difficult to identify the source. Our lawmakers have legislated some laws which may sound favorable and harmless; they have long gone and departed, but the generations to come may suffer severely for their decisions. Also, many parents who engage in cults are selling out their generations to troubles. After their death or in their old age, they see their children and grandchildren, though not joined in the cult activities, but reaping the terror of demonic attacks.

There came a time when Hezekiah, the king of Judah, was sick and was visited by Babylonian officials, who came with letters and a gift for him.

> At that time Berodach-Baladan the son of Baladan, king of Babylon, sent letters and a present to Hezekiah, for he heard that Hezekiah had been sick. And Hezekiah was attentive to them, and showed them all the house of his treasures—the silver and gold, the spices and precious ointment, and his entire armory—all that was found among his treasures. There was nothing in his house or in all his dominion that Hezekiah did not show them.
>
> —2 KINGS 20:12–13

Isaiah the prophet confronted him and declared:

> Then Isaiah said to Hezekiah, "Hear the word of the LORD: 'Behold, the days are coming when all that is in your house, and what your fathers have accumulated until this day, shall be carried to Babylon; nothing shall be left,' says the LORD. 'And they shall take away some of your sons who will descend from you, whom you will beget; and they shall be eunuchs in the palace of the king of Babylon.'"
>
> —2 KINGS 20:16–18

Hezekiah was glad for the prophetic rebuke because they were to happen "not in his days" but in the generation to come. This was same man who pleaded with God when terrified by the king of Assyria, "rent his clothes, covered himself with sackcloth, and went into the house of the LORD" (19:1, KJV). This was the king to whom the prophet Isaiah declared, "Set your house in order, for you shall die, and not live" (20:1). Even though he was sick unto death, he turned to God and pleaded his case. His prayer was so effective that before Isaiah could get out of the middle court, God turned him back to prophesy healing and reversed the ordinances of death. Fifteen more years were added to him (20:5–6). This same king, who could have sought the face of the Lord regarding the consequences of the Babylonian embassy to reverse the prophesy of desolation, did not, because he would die before the fulfillment of the prophesy. He made no effort because he would not be affected. He sowed this into his generations to come. His son Manasseh was the longest serving king of Judah; he reigned for fifty-five years (21:1). The prophesy of desolation started showing up from the fourth king after Hezekiah—eighty-eight years after. By the reign of the seventh king, the consummation of captivity was fulfilled—one hundred and thirteen years, three months.

> And he carried out from there all the treasures of the house of the LORD and the treasures of the king's house, and he cut in pieces all the articles of gold which Solomon king of Israel had made in the temple of the LORD, as the LORD had said. Also he carried into captivity all Jerusalem: all the captains and all the mighty men of valor, ten thousand captives, and all the craftsmen and smiths. None remained except the poorest people of the land.
>
> —2 KINGS 24:13–14

It was like a curse waiting for a maturity time to manifest. As long as the trouble would not be in Hezekiah's days, no effort was made to contend with it. Prayer is needed to combat curses due to manifest in our own time. However deep they are, the Almighty God is the Ancient of Days, who will annul the consequences and root out the evil.

Proverbial Curses

Some curses are proverbial in nature. This is when somebody is expressing evil, but it seems not to be directed at the person concerned; and it may come up as a story, jesting, joke, or negative comment. Most times the person concerned may even laugh along, being ignorant of the implications. It is done so that the person concerned is unaware, so as not to take action. The most difficult part of this type of curse is that it hits the victim unprepared and undefended. It is an explosive-coated curse. I was in a house-warming ceremony—praying and partying over a new house. We all were in a relaxed mood, talking and eating. One of us shared a story of someone he knew who bought a house, and within a year he had a car accident, lost his job, and later lost the house. I objected and rebuked him immediately. Others said it was just a story and that I was taking things too seriously. A year later, one of the people at the housewarming ceremony called me and said our friend had a car accident, reminding me of how I rebuked the story. Thank God for divine intervention through prayers. Our prayer strategy for him was to recall the day and the gathering; annul the evil intent. God truly answered and our friend recovered; he never lost his job or house.

I considered when God sent the prophet Nathan to David to pronounce judgment on him because he took Uriah's wife for himself. Nathan was not direct with his judgment, but he gave a parable, allowing King David to judge himself.

> Then the LORD sent Nathan to David. And he came to him, and said to him: "There were two men in one city, one rich and the other poor. The rich man had exceedingly many flocks and herds. But the poor man had nothing, except one little ewe lamb which he had bought and nourished; and it grew up together with him and with his children. It ate of his own food and drank from his own cup and lay in his bosom; and it was like a daughter to him. And a traveler came to the rich man, who refused to take from his own flock and from his own herd to prepare one for the wayfaring man who had come to him; but he took the poor man's lamb and prepared it for the man who had come to him." So David's anger was greatly aroused against the man, and he said to Nathan, "As the LORD lives, the man who has done this shall surely die! And he shall restore fourfold for the lamb, because he did this thing and because he had no pity." Then Nathan said to David, "You are the man! Thus says the LORD God of Israel: 'I anointed you king over Israel, and I delivered you from the hand of Saul.'"
>
> —2 SAMUEL 12:1–7

He was given the rope to hang himself. How often have we hastily affirmed what was to condemn us, especially when it is framed in such a way that it would be difficult to understand the concealed intention?

How about a prophet condemning King Ahab? He disguised himself and came up with a scenario allowing the king to judge and condemn.

> Then the prophet departed and waited for the king by the road, and disguised himself with a bandage over his eyes. Now as the king passed by, he cried out to the king and said, "Your servant went out into the midst of the battle; and there, a man came over and brought a man to me, and said, 'Guard this man; if by any means he is missing, your life shall be for his life, or else you shall pay a talent of silver.' While your servant was busy here and there, he was gone." Then the king of Israel said to him, "So shall your judgment be; you yourself have decided it." And he hastened to take the bandage away from his eyes; and the king of Israel recognized him as one of the prophets. Then he said to him, "Thus says the LORD: 'Because you have let slip out of your hand a man whom I appointed to utter destruction, therefore your life shall go for

his life, and your people for his people.'" So the king of Israel went to his house sullen and displeased, and came to Samaria.

—1 KINGS 20:38–43

Oh, what a trap! So are proverbial curses. They are so disguised, but would set the direction at which life would follow. It could be a symbolic action; words may not be added, but it is transmitting a message. Body language is a form of communication—a nonverbal communication—which can consist of body posture, gestures, facial expressions, and eye movements. This can amplify, modify, confirm, or subvert verbal utterance, expressing meanings which elude or surpass verbal language. Therefore, whether by words or actions, unveiling the meanings and abolishing the effects give breakthrough to the concealed traps.

Generational Curses

Curses are transferable and can remain in a family for a very long time, if not broken. Gehazi, the servant of Elisha, coveted Naaman's treasure and lied to his master. He was cursed and his descendants also. "'Therefore the leprosy of Naaman shall cling to you and your descendants forever.' And he went out from his presence leprous, as white as snow" (2 Kings 5:27). The innocence of his descendants could not stop the curse from manifesting, because it was "and your descendants forever." The Gibeonites deceived the princes of Israel into making an oath, which when discovered attracted a curse. "Now therefore, you are cursed, and none of you shall be freed from being slaves—woodcutters and water carriers for the house of my God...And that day Joshua made them woodcutters and water carriers for the congregation and for the altar of the LORD, in the place which He would choose, even to this day" (Josh. 9:23, 27). The generations of the Gibeonites were accursed slaves forever. How does this work? "Even Levi, who receives tithes, paid tithes through Abraham, so to speak, for he was still in the loins of his father when Melchizedek met him" (Heb. 7:9–10). According to verse nine, "Levi receives" while "Abraham paid." Abraham was the great-grandfather of Levi. While still in the loins of Abraham, not yet born, Abraham paid. He received what his great-grandfather had paid. Thank God this was a blessing. Therefore, as we have generational blessings, so are generational curses.

Also let's consider how barrenness plagued Abraham's generation. Abraham waited twenty-five years before receiving the promised child, Isaac, while Isaac waited twenty years for Jacob and Esau. Jacob and the love of his life, Rachel, had years of waiting before conceiving Joseph. Barrenness was like a stronghold in the family. Generational curses may manifest in different ways in a family line. It could affect marriages, finances, or health, bringing poverty or a particular affliction in a family. Some problems are peculiar to a family; it is like a stronghold that is difficult to break free and easy to be trapped in. However, we have a great assurance in God, our eternal Father, through whom all blessings flow. Just like evil can flow and affect generations to come, so also can blessings. How? Through our lineage. As a result of our covenant relationship with God, through our Lord Jesus Christ, we are connected to the flow of divine resources. "For whatever is born of God overcomes the world. And this is the victory that has overcome the world—our faith" (1 John 5:4).

Territorial Curses

A curse can be upon an environment, a property, a city, or nation. If so, the dwellers will be in perpetual trouble unless it is taken away. The city of Jericho was a major hindrance to God's people on their way to the Promised Land. After the fall of the wall, Joshua placed a curse on the walls and the gates of the city on whosoever would raise it up. "Then Joshua charged them at that time, saying, 'Cursed be the man before the LORD who rises up and builds this city Jericho; he shall lay its foundation with his firstborn, and with his youngest he shall set up its gates'" (Josh. 6:26). Several years later, somebody tried building the wall. The consequence: "In his days Hiel of Bethel built Jericho. He laid its foundation with Abiram his firstborn, and with his youngest son Segub he set up its gates, according to the word of the LORD, which He had spoken through Joshua the son of Nun" (1 Kings 16:34). It was this same city,

> Curses should not take hold of us, neither should they show superiority over us, nor should we be gripped by fear. God is glorified in us when we walk in confidence of His power.

Jericho, which the inhabitants cried unto Elisha to pray for their bad condition. "Then the men of the city said to Elisha, 'Please notice, the situation of this city is pleasant, as my lord sees; but the water is bad, and the ground barren.' And he said, 'Bring me a new bowl, and put salt in it.' So they brought it to him" (2 Kings 2:19-22). Nations of the world are going through crisis due to curses invoked on the territory. When these are taken away, joy will be restored.

There could be many types of curses, but the important thing is that however deeply rooted a curse may be, it can be broken. We can be free from the bondages of curses. God has made a way to buy us out of curses:

> Christ has redeemed us from the curse of the law, having become a curse for us (for it is written, 'Cursed is everyone who hangs on a tree'), that the blessing of Abraham might come upon the Gentiles in Christ Jesus, that we might receive the promise of the Spirit through faith.
> —GALATIANS 3:13–14

We can apply the finished work of our redemption as we expel, overthrow, and make void curses through the power of the name of Jesus and the wonders of His blood. We can be restored to blessings as we keep faith and trust Him. Curses should not take hold of us, neither should they show superiority over us, nor should we be gripped by fear. God is glorified in us when we walk in confidence of His power.

Chapter 3

KNOWING YOUR ENEMIES

WE ARE IN a world of hostility, where people oppose the purposes or interests of one another. It is almost unavoidable. Great friends have betrayed one another; confidants have turned out to be foes. Strife and profanity among family members have caused great stress and trouble in keeping relationships. People are hard to deal with and hard to bear. I ask myself, where is love in this? People are self-centered, greedy, and abusive; and it seems to be an unending journey as they become callous and inhuman. I wonder at times if this could be as a result of the pressures of life that make us see things differently. Some see life as competition, so they struggle for superiority, while others see it as battlefield and a fight for survival. Others see it as a courtroom where everyone must be prosecuted, judged, and condemned.

I took comfort in the Word of the Holy Scripture, "And that we may be delivered from unreasonable and wicked men; for not all have faith" (2 Thess. 3:2). This has ever been my prayer since the day God opened my eyes to this verse of the Scripture. I now understand very clearly that people can be relentless, unreasonable, and provoking. Apostle John concluded: "We know [positively] that we are of God, and the whole world [around us] is under the power of the evil one" (1 John 5:19, AMP). So, it is impossible to live in a world free of evil ones.

Types of Enemies

Enmity among people gets stronger because the same adversary can manifest in different ways unidentified. A child who suffered from bullying in his elementary school, if unattended to, may look for ways of fighting back. He may give in to peer pressure in order to fit in. He becomes negatively influenced, and the result may be getting involved in drugs and alcohols later in life. If the child pushes hard through college, he may find it hard to cope with his career due to low self-esteem. It may be hard to keep relationships, and he may be wrapped up in loneliness and depression. If he succeeds in getting married with the past unresolved, such a marriage will go through rough times due to insecurity. It is the same enemy but appearing in different forms with the same intention—"to steal, to kill and to destroy" (John 10:10). Identifying various ways by which the enemy of our soul operates will establish victories in all areas of our lives.

Personalized Enemies

My understanding of spiritual warfare was sharpened when I began to study with interest how some people refer to their adversary as "my enemy." It is like saying this belongs to me and is associated with me. Saul referred to David as "my enemy" (1 Sam. 19:17); Ahab called Elijah "my enemy" (1 Kings 21:20); Job responding to his friend said, "mine enemy" (Job 16:9, kjv); and prophet Micah called for his enemy not to rejoice over him: "Do not rejoice over me, my enemy; When I fall, I will arise; When I sit in darkness, The Lord will be a light to me" (Mic. 7:8). Hannah magnified God over her enemies who relentlessly provoked her. "And Hannah prayed and said: 'My heart rejoices in the Lord; My horn is exalted in the Lord. I smile at my enemies, Because I rejoice in Your salvation'" (1 Sam. 2:1). David was a man to whom God gave multiple victories:

> I will call upon the Lord, who is worthy to be praised; So shall I be saved from my enemies…I have pursued my enemies and destroyed them; Neither did I turn back again till they were destroyed…You have also given me the necks of my enemies, So that I destroyed those who hated me…He delivers me from my enemies. You also lift me up above those who rise against me; You have delivered me from the violent man.
>
> —2 Samuel 22:4, 38, 41, 49

At desperate moments, he would cry out to God to save him from his enemies, to avenge them, or judge them:

> Arise, O Lord; Save me, O my God! For You have struck all my enemies on the cheekbone; You have broken the teeth of the ungodly.
>
> —Psalm 3:7

When the wicked came against me To eat up my flesh, My enemies and foes, They stumbled and fell. Though an army may encamp against me, My heart shall not fear; Though war may rise against me, In this I will be confident

—PSALM 27:2–3

It is a terrible thing for someone to be raised specifically and particularly to attack and afflict an individual. It is like being set up not for any other person, neither for any other assignment, nor for any other thing, but for one thing—such is a personalized enemy, an enemy with major assignment without distraction and well equipped for the purpose.

It could be to an individual, family, community, race, or nation. It is like receiving an order to mark closely, devotedly committed to the assigned work. This type of enemy rarely gives up. They are so obsessed with the mandate given that they take risks and despise danger. They are difficult to contend with because they can discover the strengths and weaknesses of people, hence determining the right strategy of operation. Other things are minor and unimportant to such an enemy. It could be a lifetime project. Even if they are losing, they do not give up.

In my high school days, I enjoyed playing and watching soccer. My school was playing another school in a soccer competition. A player from our opposing team was a deadly striker, with a reputation of scoring goals no matter what. I heard my school soccer coach say to one of our defense players: "You're assigned only unto the player with jersey number nine; mark him hard and prevent him from scoring." As the game began, I watched this guy carrying out the instruction, standing by him, running after him, and jumping together, just to be a major obstacle. He was assigned mainly to this man to frustrate him. While other players freely moved about in the field and could tackle any other player, he was under mandate to carry out this specific assignment.

Low moments can cause us more pain and agony than the problem that struck us down because the enemies fight hardest at such times.

He was never deceived into facing other players, knowing the worth of his assigned opponent. If left unmarked, he could bring down any team. This is how a personalized enemy—"my enemy"—works.

David was a threat to Saul, so was Elijah to Ahab. Hannah rejoiced in God over her personalized enemies because God made her triumph over those who laughed her to scorn. A woman approached me for prayers, asking God to forgive her for what she did in bringing down a minister of the gospel. She told me how determined she was to ruin his ministry. She joined the ministry and walked her way to the top with a mission. This took her eight years to carry out her assignment. She succeeded in scattering the flock and pulling down the man of God. According to her, when the deed was done, it was like the veil was removed and she saw the evil she had done; but it was too late. Guilt set in and her own frustration began. She was in the ministry for this purpose. So are personalized enemies, they aim at their prey, pursue their goals, and never lose focus until the mission is fulfilled. We can take advantage of the ministry of angels to prevent them in their mission. Know that God also watches over His own; we can walk confidently in His grace and mercy.

Strong Enemies

Not all enemies are strong, even though they are wicked and full of hatred. They may be full of terror but weak, still not giving up. Nonetheless, some are strong and capable of withstanding forces, not easily weary or shaken. Losing everything means nothing to them until the mandate is fulfilled. Their attacks can be fierce and unmistakable because they are determined to hunt and destroy.

When people come under attack, sometimes we endure, but some attacks are difficult and hard to cope with. We groan due to overwhelming trials that words cannot express. Many try to fight back, standing strong, but soon surrender due to a series of defeats, becoming hopeless. David the king praised God who delivered him from a strong enemy: "He delivered me from my strong enemy, From those who hated me; For they were too strong for me" (2 Sam. 22:18). Though he was a mighty man of valor, yet he considered some enemies as "strong." He understood their strategies and said, "They attacked me at a moment when I was in distress, but the Lord supported me" (v. 19, NLT). Low moments can cause us more pain and agony than the problem that struck us down because the enemies fight hardest at such times.

I interestingly watched a wrestling tournament, in my youth days, of a man who had defeated all his opponents but one. After being knocked out, he spoke to the press and commented, "He is strong. I tried pushing hard but could not move him." Many today are knocked out by those they consider strong and mighty. They feel they are no match, but I have good news—the Almighty God is strong and mighty. "Who is this King of glory? The LORD strong and mighty, The LORD mighty in battle" (Ps. 24:8). At His presence the strong become weak; they melt like wax. At the voice of the Almighty, the foundations of the strong are shaken; they loose their hold on the prey and are rendered captive in turn.

> Shall the prey be taken from the mighty, Or the captives of the righteous be delivered? But thus says the LORD: "Even the captives of the mighty shall be taken away, And the prey of the terrible be delivered; For I will contend with him who contends with you, And I will save your children. I will feed those who oppress you with their own flesh, And they shall be drunk with their own blood as with sweet wine. All flesh shall know That I, the LORD, am your Savior, And your Redeemer, the Mighty One of Jacob."
>
> —ISAIAH 49:24–26

Deadly Enemies

Having an enemy is bad enough, but it is even worse to have a deadly enemy. Such a one is extremely destructive and harmful. They do not just attack, but their after effect is worse than the attack. They are virulently contagious. If they operate within a community, they have a hold on the people and can influence them negatively. They are difficult to persuade and poisonous to retain. They operate without mercy. When they associate with people, their destructive goals are set from the beginning, and they never give up until total destruction is attained. They will do everything possible to get at people by networking and probing. They are injurious to the point of creating permanent damage.

David the king encountered such people in his lifetime; even now there are more of them in the world today. "Keep me as the apple of Your eye; Hide me under the shadow of Your wings, From the wicked who oppress me, From my deadly enemies who surround me" (Ps. 17:8–9). I pray that God Almighty will deliver those who are under the yoke of deadly enemies. Such enemies are deadly because they are indifferent to pain or the distress of others, and so hardened in heart that killing or destruction is the order of the day. King David likened them to greedy lions. Their eyes are all over to ensure nothing good comes out of their victim. The way to overcome them is to hide under the shadow of divine wings.

> Keep me as the apple of Your eye; Hide me under the shadow of Your wings, From the wicked who oppress me, From my deadly enemies who surround me. They have closed up their fat hearts; With their mouths they speak proudly. They have now surrounded us in our steps; They have set their eyes, crouching down to the earth, As a lion is eager to tear his prey, And like a young lion lurking in secret places. Arise, O LORD, Confront him, cast him down; Deliver my life from the wicked with Your sword.
>
> —PSALM 17:8–13

A lady had a misunderstanding with her colleague at work. She later made moves for reconciliation, but it never worked out. Her colleague saw to it that she was fired from work, but she didn't stop there; she set her up and slandered her until her marriage broke up. Still she was not satisfied; she desired to kill her. Such is a deadly enemy. God is able to deliver those who trust Him to disappoint the deadly enemies.

Serpentine Enemies

Enemies of this nature are hard to discover because they are subtle and treacherous. They are full of deceit so as to trick people into total ruin and destruction. They are characterized by vengefulness and vindictiveness, striking their unwitting victims without warning. They associate with people with the intention to promote evil. It is so unfortunate that so many people have fallen prey to them. I have seen families totally ruined by serpentine enemies who appear as friends: children lured into violent activities, fathers abandoning family responsibility and blaming their family for their misfortune, and mothers struggling with rejection and insecurity. The psalmist cried unto God for deliverance and protection over serpentine enemies.

> Deliver me, O LORD, from evil men; Preserve me from violent men, Who plan evil things in their hearts; They continually gather together for war. They sharpen their tongues like a serpent; The poison of asps is under their lips. Selah. Keep me, O LORD, from the hands of the

wicked; Preserve me from violent men, Who have purposed to make my steps stumble.

—PSALM 140:1–4

My prayer for you is that God will expose your serpentine enemies and grant you victory over them.

Fallen Among Thieves

The reason so many people are not fulfilled in the pursuit of their purpose, calling, and destiny for which they were born is because they have fallen among thieves. I have seen gifted people trapped by poverty, the rich gone down sinking in depression, and the poor forever poor. People desire blessings, but never get them because it is of no use when surrounded by thieves and robbers. A thief will cunningly and wrongfully take what does not belong to him (unauthorized taking, keeping or using another's property with the intent of depriving the owner the rightful possession of its use); whereas a robber applies confrontation, violence, and threats. This type of enemy deprives people of their joy and violates their rights.

Jesus gave a parable of the good Samaritan: "Then Jesus answered and said: 'A certain man went down from Jerusalem to Jericho, and fell among thieves, who stripped him of his clothing, wounded him, and departed, leaving him half dead'" (Luke 10:30). "A certain man" could be you or me. "Went down from Jerusalem to Jericho": that is, from the city of peace to Jericho (a major opposition to the Promised Land). This is to say that whatsoever shifts us from the dwelling place of peace will surely oppose God's promises. That which could prevent us from abounding in peace could also prevent us from inheriting blessings. When this certain man fell among thieves, they stripped him, disgraced him, shamed him, wounded him, and departed. In like manner, so many people have been wounded and abandoned, left for "half dead"—neither alive nor dead; neither rich nor poor; neither healthy nor sick; neither happy nor sad.

"Now by chance a certain priest came down that road. And when he saw him, he passed by on the other side" (v. 32). The religious people "by chance" had an opportunity to rescue the needy but failed. How sad to know how religion has disappointed many people and even helped the enemies in their wicked works. "But a certain Samaritan, as he journeyed, came where he was. And when he saw him, he had compassion" (v. 33). The despised came to the rescue of the helpless. God can use what is despised to confound the wise, so that He alone will take the glory. The same situation that people saw and ignored, made mockery about, ridiculed, and passed by on the other side, others will see and show compassion. "On the next day, when he departed, he took out two denarii, gave them to the innkeeper, and said to him, 'Take care of him; and whatever more you spend, when I come again, I will repay you'" (v. 35). The Samaritan seized the moment and shared the darkest hour, restoring hope.

I have good news for those who have fallen among thieves and are caged in the den of thieves. Jesus overthrew their tables (altar) and their seats (thrones):

> So they came to Jerusalem. Then Jesus went into the temple and began to drive out those who bought and sold in the temple, and overturned the tables of the money changers and the seats of those who sold doves. And He would not allow anyone to carry wares through the temple. Then He taught, saying to them, "Is it not written, 'My house shall be called a house of prayer for all nations'? But you have made it a 'den of thieves.'"
>
> —Mark 11:15–17

Therefore, to break free from enemies who are thieves and robbers, overthrow their altars and their thrones. Through the altars they project evil and rule through the throne. Jesus was also crucified among thieves: "With Him they also crucified two robbers, one on His right and the other on His left. So the Scripture was fulfilled which says, 'And He was numbered with the transgressors'" (Mark 15:27–28). I wonder why, out of many capital offenses, thieves were chosen to be crucified with Jesus. I personally think this may have some spiritual implications as to secretly or artfully steal all His claims to power and prevent Him from rising again as He promised. One of the thieves crucified

There are people who will take advantage of your kind and serving heart to order your life around and enslave you. They treat you with no respect; they will abuse and ridicule you. To make it worse, they don't like to be corrected.

with Him repented, thereby breaking the network of evil unity; they no longer had hold over him to steal from Him because their power of agreement was broken. He overcame the thieves, so we also can overcome enemies who come as thieves.

Enemies as Taskmasters

These are special kinds of enemies—allotters of work and exactors of tribute. They impose burdens on their victims and put demands on people's lives as they control their resources and order their days. Somehow they benefit from people as they make them use their talents and gifts, but they harvest the reward. They are very difficult to deal with in that when you survive their plots, they devise another means. Friendship is great! What are friends for? Being there for one another—showing kindness and love. I personally love to serve others; it gives me joy because people are blessed and God is glorified. However, there are people who will take advantage of your kind and serving heart to order your life around and enslave you. They treat you with no respect; they will abuse and ridicule you. To make it worse, they don't like to be corrected. They establish control over every area of your life. An enemy who is a taskmaster will always seek profit from you to your disadvantage. They literally rule your life to ruin it, never coming to terms and not moved by your complaint. Avoiding or running away may not help because they know how to get you. "Therefore they set taskmasters over them to afflict them with their burdens. And they built for Pharaoh supply cities, Pithom and Raamses. But the more they afflicted them, the more they multiplied and grew. And they were in dread of the children of Israel" (Exod. 1:11–12). Freedom from such an enemy requires wisdom and picking up your broken pieces to rediscover your worth and develop your values because it is possible to be totally lost while being used up.

Enemies as Accusers

We may be full of shortcoming or commit errors, but we are subject to change. On the contrary, an accuser is a faultfinder who affirms another's guilt or unworthiness. I have heard people complain of being accused always even when it is unnecessary and undeserved. This is my sincere counsel to them: Accusation increases when you're determined to win the battles of life with a mind-set above mediocrity. Being accused does not mean you are bad or not good enough. Since we are each wired differently, we react to things differently. The things some ignore will not go unnoticed before the eyes of others. People may complain and murmur over everything, but they might not be enemies. However, an accuser is doing the devil's job; not just to criticize but to run down, put down, and ride over you. There is nothing you do that is good enough in their eyes; they are hard to please and difficult to approach. I also discovered that the chief role of the devil is to accuse God's people.

> Then I heard a loud voice saying in heaven, "Now salvation, and strength, and the kingdom of our God, and the power of His Christ have come, for the accuser of our brethren, who accused them before our God day and night, has been cast down. And they overcame him by the blood of the Lamb and by the word of their testimony, and they did not love their lives to the death."
>
> —REVELATION 12:10–11

It is an unceasing accusation—"day and night"—which can only be overcome by the blood of the Lamb and by the word of their testimony. As we testify of God's greatness and His power and goodness over the accusers, we shall in turn triumph because the testimony of God is greater. God's testimony corrects us, encourages us, and empowers us; whereas accusations weaken and confuse us, making us doubt God, despise others, and look down on ourselves. So when accused, stand courageous; and when alone and outnumbered by your accusers, "do not fear, for those who are with us are more than those who are with them" (2 Kings 6:16). The accusers may tempt, test, and discourage; but "looking unto Jesus, the author and finisher of our faith, who for the joy that was set before Him endured the cross, despising the shame, and has sat down at the right hand of the throne of God" (Heb. 12:2).

Anti-Progress Enemies

In the midst of wonderful opportunities, a lot of people are decreasing rather than increasing, deteriorating not advancing, losing and not gaining, regressing and not improving, and having backward movements rather than moving forward in pursuing their goals. Christian

Nevell Bovee said, "The grandest of all laws is the law of progressive development. Under it, in the wide sweep of things, men grow wiser as they grow older, and societies better."[1] I see a spirit that controls this age: servant ruling the master and the master serving the servant. Inferior is upgraded while the superior downgraded. The hardworking ones serve the lazy ones. Some labor while others wait to reap.

Solomon, the wise king, shared his wealth of experience: "I have seen servants on horses, While princes walk on the ground like servants" (Eccles. 10:7). Horses are prey animals with a strong fight-or-flight instinct. They are symbol of speed, agility, alertness, and endurance. So whosoever rides on a horse is set to progress with speed. In days gone past, horses were for princes while servants walked. But King Solomon, talking out of experience, spoke about reversal of order—princes walking while servants take over the horses. Walking and riding on a horse are different even though both are making progress, but the progress by horses is rapid and exciting, whereas progress through walking is slow and tiring. We should all consider which kind of progress we are making—rapid or slow, exciting or tiring. Life goes well when we are interested in the progress of one another, but this is not always so. Some people live their lives with the attitude that other people's progress does not matter to them as long as they are progressing and happy; however, it becomes worse when such a one becomes a stumbling block to others' progress, envying when others are making it, trying to fight it and damaging the reputation.

> Accusation increases when you're determined to win the battles of life with a mind-set above mediocrity.

Somebody who is under anti-progress attack may be ignorant and not paying attention. This is when we feel we are advancing, but we are not reflecting on the progress we are making. Sometimes it is too late before we discover wasted years and profitless hard work. Regular examinations of our life and work would help us make adjustments. Our enemies succeed when we are stagnant and deteriorating, but they fail when we are improving and advancing.

Blessings Impersonators

I watched with great interest the prosecution of a man who paraded himself for a long time as a police officer. He harassed many people with the pretense of being a police officer until his arrest. A quick way for the enemy to frustrate people is to take over our personality fraudulently, imitating our voice and manner in order to take over what belongs to us. Jacob pretended to be Esau before his father and took over his blessing.

> So Jacob went near to Isaac his father, and he felt him and said, "The voice is Jacob's voice, but the hands are the hands of Esau." And he did not recognize him, because his hands were hairy like his brother Esau's hands; so he blessed him. Then he said, "Are you really my son Esau?" He said, "I am."
>
> —Genesis 27:22–24

Samuel, the seer, would have anointed Eliab instead of David if not for divine intervention. "So it was, when they came, that he looked at Eliab and said, "Surely the Lord's anointed is before Him!" (1 Sam. 16:6). Those who take the honor belonging to others will assume someone else's identity so as to take the due benefits.[2] The sole purpose is assuming the person's name or identity in order to make transactions. Not only can thieves run up bills for the victim, but also they commit crimes pretending to be the victim. An individual's identifying information is misappropriated with the intent to commit fraud. However, this runs parallel to the ancient conspiracy on mankind, when our divine identity was usurped by the ancient robber, Satan. "And no wonder! For Satan himself transforms himself into an angel of light. Therefore it is no great thing if his ministers also transform themselves into ministers of righteousness, whose end will be according to their works" (2 Cor. 11:14–15).

This type of enemy will permit opportunity to keep coming up, but they take the honor. I have seen people who perform really very well, commended by others, but are neither promoted nor rewarded. People complain saying, "I work hard, but I have nothing to show for it; when I build up, someone else shows up and takes over." Good people are not always rewarded, neither do they always take the place of honor, nor are they always appreciated. My prayer for you is in this passage of the Word of God:

They shall build houses and inhabit them; They shall plant vineyards and eat their fruit. They shall not build and another inhabit; They shall not plant and another eat; For as the days of a tree, so shall be the days of My people, And My elect shall long enjoy the work of their hands. They shall not labor in vain, Nor bring forth children for trouble; For they shall be the descendants of the blessed of the LORD, And their off-spring with them.

—ISAIAH 65:21–23

Detecting Their Operations

Understanding the enemy's attack could be a sign of victory, more so is acting on it. Overlooking and allowing attacks to pass by could be deadly. Some attacks come and go and regular life continues, whereas others leave permanent damage. While some take time to recover, others are total ruins. Some attacks can entirely change the course of life, leaving behind unforgettable memories and mind torture. The most deadly ones are silent and undiscovered, but with damaging effects. Christian Nevell Bovee, said, "Affliction, like the iron-smith, shapes as it smites."[3] Job was a man who suffered severe afflictions, but he survived, even though he was so damaged that his friends could scarcely recognized him. "And when they raised their eyes from afar, and did not recognize him, they lifted their voices and wept; and each one tore his robe and sprinkled dust on his head toward heaven" (Job: 2:12). I, therefore, will like to unfold some of the ways the enemy of our soul operates, "lest Satan should take advantage of us; for we are not ignorant of his devices" (2 Cor. 2:11).

Abolishing destructive warrant

Our lives, one way or the other, communicate something to others, and people relate to us as such. What we desire at times may not match up with what our life is communicating. There is that thing that is written all over us, which often speaks louder than we thought.

Uriah was an officer in David's army, whom David the king ordered to return from the battle and later sent back to the battle front with a letter. This letter was Uriah's death sentence, so he became the carrier of his own death sentence.

> In the morning it happened that David wrote a letter to Joab and sent it by the hand of Uriah. And he wrote in the letter, saying, "Set Uriah in the forefront of the hottest battle, and retreat from him, that he may be struck down and die." So it was, while Joab besieged the city, that he assigned Uriah to a place where he knew there were valiant men. Then the men of the city came out and fought with Joab. And some of the people of the servants of David fell; and Uriah the Hittite died also.
>
> —2 SAMUEL 11:14–17

Out of loyalty he never opened to read the letter. He delivered it to Joab, the commander of David's army, who was to execute the content of the letter. According to the letter, Uriah was to be slain in the battle. In like manner, we all carry something which when executed could bring favor or ruin, death or life. What Uriah carried gave authority to slay him. The battle had been normal until permission was given to put him to the hottest part of the battle: "And he wrote in the letter, saying, 'Set Uriah in the forefront of the hottest battle, and retreat from him, that he may be struck down and die'" (v. 15). Also ask yourself, why sudden hatred by your lovers? Why is the rejection getting stronger? Why are people changing toward you, and why are helpers withdrawing? The answer to all these questions could be what you are communicating to others; you may be carrying a destructive warrant. Unless this is abolished, it may have destructive effects. So when we start noticing signs of deep hostility and unusual withdrawal of helps, it is time to annul the negatives our lives are communicating.

Exploitation of open doors

In my capacity as a pastor and biblical counselor for over three decades, I have encouraged and given prophetic directions to many who came weeping profusely, broken down and despondent about life because what they thought to be a blessing, open door, and breakthrough turned out to be failure and great lost. It is difficult to be in such a situation because it leaves many bewildered and confused, wondering if God ever answered their prayers. I realize that when blessing comes, evil loves to take advantage and turn it bad. I have heard people say, "I got a job I always desired, but when I was about to settle on it, feeling everything was going right, I was fired"; "I got into a relationship with the person I felt I loved, and I thought he loved me, counting it to be a blessing, but it became the worst"; or "My child started out well in life, doing well in school and attending church services with me, but suddenly he lost focus and couldn't make it through high school. I'm afraid he might belong to a gang." These are the heart-breaking stories of some people. Truly God answers prayers, but retaining them is a problem to many. The enemy of our soul also engages in serious exploitation of the same opportunity that brought blessings into our lives.

The children of Israel escaped the captivity of Egypt and were confronted by the Red Sea. God commanded Moses to stretch out his hand over the sea: "Then Moses stretched out his hand over the sea; and the LORD caused the sea to go back by a strong east wind all that night, and made the sea into dry land, and the waters were divided" (Exod. 14:21). The sea parted for them to pass through. That would be an escape from the Egyptians. "And the Egyptians pursued and went after them into the midst of the sea, all Pharaoh's horses, his chariots, and his horsemen" (v. 23). These same open doors became the route of pursuit by the Egyptians. The door of opportunity that brought blessings was now to be used by the enemy of their souls. This could have made people murmur, complain, and blame God. Here is the solution that brought victory: Moses stretched out his hand over the sea to open up the sea (v. 21), and in closing it against the Egyptians, he stretched out his hand over the sea (v. 26). The implication is that the same hand that got the blessing can stop the invasion of the wicked. The Power that brought them out of captivity was abundantly able to keep them from the pursuit and destruction.

> The wicked soon forget the wickedness done to others, but the person concerned will forever nurse the wounds.

The faith to trust God and get the miracle is also good enough to stop attacks. Never mind when you come under attack at the time of blessing, rather hold steadfast to the Giver, who is able to preserve and cause blessing to abound. The Egyptians perished and never caught up with them. We should not shrink back when the enemy reinforces; rather, stand strong in the Lord. The wicked ones block chances of miracles, but when we prevail in prayer and get the required blessing, they still don't give up. They violently pursue to destroy the blessing. This is the usual satanic operation. So, never fret when you are under attack, especially when blessings are not manifesting. My counsel to you is: If they fail in preventing the blessing from happening, it is guaranteed that they will also fail in destroying the blessings.

We shall see

This is an ancient principle of warfare attack: waiting to see how dreams will be accomplished. This shows desperate determination to ruin any success plan. It is the most frustrating thing when people vow unceasing attacks, never to give up, and forbid good things from happening. Joseph was a man loved by his father but hated by his brothers. He became an object of envy, and they conspired against him saying, "We shall see what will become of his dreams!" (Gen. 37:20). So Joseph went from pit to slavery and then to imprisonment. It was as though his visions would never come to pass. Similarly, people may have to pass through these stages before attaining glorious height: pit, slavery, imprisonment, and then palace. A pit life is a lowly life where people look down on you and cast insult to ridicule; whereas slavery life is a life where one has lost his rights and privileges, and is subjected to torture and profitless hard work. Imprisonment may not be a physical imprisonment, but restraint, limitation, and confinement. These are the crisis seasons of life. We can push through pit, slavery, and imprisonment to the throne.

They conspired, saying, "We shall see what will become of his dreams!" (v. 20); and surely and truly they saw: "And behold, your eyes and the eyes of my brother Benjamin see that it is my mouth that speaks to you" (45:12). After Joseph had been exalted, his vision accomplished, and he met with his brothers, they could not recognize him, but he could recognize them. Why? They never expected him to be in such a glorious position. If he was even alive, he should have been a slave. I perceive if they had seen him as slave in the slave market, they would have easily identified him. Why could Joseph identify them? It is because the wicked soon forget the wickedness done to others, but the person concerned will forever nurse the wounds. It is also possible for his brothers to visit Egypt without seeing Joseph, but God positioned him to see their shame. The Egyptians knew Joseph as a former slave, but never knew what brought him to slavery.

It is, therefore, part of the enemy's operation to wait to see whether we will succeed or not and fulfill dreams or not, but they shall be disappointed when God's mercy pushes us and establishes us in His purposes. They said, "We shall see what will become of his dreams!" (v. 20).

After several years of toiling and almost wasting away, his dream came through. The pit could not bury it, neither was slavery strong enough to destroy his dream, nor prison able to limit his eye on the throne. They stripped him out of his coat of many colors, but God put on him a royal robe. The garment of slavery and imprisonment were but for a moment. He soon cast them off to take the garment befitting his dream. I really do not know the vows upon your life—"we shall see"—waiting to see how your marriage will work, how your children will be successful, how you will have a fulfilling career or fulfill God's calling and election. By saying, "We shall see," it is to show the level of opposition to prevent it from happening. However tough the pathway to success, those who said, "We shall see," shall surely and truly see the evil expectation not happen.

Defeating the Enemies

We need not be afraid of the enemies, neither should we be terrified by their weapons or their devices; victory can be attained notwithstanding. According to the word of Winston S. Churchill, "Victory at all costs, victory in spite of all terror, victory however long and hard the road may be; for without victory there is no survival."[4] The purpose of this book is to set you on the path of significant, noteworthy victories. In spite of losses, Sam Snead said, "The mark of a great player is in his ability to come back. The great champions have all come from defeat."[5]

> It is wrong to assume that your enemies have no fear; though appearing bold and courageous, they most times struggle with fear, but try to hide it, because they operate in deceit.

Detecting enemies' fear

It is wrong to assume that your enemies have no fear; though appearing bold and courageous, they most times struggle with fear, but try to hide it, because they operate in deceit. God called Gideon to lead His people out of the oppression of the Midianites. He thought it was an impossible thing until he sneaked into the camp of the adversary. He discovered that they were more afraid than he was; their hearts filled with terror.

Then his companion answered and said, "This is nothing else but the sword of Gideon the son of Joash, a man of Israel! Into his hand God has delivered Midian and the whole camp." And so it was, when Gideon heard the telling of the dream and its interpretation, that he worshiped. He returned to the camp of Israel, and said, "Arise, for the LORD has delivered the camp of Midian into your hand."

—JUDGES 7:14–15

On another occasion, the people of Israel were set to go forward in possessing the Promised Land, but they encountered several oppositions; one of the most challenging ones was the hiring of a prophet to curse them. Even with that, their adversary expressed doubt and probability: "Therefore please come at once, curse this people for me, for they are too mighty for me. Perhaps I shall be able to defeat them and drive them out of the land, for I know that he whom you bless is blessed, and he whom you curse is cursed" (Num. 22:6). A word to note in this verse is "perhaps," meaning possibly but not certain. We can gain courage and strength in this as we turn back our fears on the enemy of our soul.

In the days of Eli the Priest, the Philistines set war against Israel. The presence of the ark of God brought great fear upon the Philistines, but they encouraged themselves to fight strong.

Now when the Philistines heard the noise of the shout, they said, "What does the sound of this great shout in the camp of the Hebrews mean?" Then they understood that the ark of the LORD had come into the camp. So the Philistines were afraid, for they said, "God has come into the camp!" And they said, "Woe to us! For such a thing has never happened before. Woe to us! Who will deliver us from the hand of these mighty gods? These are the gods who struck the Egyptians with all the plagues in the wilderness. Be strong and conduct yourselves like men, you Philistines, that you do not become servants of the Hebrews, as they have been to you. Conduct yourselves like men, and fight!"

—1 SAMUEL 4:6-9

The truth is that the fear does not keep the enemy back from fighting; it rather encourages them to persist in the face of obstacles or discouragement, knowing that most people give up easily. I consider faith in battle as standing obstinately despite difficulties or setbacks, carrying on, going on, hanging on, and keeping on to the One who has made us more than conquerors. With this understanding that the enemy is more fearful than you are, it should encourage you to persist until victory.

Daily battles and daily victories

The Scriptures prescribe some things to be done daily: exhort (admonish and encourage) one another (Heb. 3:13), and to take up our cross daily (Luke 9:23). Also, there are some things God does for us on daily basis: He loads us with benefits (Ps. 68:19) and makes blessings available every day (Matt. 6:11). It is wise to know that we are in a constant battle every day. "Be merciful to me, O God, for man would swallow me up; Fighting all day he oppresses me. My enemies would hound me all day, For there are many who fight against me, O Most High" (Ps. 56:1–2). Hence, the psalmist cried out for God's mercy; otherwise, he would be swallowed in the midst of "daily oppression." Some of these daily battles may be rooted in the following:

> I consider faith in battle as standing obstinately despite difficulties or setbacks, carrying on, going on, hanging on, and keeping on to the One who has made us more than conquerors.

Heart Issues: Our hearts reveal who we are: "For as he thinks in his heart, so is he. 'Eat and drink!' he says to you, But his heart is not with you" (Prov. 23:7). It defines us and determines the course of life. God Himself saw that "every intent of the thoughts of his [man's] heart was only evil continually" (Gen. 6:5), so David cried, "Create in me a clean heart, O God, And renew a steadfast spirit within me" (Ps. 51:10). Jesus said, "Let not your heart be troubled" (John 14:1); so as the heart can rejoice, it can also be overwhelmed. Murder, adultery, covetousness, wickedness, deceit, and pride are all heart issues (Mark 7:20–22). We struggle with these daily, and it is a battle that must be won. Lasting victory starts from the storeroom of our hearts, because it overflows and rules our lives. If we store good, good is revealed; if we store evil, evil is revealed. "A good man produces good out of the good storeroom of his heart. An evil man produces evil out of the evil storeroom, for his mouth speaks from the overflow of the heart" (Luke 6:45, HCSB). Our heart can deceive us if not dedicated to God Almighty and filled with the word of God to check our thoughts, words, and imaginations.

The heart is deceitful above all things, And desperately wicked; Who can know it? I, the LORD, search the heart, I test the mind, Even to give every man according to his ways, According to the fruit of his doings.
—JEREMIAH 17:9–10

Setting a guard in our heart seems to be the most important thing because whatsoever rules our hearts controls our entire being. We all know how we protect what we love and cherish in order to keep it safe from danger or attack; we defend and preserve until they are secured. How much more what determines our entire life—our heart. "Keep your heart with all diligence, For out of it spring the issues of life" (Prov. 4:23). Defeat or victory, sorrow or gladness are settled from the heart.

The Flesh (Human Nature): Our body that we so much cherish, as beautiful and tender as it may be, can determine how weak or strong we are. We are made out of the dust (Gen. 2:7); the breath of the Almighty gives us life. When we die, the flesh decays and returns to the dust (3:19), but the soul and spirit return to our Maker—God. So the flesh is earthly; it was formed from the earth and remains there. Therefore, it does what pleases it, and it is not interested or excited about going to heaven or hell. It opposes the things of the spirit. Who can blame it? The flesh is just feeling at home. Jesus even said, "Watch and pray, lest you enter into temptation. The spirit indeed is willing, but the flesh is weak" (Matt. 26:41). So we need to stay alert because there is a part of us that is eager and ready for anything in God, but there's another part that is dragging behind—the flesh. It contradicts the spirit, so we have to subject it to the Word of God because it can enslave our soul and spirit. "For the flesh lusts against the Spirit, and the Spirit against the flesh; and these are contrary to one another, so that you do not do the things that you wish" (Gal. 5:17). Our daily victory can be established over the flesh as we put our confidence in who we are in Christ and allow the Word of God to change our desire, control our feelings, and guide our decisions. "For we are the circumcision, who worship God in the Spirit, rejoice in Christ Jesus, and have no confidence in the flesh" (Phil. 3:3). It is a daily battle which requires daily victory.

Adversary and Adversity: Oftentimes I wonder what makes the wicked boast, seeming to increase in strength and never willing to give up. I was puzzled until I discovered the secret. The Holy Spirit gave me some examples. If someone burns down your house and flees, and is later arrested and prosecuted—yes, you are happy that justice is executed, but the harm is done already. The adversary is arrested, but the adversity must be corrected. The adversary is the enemy, while the adversity is the distress, pain, and agony caused by the enemy. It does not matter what is done to the adversary; the effect of the attack could be a lifetime of painful memories. It stirs up days of adversity. There are those who have suffered hostility, dislike, and rejection; they often go after those who caused them harm, but the way to full recovery according to the Scripture is: the horse and its rider (Exod. 15:1); the strongman and his stronghold (Mark 3:27); the altar and the priest (Lev. 3:11); the sower and the reaper (Luke 19:21); the weapons and the warriors (Ps. 46:9); and the message and the messenger (Hag. 1:13).

If we kill the horse and let go of the rider, he will get another horse for battle; or if we destroy the rider and leave the horse, someone else will ride the horse. If we attack the strongman and leave the strongholds where goods are kept, of what advantage is the fight if there is no recovery of goods? And if our target alone is the stronghold—getting back the goods—the strongman will reinforce his defenses. Also if the altar and the sacrifice are destroyed without the priest, another altar will be erected; and if the priest is destroyed without the altar, someone else will sacrifice upon the altar. If there is a sower, there must be reaper; and there cannot be a reaper without the sower. The warriors use the weapons, and weapons are useless without the users. Messages are not communicated without the messengers.

> Lasting victory starts from the storeroom of our hearts, because it overflows and rules our lives.

Therefore, a sure victory is when the enemies are dealt with and also the effects of their attacks. When they attack, it leads to a season of chaos and affliction, which also must be worked upon for proper deliverance. The victory strategy, therefore, is to establish dominion over the adversaries and their adversity.

Let Me Not Fall into the Hand of Man: The terror of man can stir up great wrath beyond repair. Human beings, men and women alike, as loving as we are, can be very destructive. I once commended a brother in the church for his devotion and dedication; he smiled and commented, "You don't want to see my other side." Surely and truly, the day he showed his other side, I went into prayers and fasting for God to truly save him.

David the king sinned against God, and he had three choices of punishment from God: famine for seven years, flee for three months before his enemies, or three days of pestilence (2 Sam. 24:13). He was in deep distress with all the available options, so he pleaded with God. "And David said to Gad, 'I am in great distress. Please let us fall into the hand of the LORD, for His mercies are great; but do not let me fall into the hand of man'" (2 Sam. 24:14).

Famine was not an option because he would be dependent on other nations. Neither was war the best to choose, because they would be at the mercies of their conqueror, nor pestilence because of shame and lost. He had seen the wrath of men and never wished for that to happen again. God eventually had mercy on him. Oh, for a great prayer to pray: "Do not let me fall into the hand of man." If we must see good days and enjoy long life, this should be our heart cry unto the Lord. As good as we are, as long as we are in the flesh, we should "have no confidence in the flesh" (Phil. 3:3). A well-behaved person today may turn out to be the worst criminal. This is why we should mortify the flesh (Rom. 8:13) and not yield to its craving lust. Since we still have to work with one another, it will be difficult to avoid offenses; it will surely come, but forgiving one another, being tender hearted, and allowing the love of God to flow through us will help maintain a joyful and peaceful relationship.

Persecuted but Not Wasted: Suffering, persecution, and trials are bad, but worse when we are overwhelmed by them, worse still when we are destroyed by them. Persecution may be targeted to reproach, blaspheme, and ridicule, but can also turn to joy. God's people are assured of being persecuted in this world (Matt. 5:10–12). There is an outrage on us because of the faith we profess. It is sad to say, but it will get worse. Is it avoidable? No! If only we continue and persist in faith, we will overcome at last. Apostle Paul gave us a strategy on how to withstand persecution. He was a man that was truly persecuted, but he was never overcome by it, even though he persecuted others before his conversion. He shared on how he persecuted and wreaked havoc on the church: "For ye have heard of my conversation in time past in the Jews' religion, how that beyond measure I persecuted the church of God, and wasted it" (Gal. 1:13, KJV). He truly persecuted them beyond measure, unto death, putting them in chains, imprisoning them, whipping them, blaspheming, being exceedingly mad against them, and pursuing them to strange cities (Acts 22:4; 26:11). He was licensed to kill and consented to Stephen's death (Acts 9:1-2). He indeed persecuted and wasted many people's lives.

Ask yourself what level of persecution, trials, and troubles you are going through. However tough the persecution, be sure you are not wasted. It is to strengthen us, looking unto "the author and finisher of our faith" (Heb. 12:2). Apostle Paul later expressed his ministry of suffering about how he was "persecuted, but not forsaken" (2 Cor. 4:9). The point I'm bringing up is that he who persecuted and wasted others, though persecuted also, refused to be wasted or forsaken. The difference is not allowing persecution to push you to the point of worthlessness and faithlessness. He knew the secret; so after his conversion, he was prepared for persecution, but not to be wasted. In the face of persecution, we should never lose focus on whom we believe, why we believe, and our hope in serving Him. The strategy of continuing in faith and possessing the crown is never to allow persecution to weaken us to the point of denying the faith. Stand strong no matter what!

Outwardly and Inwardly Protected: The search for protection is a desperate need for mankind, even more in our time. People will do anything whatsoever, not minding what it will cost them, to get protected. I boarded a taxi in New York City, sometime back in September 1999, and I noticed some religious symbols hanging on the rearview mirror. Out of curiosity, I asked the taxi driver what each symbol represented. He told me, one for each religion powerful enough to protect him; there were five of them. I was sincere with him as to point out the confusion of his heart and that Jesus Christ is the only way (John 14:6). Because of fear within and terror without and an increase in expectation of danger, people are frightened.

Amos the prophet gave us a picture of how it will be: "It will be as though a man fled from a lion, And a bear met him! Or as though he went into the house, Leaned his hand on the wall, And a serpent bit him!" (Amos 5:19). The man ran away from a lion but was attacked by a bear at the other end. Because of his desperate need for safety, he ran into the house and rested on the wall for support, but there was a serpent by the wall. Where else could he run to? Where else is safe? If outside is not safe, even inside is a death trap. I feel this is the best illustration that can describe our age. Lion and bear are outside, while the serpent is waiting inside. Nothing is secured. What worked out yesterday will fail today and cannot stand the future. The lion devours while the bear has large, strong, non-retractile claws for catching prey and for digging. Their teeth are adapted for grinding as well as tearing. They can climb and swim. So, how do we face such an opponent and overcome? David confronted both lion and bear and prevailed.

> Moreover David said, "The LORD, who delivered me from the paw of the lion and from the paw of the bear, He will deliver me from the hand of this Philistine." And Saul said to David, "Go, and the LORD be with you!"
>
> —1 SAMUEL 17: 37

Similarly, there are lion-like and bear-like opponents waiting to terrify us to death. Unfortunately, there are serpents in the wall—deadly enemies at the place of safety.

Naiveness of this truth can jeopardize our lives, but being protected inwardly and outwardly can secure victory. Notwithstanding, it is good to know that God is more enthusiastic and devoted to the cause of protecting His people. He is tirelessly diligent in watching His Word come to pass. I am excited that the Almighty God is personally committed to my care and safe keeping. What a joy to know the price paid for our redemption and protection! He shed His blood, defeated darkness, stripped them of the authority usurped from mankind, and proclaimed, "It is finished." We can rest on this assured word and be thankful forever that we are inwardly and outwardly protected.

Chapter 4

CUTTING OFF WITCHCRAFT

IN OCTOBER 1986, I was invited by an elderly friend who operated an animal farm in Lagos, Nigeria, to pray for his dying animals. This man reared different kinds of animals and was very prosperous until he had a quarrel with a family friend who, in revenge, cast a spell on his farm. More than 90 percent of the animals were sick near to death. He did all he could and brought in some experts, but to no avail. His heart was failing him because of the fear of losing his livestock. This was the time he invited me to pray over his farm, believing God to heal and save his animals. At first, I wanted to refuse him, thinking there might be no need to pray, but the Spirit of God rebuked me and persuaded me to go with him. I comforted and encouraged him that "all will be well." My heart was filled with compassion when I saw the deadly attacks on the livestock. The compassion I had was not just of how much my friend would lose, but for the animals. I asked God to put His word in my heart to speak. He laid an amazing scripture in my heart that I argued in my spirit until I got the revelation; I didn't want to misapply or misinterpret the scripture. After a few minutes of trying to reason it out, I obliged. What scripture was it? "And it shall come to pass afterward That I will pour out My Spirit on all flesh; Your sons and your daughters shall prophesy, Your old men shall dream dreams, Your young men shall see visions" (Joel 2:28). God's Spirit poured upon all flesh, including animal's flesh. I opened and read this verse of the Scripture, stretching my right hand over the farm, and then I commanded the Spirit of the Living God to bring life back to the animals—lo and behold, strength came upon the animals. Some could eat, while some tried walking, and others made some noise. Two weeks after the prayer, to the glory of God, all the livestock were back to life again; none had died. It was a witchcraft attack on the farm because his competitors were determined to ruin his business and bring him down.

In June 1998, a brother approached me to pray that he might be able to sell his house in Mississauga, Ontario, Canada, which had been on the market for over a year. He explained that houses in the area sell fast. Four other houses in his street were sold within weeks. He lowered his price and renovated, but there was no buyer; no one even came to check it out. A spell had been cast on it. I visited the property and immediately I could perceive a high level of evil trafficking over the property. I pleaded the blood of Jesus, rebuked the evil hold, casting them out and praying God's presence. I believed God for a glorious testimony because "the earth is the LORD's, and all its fullness, The world and those who dwell therein" (Ps. 24:1). Thanks be to God who always answers prayers. As I was opening the door to my house, my phone rang and the brother told me about someone who had just walked in and was ready to buy the house. Why was there a spell on the house? He had boasted before his colleagues in the office about moving to a bigger house. One of his colleagues had said, "How is it going to happen? What if there is no buyer for the present property you're occupying?" He did not take his words seriously. He thought he could rent or sell, but neither worked out. It was after the sale that he announced in the office that this same guy exclaimed, "It is not possible!" He smiled and said, "God did it!"

The purpose of this writing is not to exalt witchcraft, but to establish that the Almighty God is greater and He is the most powerful. Although witchcraft has caused havoc, there is deliverance through the blood of Jesus. It is unfortunate that witchcraft is gaining popularity in our time, regarded as a religion to entice and initiate more people, especially the youth. Hence, this has structured our educational system with curricula to develop a mind-set that opposes God. The media is playing no small role in communicating witchcraft agenda. It is a voice that rules our home, controls our lives, and confuses our spirit. It gives direction and training to our children, because many parents are not available to give what it takes in raising up their kids. Witchcraft has taken over the arts and entertainment with a conspiracy from the pit of hell to go through the cycle of fame, depression, drugs, and suicide. Witchcraft is rebellion against God and His people; it is resisting and defying God's authority, and expressing disagreement to anything about God and His kingdom (1 Sam. 15:23).

Families and governments are the major targets of witchcraft domination (Nah. 3:3). If the families fail, the nation cannot survive. Also, healthy families produce a healthy nation. When witchcraft controls governmental seats, they produce laws that will make people sigh by reason of bondage. This will cause financial collapse with the intention of subjecting people to fear and control. As witchcraft has taken control of major aspects of life, the consequence is raising an abusive, blasphemous, and profane generation. Being loose in morals and conduct, and lovers of sensual pleasures, is the order of the day.

Attacks of witchcraft can cast hindrances on people's progress, causing vain labor, thereby consumed by troubles. I can personally define witchcraft as "being in a league with the devil to manifest evil spirits and effect wickedness." Is there hope for the righteous? Absolutely, yes! I sincerely believe that in the midst of this, God is raising a people unto Himself who will operate in the power of His might, whose lives will testify of His goodness and greatness.

Types of Witchcraft

Witchcraft can manifest in many ways, but whichever way, it still does not glorify God.

> "There shall not be found among you anyone who makes his son or his daughter pass through the fire, or one who practices witchcraft, or a soothsayer, or one who interprets omens, or a sorcerer, or one who conjures spells, or a medium, or a spiritist, or one who calls up the dead. For all who do these things are an abomination to the LORD, and because of these abominations the LORD your God drives them out from before you."
> —DEUTERONOMY 18:10–12

Blind witch

These are those who are under the yoke of witchcraft but are ignorant of it. They are unaware of being part of it, because it is covered, and they truly do not know. These ones are very dangerous, as they attack without restraint; but when their victims fire back, they are also defenseless, unlike those who know what they are into and can reinforce their defenses. These kinds of witchcraft are the people who are under mind control and will manipulation.

Hard-hearted witchcraft

These sets of people are conscious of being witches. They know it and they do not hide it. Their hearts are as hard as stone, resolving to do wickedness. They are deadly to friends and family, sparing no one, and are difficult to appease, stopping at nothing until total destruction is achieved. Delighting in wickedness, hurting their prey, and destroying the innocent are the rules of the day. It takes vigilance and steadfastness in the spirit to overthrow and conquer them.

Well-favored witchcraft

This is the most delicate witchcraft because it is not a clear-cut evil, but it is assisting, helping, laboring, and spending for people with the intention of reaping with interest. There is always a payback; nothing is free. They put demands on people's lives because of favor they have shown. They are quick to render help so as to forbid help coming from elsewhere. They appear harmless in order to ensnare. True help comes from God, "a very present and well-proved help in trouble" (Ps. 46:1, AMP).

Generational witchcraft

Our foreparents knowingly or unknowingly made choices which now enslave their bloodline. Just like Joshua, the leader of Israel, made vow to service the Lord, and he covenanted his house (their consent probably not necessary): "But as for me and my house, we will serve the LORD" (Josh. 24:15). In like manner, our foreparents yoked themselves with things that are ungodly, which opened doors to invasion of evil. Unless careful repentance is made and rededication to God Almighty, the consequences of these vows keep tormenting us. Witchcraft is a stronghold in some families, which gives legal hold to the oppressors of our souls. "Also he caused his sons to pass through the fire in the Valley of the Son of Hinnom; he practiced soothsaying, used witchcraft and sorcery, and consulted mediums and spiritists. He did much evil in the sight of the LORD, to provoke Him to anger" (2 Chron. 33:6). The trouble with witchcraft transfer from generation to generation is that the family members are under witchcraft influence, and those who refuse, turn their back, and are not willing to partake are under constant spiritual warfare. If such will always trust the Lord God through the atoning blood of Jesus, they will prevail. "I have set the LORD always before me; Because He is at my right hand I shall not be moved" (Ps. 16:8).

Territorial witchcraft

Witchcraft can have a hold over communities by influencing decisions, laws, and orders, thereby subjecting the whole environment to the reign of evil and wickedness. Jezebel, the wife of King Ahab, through witchcraft manipulated her husband, and then controlled the nation. She cut off God's prophets, took over people's (Naboth's) inheritance, and sold out the nation (1 Kings 18:4; 21:5–16). The network of witchcraft upon the land makes the heaven brass to resist righteousness. When witchcraft invades the land, people groan in oppression, labor under affliction, and are tormented with fear. But deliverance comes: "If My people who are called by My name will humble themselves, and pray and seek My face, and turn from their wicked ways, then I will hear from heaven, and will forgive their sin and heal their land" (2 Chron. 7:14).

How Witchcraft Operates

They operate as powers behind the scene. What we see manifesting may not be the actual battle; the real battle is what is supporting or supplying the strength, which is oftentimes hidden or unknown to us. Oftentimes those who declare war don't engage in the actual battle. They give orders and release the troops. "Then they said to him, 'Who are you, that we may give an answer to those who sent us? What do you say about yourself?'" (John 1:22). Priests and Levites were sent to Jesus to inquire about who He was. They pressured Him for answers which they would relay to those who sent them—so there are powers behind the scene. Those who came to Him were under the mandate of their senders. The information they got would be good enough to use against Him. Effective warfare, therefore, is to breakdown the powers behind the scene and their subjects.

The familiar spirit spies individuals, families, or environments while the witchcraft enforces the attack based on the information. It is safe to know that the familiar spirit is a spirit that is well acquainted and intimated with an environment, a family line or association. The spirit is well informed even to the deepest secret. It holds a record of events and occurrences in a family line or in an environment. It is a demon spirit-possessing medium, making predictions. It promotes enchantments, witchcraft, sorcery, soothsaying, and necromancy. The reason why witchcraft attacks seem to be difficult to handle by many is because they easily change the battlefront. It is the same battle but with different faces. The battlefront is the area where opponents meet or clash; it is a decisive place where armed forces engage in combat. It can be upon the mountain or valley or plain, water, air, or wherever. So with the information of a familiar spirit, witchcraft stirs up a confusing situation at work, disorderliness at home, and health problems; it is the same battle but with different fronts. No wonder when victory is achieved in one aspect of life, trouble shows up in another.

My heart goes out to those who never wanted anything to do with witchcraft, yet a mark is put upon them. This mark subjects them to mischief and sabotage. Their helpers are not spared at all. I had the opportunity to meet a man a while ago, and the Holy Spirit laid it upon my heart to help him. I obeyed and followed divine guidance and leading. I indeed helped him financially, and supported and encouraged his family continuously for thirteen months until they could stand strong. He told me something that shocked me after a year of standing with him: "You're the very first person who helped me for this long. Others tried but couldn't continue because of sudden problems that overwhelmed them; they always got into trouble." I affirmed to him that it was because God instructed me to do so and He defended me. I did feel the attacks, but that could not stop me from helping him. His wife said that

> The trouble with witchcraft transfer from generation to generation is that the family members are under witchcraft influence, and those who refuse, turn their back, and are not willing to partake are under constant spiritual warfare.

for the last person who tried to help them "hell broke loose." Thank God they are doing wonderfully well now to the glory of God. I identified it as a witchcraft attack against their helpers. I also discovered that it is a witchcraft operation to tarnish people's reputations because they hate to see people prosper; they put a blemish on people's character and make them fall from a dignified position. It is like Benjamin Franklin's saying: "Glass, china, and reputation are easily cracked, never mended well."[1] But only the precious blood of Jesus can and will surely mend it. Another deadly attack of witchcraft is to program error into people. Such people act or think, though unintentionally, deviating from what is correct, right, or true. They make mistakes, misstep, and slip into wrongdoing. A mistake could be an error caused by a fault due to carelessness or forgetfulness, but it is much more pronounced through witchcraft. I am glad that the blood of Jesus can annul and correct all these.

Witchcraft Remnants

Why do I say witchcraft remnant? I do so as I consider the mistress of witchcraft—Jezebel. After she had been thrown down, her bones were shattered and dogs feasted on her, to fulfill the prophesy of Elijah the prophet. While other parts of her body were eaten up, some parts were left. "So they went to bury her, but they found no more of her than the skull and the feet and the palms of her hands" (2 Kings 9:35). I ask myself, why the skull, the feet and the palms of her hands? How about other bones of her body? Perhaps the dogs carried them away with their teeth. However, I perceive there are spiritual significances to this, considering the functions of these parts of the body. The skull protects the brain and gives shape to the face. How about the feet? Our feet support our body. We stand and move with our feet. We hold things with the palms of our hands, and we shake hands in greeting each other.

Regardless of her shattered bones, her witchcraft stronghold remained, so was her influence on the land and the people. If the Bible was so specific with the palm of her hand, I ask, why would some people read the palms in order to foretell the future? "And I will cut off witchcrafts out of thine hand; and thou shalt have no more soothsayers" (Mic. 5:12, KJV). Witchcraft in the hand? May I also ask, what is the symbol for a danger sign? Is it not with a human skull and crossbones? Anywhere we see that sign, it indicates dangers posed by poisons, toxins, and hazardous materials. Does witchcraft not pose danger to us and our society at large? The feet reflect conquest. Didn't she subdue the nation with her witchcraft reign? So, when Jezebel was thrown down and eaten up by dogs, her skull, feet, and the palms of her hands were not devoured.

As the skull protects the brain, which is the seat of the faculty of intelligence and reason, so is their craftiness of doing evil. With the palms of their hands, they capture lives and establish conquest with their feet. It is, therefore, safe to pray against witchcraft remnants. Though Jezebel was dead, her witchcraft remained in the land. The power of the Cross of Jesus can break their reasoning and annul their deceit. Then, they shall lose their grip on their prey. I, therefore, pray that the witchcraft remnants over your life be abolished by the power of His Cross.

Jesus demonstrated victory over the wicked world to set the captives free. When He paid the price to ransom us from sin and oppression, He was crucified in the place called Golgotha, the place of a skull (Matt. 27:33). I picture the cross lifted up and piercing through the "place of a skull"; He broke the skull. He also wore a crown of thorns on His head, pressing through His skull. The nails went through His feet and hands. His blood shed through His head (skull), hands, and feet destroyed the hold and claim of witchcraft. May we rest upon this victory and forever hush witchcraft attacks.

Conquering Witchcraft

Thank God for His grace upon me as a prophetic intercessor. Through many years of ministering deliverance to the captives, I have seen the forces of witchcraft bow to the lordship of Jesus, their works nullified and captives set free.

Witchcraft should not be feared, neither their activities, because it is part of the devil's devices that were defeated at the cross, when Jesus said, "It is finished!" (John 19:30). Through the death and resurrection of our Lord Jesus Christ, we have been equipped to walk in victory over all the works of the devil. Our spiritual weapons should never be ignored or underrated because they are "mighty through God to the pulling down of strong holds" (2 Cor. 10:4, KJV).

Applying the Cross of Jesus against a witchcraft attack is very valiant, because to them it is mockery, but to those who believe the perfect sacrifice at the Cross it is the power of God to deliver (1 Cor. 1:18). Remind them that the suffering and eternal sacrifice of our Lord Jesus Christ are not in vain over you. The power of the blood of Jesus is a deathblow to witchcraft. Their covens, gatherings, and weapons scatter at the persistent pleading of the blood of Jesus. While the blood of Jesus gives life to those who love and obey Him, the same brings terror and disaster to the works of darkness. The blood of Jesus is like lightning and thunder against witchcraft. Apply this and walk in victory.

I have also learned by experience how powerful the Word of God is in deliverance, especially against witchcraft attack. As destructive as their incantation can be, it cannot withstand the power of the Word of God.

A regular declaration of the Word of God brings victory over witchcraft activities. As the Word fills our heart, it empowers our spirit to bring wonderful results. In their strongholds many witches and wizards have confessed sudden lightning, thunder, whirlwind, and confused noises. All these happened when God's people—the redeemed and the sanctified—unceasingly proclaim God's eternal Word. They may try firing back but shall not have hold as we remain and abound in Him.

Mock Their Prophets

Witchcraft ridicules people because it is a counterfeit spirit that frustrates the hope of people. A witch or wizard is only fulfilled when things are not going well with others, though they sympathize with you. They abhor progress and success, so they cast the spell of bad luck on people to limit their chances of excelling. Purposeful disparagement weakens the morale of people to discourage good performance. When your good intention is hatefully laughed at, it is to devoid you of dignity and make you look down on yourself. So witches and wizards enjoy mocking others, but hate mockery.

Prophet Elijah demonstrated this when he had an open confrontation with the prophets of Baal and of the groves. The two sides—Elijah, the prophet of God, and the Baal prophets—agreed to offer sacrifices; "and the God that answereth by fire, let him be God" (1 Kings 18:24, KJV). Even all the people agreed to the contest, ready to watch the show. The Baal prophets started off, prepared their offering, "and called on the name of Baal from morning even until noon, saying, "O Baal, hear us. But there was no voice, nor any that answered. And they leaped upon the altar which was made" (1 Kings 18:26, KJV).

As Elijah the prophet of God, watched them, they cried out loud, cutting themselves "with knives and lancets, till the blood gushed out upon them" (v. 28, KJV). He resolved to mock them. "And it came to pass at noon, that Elijah mocked them, and said, Cry aloud: for he is a god; either he is talking, or he is pursuing, or he is in a journey, or peradventure he sleepeth, and must be awaked" (v. 27, KJV). I believe this mockery was not just to taunt them but had some prophetic interpretations. When he derided them to cry aloud, he twitted them about the activities of their gods saying: "talking," "pursuing," "in a journey," and "sleeps and must be awaked."

"Talking": The intent of idol worship is to communicate something to their worshipers. They may not talk but transmit demons to their victims, thus having mastery over them. This explains why people are slaves to idol worshiping. So Elijah mocked them and by so doing annulled evil transference. Transfer of evil takes place when people try to relate or talk to demonic entities; this subjects them to continuous afflictions until such covenants are renounced and broken. We can withdraw and cancel every way we have ever communicated with demons, ranging from communication with the dead, stargazing, palm reading, and so on. The blood of Jesus speaks better things (Heb. 12:24) than any other voice. We can apply this to silence any other voice in our lives.

"Pursuing": Can you answer these questions: "Why are people's thoughts overtaken by evil? Why do people feel being followed or monitored, even when nothing is around them? Did not Pharaoh, the king of Egypt, send his host against the people of Israel when they left the Promised Land? Indeed they pursued after them even unto the sea, but God drowned them. So Elijah understood the pursuit of evil and mocked them, implying that their pursuing strength was cut off. We also can speak against the pursuit of the enemies over our lives and cut off their strength. "The evil will bow before the good, And the wicked at the gates of the righteous" (Prov. 14:19).

"In a Journey": Even though they do not move, their spirits traffic and network. Distance is no barrier in the spirit. Long or short distance, a spirit can cover it easily. Demonic priests do send demons on errands—a trip taken to perform a specified task. Such are carried out with specific instructions, and directions are given as to how it must be done. Demons are afraid to go back to their master without carrying out the assignment, so they persist and keep attacking even when defeated. This explains why they don't give up, because they fear the wrath of their master and the ridicule of being demoted.

> Demons go into a death sleep at the voice of the blood of Jesus.

Demonic entities have been sent to people to invade homes, destroy careers, afflict health, and subject people to fear. After several unsuccessful attempts, they move aimlessly with intention to take vengeance on someone else. This they do to stir up provocation, to test the potency of their weapons, because oftentimes they are rendered ineffective after being used against the righteous. So they need to try it on someone else to see if it still works. This is why I always encourage God's people never to give up on God, even when things don't work out as expected. Many weapons of the wicked have become useless due to our prayers. Though weak on us, they are strong when applied to those not under the protective blood of Jesus. So Elijah mocked them by making it known that the errand imposed on their demons would not work. We also can taunt every evil assignment by terminating their strength and canceling their missions.

"Sleeps and must be awaked": Demonic operations vary; some are more active in the dark, others at day time. Some operate so well in the water, air, forest, desert, firmament (sky), the sun, the moon, and the stars. "You shall not be afraid of the terror by night, Nor of the arrow that flies by day, Nor of the pestilence that walks in darkness, Nor of the destruction that lays waste at noonday" (Ps. 91:5–6). Based on this passage of the Scripture, the terror takes hold of the night; fiery darts fill the day; while there is pestilence advancing in the dark and destruction at broad daylight that wastes lives. Believers in Christ Jesus can take charge rather than allowing the enemies to control the day, noon, and night. So Elijah mocked the inactiveness of the demons because the power of the Almighty God had put them into a death sleep.

This mockery hurt them so badly that they cried out loud all the more, but there was no voice, nor any movement. The Baal prophets thought shedding of their own blood would help awaken their gods but to no avail, so they cut themselves "till the blood gushed out upon them" (1 Kings 18:28, KJV). Their god shamed them and could not perform. May we also proclaim the power of the blood of Jesus as our eternal sacrifice because demons go into a death sleep at the voice of the blood of Jesus. I encourage you to never underestimate the greatness of the efficacious blood of Jesus.

Elijah sealed up the mockery by repairing the Lord's altar that was broken down. Our broken relationship with God must be repaired and true communication restored. Elijah gathered wood, cut the sacrifice, soaked it with water, and waited until the "time of the offering of the evening sacrifice" (v. 36, KJV) before calling on the God of Abraham, Isaac, and Israel. He did all these before the people in order to reconnect them back to God and to the worship of His name. God answered and fire fell. With a repentant heart, we can walk in boldness and be confident of the Holy Spirit to overcome all witchcraft attacks.

Freedom for Witchcraft Victims

Witchcraft has made so many people suffer in undeserved ways. Why would people suffer hardship and bad luck despite their hard work to attain excellent goals? The intent of the witchcraft attack is to make people feel like or actually live their lives as losers, unqualified for blessings and useless. To be a victor and not a victim, we need to recognize that witchcraft has mandates just like their father the devil—to steal, to kill, and to destroy (John 10:10). People's virtues have been stolen; whatever should profit them and make them great has been stolen, killed, and destroyed. But thank God for our redeemer Jesus Christ who has come that we might have life and that we might have it more abundantly (John 10:10).

Therefore, for the victims to become victors, the following witchcraft authoritative commands must be overcome:

1. This is a witchcraft saying to their victims: "Even if people know that they're under attack, it won't matter to them, and they would not be determined enough to be free."

Ignorance has plagued so many lives today, "lest Satan should take advantage of us; for we are not ignorant of his devices" (2 Cor. 2:11). It is not that we seek to know what witchcraft is all about, No! Rather, we seek to know the greatness of God, the Holy One of Israel. Our knowledge of God annuls the devices of the wicked. Those who are oppressed and afflicted, but not determined enough to overcome, end up in deep trouble. So many people start great, but soon give up and can't press through to victory. So, I ask you, are you determined well enough to wait upon the Lord until victory is attained? Like the woman with the issue of blood for twelve years who came from behind because she was determined to touch the hem of His garment—the crowd couldn't stop her. You also can come from behind, however far back you are, and become a victor.

2. This is another witchcraft saying: "If people choose to pray religious, a spirit would replace the actual divine encounter."

As good as it is to pray and get committed to God, people soon lose focus on God and are controlled by the tradition of men. This is a religious spirit and it kills. As powerful as prayer is, if not led and guided by the Holy Spirit with the right unction, it avails to nothing. But if we pray the will of God, as it is written in His Word, and not be hearers only, but doers of His Word, there is no power that can resist our prayer. "The earnest (heartfelt, continued) prayer of a righteous man makes tremendous power available [dynamic in its working]" (James 5:16, AMP).

3. Another important authoritative command of witchcraft is to yoke their victims with friends that are of the same foundational bondage.

If a community of ten thousand people are left to mingle freely with one another, within a few weeks, people will find their level. Those who are into drugs would easily identify themselves and flock together. Fraudulent people wouldn't take time to form their own group. The godly would perceive the aroma and link up. People will always find their level. This explains why you may be surrounded by people who can't offer any help, encouragement, or inspiration in time of trouble. You can prayerfully break free and be yoked with Christ Jesus to enjoy His peace and rest.

4. Here is the most important one: that he who puts you in bondage may not be strong enough to bring you out.

"Although our flesh is the same as that of our brethren and our children are as theirs, yet we are forced to sell our children as slaves; some of our daughters are already being thus sold, and we are powerless to redeem them, for others have our lands and vineyards" (Neh. 5:5, AMP). Truly, everyone, including powers, spirits, and personalities, are "powerless to redeem." Once the evil is done, it is not in their power to redeem or restore. Only the eternal blood of Jesus can repair the damages and reconcile us unto our heritage. May we learn to trust God always, at all times, and in all situations.

Chapter 5

BREAKING THROUGH OR BREAKING DOWN

THIS IS THE title I sought the face of the Lord for because of the multiple ways the word *breakthrough* is used. I have personally attended "breakthrough meetings," "breakthrough seminars," "breakthrough camping," "breakthrough revival," and "breakthrough crusades." I get excited about the meeting but return to what I was before. Then I decided I would seek God's face about the subject. The result of my divine encounter is what I am sharing now. Breakthrough is an act of overcoming or penetrating an obstacle or restriction, and ready to be at the offensive in penetrating what has held us bound. The word sounds like something sudden or quick despite the obstruction, yet advancing. The good thing about it is, when achieved it permits further progress.

> Challenges may come, but maintaining a winner's attitude while overcoming the most difficult circumstances is a way to break through.

In seeking God's face, the Spirit of God asked me questions when I was demanding answers to my problems. The first question was, "When problems refuse to go and obstacles prevent you from achieving success, how do you respond?" My responses are: Sometimes I turn back and sometimes I wait or stop. Long waiting without action or not knowing what to do may result in frustration, which may end up in defeat. In rare times, I allowed the obstacle to change my course, which reduced the chances of success. My final response was that I sometimes summon courage and confront to overcome.

Then the Spirit of God began to deal with me further, and I understood that the same sun that hardens the clay melts wax. We may all be subject to the same opportunities, but while some fail others succeed; some have breakthroughs while others break down. Moses sent twelve spies to the Promised Land. They all were given the same instruction (Num. 13:17–20). They all returned from the search after forty days and came back with the fruit of the land. Caleb was excited to go up and take the land along with Joshua, but others were not willing because they counted themselves "not able." They broke down while Joshua and Caleb were ready to break through despite the giants in the land. Same opportunity, same exposure, but not the same outcome.

Jacob and Esau were born of the same parents, and can be regarded as twins. They were raised up together, but Jacob had his breakthrough of blessing while Esau had a breakdown (Gen. 25:24–26).

When Joseph was imprisoned in Egypt along with the chief butler and chief baker of Pharaoh, they both had dreams that they shared with Joseph for interpretation (Gen. 40). They both served Pharaoh and were imprisoned together, yet one had a breakthrough while the other broke down. So we see people of the same background and the same carrier opportunities and exposure; while some fail others succeed. The difference between those who have breakthroughs and those who break down is that while those who break down fear that they may fail, those who break through fear rather that they might never succeed if they do not dare to try. Those who break down fear that someone may laugh at their mistakes while breakthrough people see laughter as an envious attack to be ignored. Those who break through discover their strength in the midst of adversity, but those who break down fear oppositions and accusations. Challenges may come, but maintaining a winner's attitude while overcoming the most difficult circumstances is a way to break through. When you break down, it doesn't mean life is over or you are a fool or inferior, rather it does mean you have to do something different and might have to learn some lessons to correct your ways.

Pass Through It or Take It Away

Everyone prays not to have problems, but this seems impracticable because it is part of life. And when we do have a problem, most people's desire is for God to take it away. We seek for solutions, pray for answers, but oftentimes the problem persists. This keeps us wondering if God still loves us or still answers prayers. No one wants problems to last long without a way out or a solution to end the problem. We cannot ignore it, neither can we run away from it; it will pursue us wherever we go. Is there hope for us in the way we handle problems? I would like to be honest with the readers of this book; you either go through the problem or it is taken away. If you try hard to get rid of it, and it is not going away, you might have to go through it. And if you have to go through it, be it known to you that you cannot jump steps. Also there might be lessons to learn; if you refuse to get the lesson and experience for each stage of the problem, repetition is guaranteed. This fortifies you well enough to confront any future problem.

Jesus, the Son of God made manifest in the flesh, was faced with two options when confronted with His greatest trial—abandon the cross or face it. He earnestly prayed to God because He never wanted to yield to the weakness of the flesh.

> He went a little farther and fell on His face, and prayed, saying, "O My Father, if it is possible, let this cup pass from Me; nevertheless, not as I will, but as You will."…Again, a second time, He went away and prayed, saying, "O My Father, if this cup cannot pass away from Me unless I drink it, Your will be done."
>
> —MATTHEW 26:39, 42

He desired that it could be taken away and He would not have to pass through it because the agony and torture of death were unbearable. As wonderful as God's love was for Him, He made Jesus pass through it, never taking it away. David, the shepherd and king of Israel, said, "Yea, though I walk through the valley of the shadow of death, I will fear no evil; For You are with me; Your rod and Your staff, they comfort me" (Ps. 23:4). Even though it was a valley full of death traps, he fearlessly walked through it because God was with him. My understanding used to be that if God is with me, He will not let me walk through such a deadly valley. He will make another route. Yes, of course, He's a way maker, but His will must be accomplished. I just have to trust Him. If He permits it, there must be reasons beyond my understanding. When David walked it through, he became a better man to lead the people of God.

Apostle Paul wrestled with a situation he referred to as a "thorn in the flesh, the messenger of Satan" (2 Cor. 12:7, KJV). This was a great torment for him, and he sought the face of God three times to take it away from him; but the divine response was, "My grace is sufficient for thee: for my strength is made perfect in weakness" (2 Cor. 12:9, KJV). The reason God allowed it was to keep him from exalting self. Here was a man who loved God and was dedicated to His work, but God permitted him to go through it. Does God still love him? Absolutely! Will God still use him to help others? Yes, even mightily.

Job in the Bible can be considered a man who experienced breakthrough and also had a breakdown; his breakdown was but for a moment, and he broke through again. I have seen people rise and fall, and never rise again. I have also seen people who were down never rise, and those who rise no matter what comes their way. Job was a man noted for multiple afflictions, great loss, and repeated tragedies. He was a man who sought God in his deep trials; but as though God was afar, difficult to appease, and impossible to reach. He was mocked by friends and abandoned by relatives. He was a godly man who led his family in the way of the Lord, and a man whom God could boast of as being upright and perfect (Job 1:8). He likened his multiple afflictions to being stripped of God's glory and his crown taken from his head (19:9). The devil felt that if anyone is a victim of a series of trials, they will abandon faith; but this was not true with Job. Even today, the righteous are going through multiple trials; at such times God seems to be unreachable, and peace becomes the hardest thing to ever imagine.

> I have learned not to despise any man's problem, because what is no problem to me might be a worse experience to another.

The hardest part for Job was when his wife counseled him, "Curse God and die" (2:9). He was visited by friends whom he termed "miserable comforters" (16:1–2). They were indeed troublesome in their approach, which was never helpful to Job. Eliphaz's approach was based on human experience, while Bildad focused on human tradition, and Zophar on human merit. Elihu's concern was different, and he charged Job with wickedness and folly. Human experience, however good, may not provide enough evidence to condemn anyone because God's ways are not our ways. Beliefs and customs may not apply to every trial, while judging based on ability and achievements may be a wrong way to go.

How was Job able to break through despite his breakdown? This is a great lesson for us who desire nothing but breakthrough. He began by acknowledging the greatness of his past, the humiliation of his present, and desiring God to answer him. When our past cannot help us and neither can our present, then it is time to turn it all to God who can make our future better. I learned from Job's life how to handle breakdowns: never justify myself, rather justify God; do not to speak rashly; and never rebel against sovereign justice. He overcame at last. He was restored to honor and dignity. However long affliction may last, we can surely outlast it with shouts of triumph. "Many are the afflictions of the righteous, But the LORD delivers him out of them all. He guards all his bones; Not one of them is broken" (Ps. 34:19–20).

Confronting the Adamant

I love rocks, and I enjoy the view. I had a tour of Northern Ontario, Canada, and observed that the rocky landscape along with the deep green forests and shimmering lakes are the images that define northwestern Ontario. Rocks vary in sizes, shapes, and hardness. As hard as rock is, flint is harder, and adamant is another type, harder than flint. If problems are likened to the hardness of rocks, I perceive some are harder than others. No problem, however easy we think it is, is solved without mind troubling. I have learned not to despise any man's problem, because what is no problem to me might be a worse experience to another. Therefore, regarding it with utter contempt could be an unacceptable behavior.

Rocks have their own usefulness. We can make implements of war from flint, it produces sparks when struck against steel, and it can be used for cutting. Adamant is impenetrable in its hardness and is an extremely hard substance. If problems are likened to rock, flint, or adamant, different approaches will be required for a solution. There might be delays or opposition, but a flint-like problem cuts deep into several areas of life. Sparks consume our strength so that moving toward achieving goals will almost be impossible. On the other hand, an adamant-like problem is like being confronted with equally unpleasant alternatives and few or no opportunities to evade or circumvent them. These are stubbornly unyielding situations with resistance to pressure, and there is no clue of a solution. The way out is unthinkable and unworkable, and choices set before us are not good enough.

I meditated deeply on this and asked God how to overcome flint-like and adamant-like problems. God's word to prophet Ezekiel came alive in me: "Behold, I have made your face strong against their faces, and your forehead strong against their foreheads. Like adamant stone, harder than flint, I have made your forehead; do not be afraid of them, nor be dismayed at their looks, though they are a rebellious house" (Ezek. 3:8–9). God equipped the prophet for the hard work before him. He would have to be bold, hard, stubborn, and unyielding to be able to cope with these hard and stiff-hearted people. This was so, so as to be able to cut the hard hearts to the core. We should never be overwhelmed by thoughts of impossibilities, rather we should reflect on the greatness of God.

I take consolation in the fact that Jesus is the Rock, harder than flint or adamant. "And all drank the same spiritual drink. For they drank of that spiritual Rock that followed them, and that Rock was Christ" (1 Cor. 10:4). He is the Rock of our salvation: "He only is my rock and my salvation; He is my defense; I shall not be moved. In God is my salvation and my glory; The rock of my strength, And my refuge, is in God. Trust in Him at all times, you people; Pour out your heart before Him; God is a refuge for us" (Ps. 62:6–8). Like prophet Ezekiel, God can fortify us so much with strength to be stronger than any problem or situation that confronts us. Rather than breaking down we can break through because other rocks break in pieces before our Rock.

Breaking Down?

How we perceive a problem and the way we express it will determine the way out. I do ask myself some mind-probing questions about how I qualify problems. When I get into trouble, what do I relate it to? Some people will say, "I'm going through hell," or, "It is like I'm being imprisoned." Others consider a problem to be a "mountain," "valley," "storm," or "wind that passed away." The psalmist considered problems to be "sink in deep mire," "deep waters," and "floods" (Ps. 69:2; 14–15).

Whatever way is classified, it is a need yearning for a solution. I like to consider a breakdown as a ditch in the valley. The valley can be deep enough, but the valley full of ditches is an indication of deep issues to be resolved. This was the prophetic order given by prophet Elisha: "And he said, 'Thus says the LORD: "Make this valley full of ditches"'" (2 Kings 3:16). Ditches in the valley? Yes it is a valley but not deep enough. Several years ago, the Lord spoke to me saying, "Make more room in your valley, for I will turn your valley state to victory ground." This bothered me for a few days, saying how much room I could make in this valley state! I prayed about it and discovered that it is possible to need God and not have enough room for Him. When God occupies our valleys and fills it with His fullness, it will not be deep enough to contain His glory. Yours could be a void, a need, low self-image, or deep wounds; the prophetic fulfillment is: "For thus says the LORD: 'You shall not see wind, nor shall you see rain; yet that valley shall be filled with water, so that you, your cattle, and your animals may drink'" (v. 17). However complicated the matter may be, it is "but a light thing in the sight of the LORD" (v. 18, KJV). There was no sign of rain, flood, or wind, but both valley and ditches were filled with water. Oh, for a generation that seeks for signs! There was no outward demonstration; the solution came quickly. Even though I personally enjoy seeing things shaking and stirred up, I have learned by experience that it may not always be by noise, shaking, jittering, or unnecessary quietness that bring miracles. Rather it is by God's determinate will and purpose. His will and purpose are far different from ours. He chooses what pleases Him. The day brought sunlight shining upon the water and becoming red as blood in the sight of Moabites (v. 22). The water was to quench their thirst and meet their needs. God's glory shone upon the water. The glory of God filled the valley and the ditches, and it became a trap to the enemies. What refreshes us when incubated in glory can bring the destruction of our adversaries. So, seek for God's glory to fill your valley, and your needs shall be met while joy is restored.

Breaking Through—How?

I am grateful to God Almighty on how He has helped me to achieve breakthrough in various aspect of lives. The way breakthrough comes is not similar in each situation. Of course, it differs, but I am putting the sum of my experiences together on how I overcame in different areas of life. I pray the following will be of great help to you:

Holy Spirit conviction

This is a great way to start, as the Holy Spirit brings to our awareness areas we need to work on. If we allow Him, He encourages us not to lose hope. It all begins by asking, presenting the need, and asking Him to search out and reveal the way forward.

> Likewise the Spirit also helps in our weaknesses. For we do not know
> what we should pray for as we ought, but the Spirit Himself makes
> intercession for us with groanings which cannot be uttered. Now He
> who searches the hearts knows what the mind of the Spirit is, because
> He makes intercession for the saints according to the will of God.
>
> —Romans 8:26–27

Whatever is hidden to us, it is not so with the Holy Spirit. He can
reveal and strengthen to overcome.

Getting rid of wilderness mentality

The children of Israel left Egypt, but they had to pass through the
wilderness. It is so unfortunate that so many people perished in the wilderness and never made it to the Promised Land. To them, the wilderness was like a trap; they couldn't return to Egypt, even though they
attempted it, but it was impossible because there was the Red Sea to cross
and any other way was a war zone, occupied by other nations. Neither
could they move forward to the Promised Land because giants abounded
in the land. So they were trapped in the wilderness. So are we also today;
the world cannot absorb us, and we seem not to know the way forward.
Therefore, the wilderness mentality is to always look back to our years
of captivity and never have a vision of the Promised Land. Even though
they witnessed God's miracles, signs, and wonders, they were unappre-
ciative and despised divine provision; so they wandered in the wilderness until they perished. Wilderness mentality makes us go through life
in circles, never reaching our promised land.

How do I know I have wilderness mentality? I can tell based on experience that it is when I am becoming godless in thinking with vain imaginations; these are signs to watch out for. Also it is when I am fearful of
the past, having no confidence about the future and discouraged about
the present. Then I know I have to shake off the dust of the wilderness. I
wouldn't allow it to stick to me for too long, or else I am trapped.

How do we break free from wilderness mentality? I strongly believe
that our knowledge of God is a mighty weapon. I carefully studied the "I
know" of some individuals in the Bible and discovered that it was a key
to their deliverances. What we know saves us from ignorance:

Job:

- "What you know, I also know; I am not inferior to you" (Job 13:2). Hence, through knowledge he broke the bondage of inferiority.

- "See now, I have prepared my case, I know that I shall be vindicated" (v. 18). Applying what he knew established justice.

- "For I know that my Redeemer lives, And He shall stand at last on the earth" (19:25). His knowledge about the Redeemer gave him the assurance of victory and recovery of lost heritage.

- "I know that You can do everything, And that no purpose of Yours can be withheld from You" (42:2). Knowing God can do everything, however hard or difficult, refreshes the soul and breaks the wilderness mentality.

The Psalmists:

- "By this I know that You are well pleased with me, Because my enemy does not triumph over me" (Ps. 41:11). Satisfying divine pleasure is a key to victory.

- "When I cry out to You, Then my enemies will turn back; This I know, because God is for me" (56:9). Knowing that God is for you terrifies the enemies. Moreover, when you cry to Him, the wicked flee.

- "For I know that the LORD is great, And our Lord is above all gods" (135:5). Knowing God's greatness empowers your soul.

Jesus:

- "Jesus answered and said to them, "Even if I bear witness of Myself, My witness is true, for I know where I came from and where I am going; but you do not know where I

come from and where I am going" (John 8:14). Jesus knew
His purpose, and He could not be distracted, neither could
He abandon it; but He pursued it with all His might.

Apostle Paul:

- "For this reason I also suffer these things; nevertheless I
  am not ashamed, for I know whom I have believed and am
  persuaded that He is able to keep what I have committed
  to Him until that Day" (2 Tim. 1:12). Knowing whom you
  believe takes away shame to establish unwavering faith of
  bringing to pass what you have trusted Him for.

- "And we know that all things work together for good to
  those who love God, to those who are the called according
  to His purpose" (Rom. 8:28). Ask yourself: Do I love God?
  Am I called according to His purpose, even the eternal
  purpose of salvation? Then all things will surely work for
  your good.

What we know of God makes us celebrate His goodness and greatness;
we can live each moment of our lives with gratitude because "knowledge
is power." I counsel that you desire to know more about God and pursue
His presence and He will reveal Himself to you. His knowledge destroys
wilderness mentality.

Living by faith
No one can break through without faith. It takes faith to confront
your problem. Faith is needed to despise the shame of failure and to keep
holding on to God with thanksgiving and praise. Faith assures success.
It is both a defensive and an offensive weapon. We are justified by faith
(Rom. 5:1), and without it we cannot please God (Heb. 11:6). Faith in God
is not the imagination or the wishing of things, rather it is the conviction of the reality. "Now faith means that we have full confidence in the
things we hope for, it means being certain of things we cannot see" (Heb.
11:1, PHILLIPS).

Pressing unto completion

Breakthrough is having all that is needed to finish well. Contrary to this, so many people become wary and can't hold to the end. "Finishing is better than starting. Patience is better than pride" (Eccles. 7:8, NLT). I also love this: "Endings are better than beginnings. Sticking to it is better than standing out" (v. 8, THE MESSAGE). I am intrigued by nameless stories of those who started well and finished well. One of my favorites was Zerubbabel, the governor of Judah, "The hands of Zerubbabel Have laid the foundation of this temple; His hands shall also finish it. Then you will know That the LORD of hosts has sent Me to you" (Zech. 4:9). Jesus came to do His Father's will and completed it: "Jesus said to them, 'My food is to do the will of Him who sent Me, and to finish His work'" (John 4:34). And surely He did.

> As we rejoice seeing the beginning of a thing, we should not give up when challenges arise but rather be certain, pressing on until there is a flourishing finish.

I have learned by experience never to despise days of new beginnings (Zech. 4:10), when things look rough as though there is no future in it. Be it known to you that the formative stage of a life, as crucial as it is, is always not impressive. As we rejoice seeing the beginning of a thing, we should not give up when challenges arise but rather be certain, pressing on until there is a flourishing finish. Move to each step having in mind your glorious ending. "Being confident of this very thing, that He who has begun a good work in you will complete it until the day of Jesus Christ" (Phil. 1:6).

Chapter 6

SELF-DELIVERANCE

I HAVE CONQUERED AN empire but I have not been able to conquer myself."[1] This was the saying of Peter the Great, the Russian czar who transformed Russia from an isolated agricultural society into an empire on par with European powers. Victory is not total until the internal battles are won. As terrible as external battles could be, the war within, struggling with self, is fiercer. Someone may appear peaceful, but inwardly he or she is struggling with thoughts of defeat, dreadful imaginations, fear of tomorrow, and fear of the unknown. It is possible to study others and read them like letters, but never to understand oneself. Stephen R. Covey said, "Private victories precede public victories. You can't invert that process any more than you can harvest a crop before you plant it."[2] This is so true because real victory is self-conquest. Plato said, "Self conquest is the greatest of victories."[3]

> But now, it is no longer I who do it, but sin that dwells in me. For I know that in me (that is, in my flesh) nothing good dwells; for to will is present with me, but how to perform what is good I do not find. For the good that I will to do, I do not do; but the evil I will not to do, that I practice. Now if I do what I will not to do, it is no longer I who do it, but sin that dwells in me. I find then a law, that evil is present with me, the one who wills to do good. For I delight in the law of God according to the inward man. But I see another law in my members, warring against the law of my mind, and bringing me into captivity to the law of sin which is in my members. O wretched man that I am! Who will deliver me from this body of death? I thank God—through Jesus Christ our Lord! So then, with the mind I myself serve the law of God, but with the flesh the law of sin.
>
> —ROMANS 7:17–25

In this short passage, "I" was mentioned multiple times, indicating Paul's struggle with self until victory through the Holy Spirit. Then he proclaimed, "There is therefore now no condemnation to those who are in Christ Jesus, who do not walk according to the flesh, but according to the Spirit" (8:1).

Our struggle with the flesh may result in: self-abasement, self-condemnation, self-deception, self-justification, self-pity, self-will, self-centeredness, and self-righteousness.

- Self-abasement: degradation or humiliation of oneself, especially because of feelings of guilt or inferiority

- Self-condemnation: condemnation of one's self by one's own judgment

- Self-deception: the act of deceiving oneself or the state of being deceived by oneself

- Self-justification: showing the need to justify our actions and decisions, especially the wrong ones

- Self-pity: a feeling of sorrow (often self-indulgent) over your own sufferings. Comparing it to boasting, while boasting is the response of pride to success, self-pity is the response of pride to suffering. "Boasting is the voice of pride in the heart of the strong. Self-pity is the voice of pride in the heart of the weak."4

- Self-will: willfulness, especially in satisfying one's own desires or adhering to one's own opinions. Such a one may be habitually disposed to disobedience and opposition.

- Self-centeredness: engrossing in oneself and one's own affairs. Such a person is said to be selfish and absorbed in his or her own interests or thoughts.

- Self-righteous: righteous in one's own esteem, proving "holier than thou" and superior, whereas such a one is invalid before God

There are lots of unhealed memories that so many people are struggling with; in trying to suppress them, flashbacks of hurtful events occur and this usually results in even greater fear of the memories. It has resulted in self-hate and apportioning blame on everyone around them, to the point that when people try to determine the root of their problems, they point to external pressures: my spouse is uncooperative, my job is stressful, my children are rebellious, my parents neglected me, my friends don't know how to relate to me, my boss is intimidating, and many more.

It is sad to know that problems that appear simple may have deep-rooted issues. And unless they are treated from the root, the trouble continues. Who has wounds without a source? Some of the past injury we have had may be from when our understanding of life and its twists and turns had not yet developed. These wounds can become infected if not well treated, and worse still, people feel they are incurable. I figured out that inflicted wounds relating to our emotions and mind seem incurable when our security is not first in God, but in what people think of us. Allowing this to control us may run down our feelings.

> **Victory is not total until the internal battles are won.**

"Why is my pain perpetual And my wound incurable, Which refuses to be healed? Will You surely be to me like an unreliable stream, As waters that fail?" (Jer. 15:18). Untreated wounds may rob us of our sense of security and values—feelings of worthlessness, inadequacy, shame, guilt, fear, rejection, anger, resentment, bitterness, and even addictions. Nonetheless, deep wounds require deep healings. When attacked from within, we are weak to confront life issues, and this may affect not only us, but also the people around us. What we hear, see, taste, feel, think, imagine, or partake in could affect us to the degree of being wounded. Nehemiah served under King Artaxerxes and heard the news about the ruins of the walls of Jerusalem; he wept and mourned until the king noticed it. "Therefore the king said to me, 'Why is your face sad, since you are not sick? This is nothing but sorrow of heart.' So I became dreadfully afraid" (Neh. 2:2). Oftentimes, when wounded or sorrowful, we feel no one can detect it until it starts affecting our work and people around us. Nehemiah received help because he had first communed with God about the matter before reasoning out with men.

Elijah the prophet, a man greatly used by God, when threatened by Jezebel made a remark and requested that he might die: "It is enough! Now, LORD, take my life, for I am no better than my fathers" (1 Kings 19:4). How many of Elijah's forefathers were fed by ravens or raised the dead? Which of them sealed up the heaven that it might not rain and later prayed rain to come forth? Who among them called down fire? Yet he said, "I am no better than my fathers." This is what happens to us when persistent waves of frustration hit us and we become depressed and consider ourselves worthless. I would like to ask, have you ever come so low as to wish yourself dead? Seeing no reason to live? Hopeless about tomorrow? Even if everyone has failed you, including yourself, you can count on God. He knows you to the thinnest fiber and can cure you. "He heals the brokenhearted And binds up their wounds" (Ps. 147:3). "'For I will restore health to you And heal you of your wounds,' says the LORD, 'Because they called you an outcast saying: "This is Zion; No one seeks her"'" (Jer. 30:17).

Raising children is always a great task. Children are very playful without restraint and sometimes get injured. They develop a sensitive area around the wound and guard it so it won't hurt them. So are offenses and rejection. Wounds can be simple or complex, superficial or deep, accidental or intentional, self-inflicted or inflicted by friends or enemies. Wounds by friends are more painful. However defensive we are, we pay less attention, hence they stab when least expected. "And one will say to him, 'What are these wounds between your arms?' Then he will answer, 'Those with which I was wounded in the house of my friends'" (Zech. 13:6).

May I probe a little deeper with these questions? Do you take remarks (that others would laugh at) personally, seeing such as an insult or slight? Do you require special invitation or encouragement to participate in things that others would just join in? Do you see others in the light of the person who hurts you? That is, if hurt by a man, then all men are "pigs." If hurt by a woman, then all women are bad. If hurt by a child or someone younger, then all youths are rebellious; and if hurt by authority figures (boss, father, etc.), then all authority figures are seen as threats. All unhealed memories, flashbacks, dreadful thoughts, and imaginations can be overcome through intense studying, meditating, and confessing the Word of God. I am a living witness of how efficacious the Word of God is in calming a soul when overwhelmed by storms. Engaging our mind with the Word of God can empty us of the strongholds' hurts and

offenses it has cost us. Continuous in-depth study of God's Word elimi-
nates our fears and builds our trust in the unfailing grace of God. This
should not be just reading to quiet our conscience or being religious about
it, rather it is allowing the holy fire of His presence to devour doubts and
melt our fears. Intense study of God's Word releases the sword of the
Spirit to cut asunder the ties that bind us. More so, the unfailing love of
God is revealed on every page of the Scriptures as we study with a teach-
able spirit—readiness and willingness to be taught—for this is profitable
in all things.

> For the Word that God speaks is alive and full of power [making it
> active, operative, energizing, and effective]; it is sharper than any two-
> edged sword, penetrating to the dividing line of the breath of life (soul)
> and [the immortal] spirit, and of joints and marrow [of the deepest
> parts of our nature], exposing and shifting and analyzing and judging
> the very thoughts and purposes of the heart.
> —HEBREWS 4:12, AMP

However deep the wounds, hurts, and offenses, the power of God's
Word can identify them and root them out. You can begin the process
now; when you stumble or cannot keep your commitment, do not let that
discourage you, rather continue from where you fell. His Word is truth
(John 17:17). Every other thing around you may be false and unreal, but
the Word of God is proved and well tested to be eternally true and secure.
God's Word restores confidence to the weary and strength to the weak.

> Let the Word [spoken by] Christ (the Messiah) have its home [in your
> hearts and minds] and dwell in you in [all its] richness, as you teach
> and admonish and train one another in all insight and intelligence and
> wisdom [in spiritual things, and as you sing] psalms and hymns and
> spiritual songs, making melody to God with [His] grace in your hearts.
> —COLOSSIANS 3:16, AMP

Breaking the Circuit

Untreated wounds make people go through their lives in circuit—a
journey that ends where it began or repeats itself. Every effort to turn
things around may not work out until deep-rooted healings are accomplished. We know the healing process has begun when we can look back

on things that hurt us with gratitude as we consider the scars as lessons preparing us for a better tomorrow and to help those who have suffered the same. Else, this may prevent us from arising or even expose our weaknesses regardless of the position we attain.

Jesus had a great reputation of being called the "Man of Galilee." I often wonder why. Galilee by interpretation means "circuit." Many times people have divided opinion about Jesus, even today, but on one of those occasions the Pharisees remarked, "They answered and said to him, "Are you also from Galilee? Search and look, for no prophet has arisen out of Galilee." And everyone went to his own house" (John 7:52–53). Why did people depart without giving answer to the charge: "Search and look, for out of Galilee arises no prophet." The Pharisees challenged those who wanted to search, investigate, study closely, observe, and inquire into details—checking into thoroughly and ignoring nothing, that prophets never arise from Galilee. I love this translation: "They answered him, Are you too from Galilee? Search [the Scriptures yourself], and you will see that no prophet comes (will arise to prominence) from Galilee. And they went [back], each to his own house" (John 7:52–53, AMP). The trouble, therefore, is that they do not rise to prominence—fame, prestige, renown, distinction, or being outstanding. What is it about Galilee that made people never arise or be exalted with honor or recognized in importance?

Galilee means "circuit"—a journey that ends where it began (repeats itself). So, it doesn't matter the measure of giftedness, which may look like things are working out, but such a one will always get back to where he or she started. It may look as though it is getting better, but soon they come back to the degrading position. The Pharisees were so sure of what they were saying, and even the people knew that about Galilee. During Jesus' time, the province of Galilee was comprised of these tribes: Issachar, Zebulun, Asher, and Naphtali, which by interpretation are Issachar ("reward"), Zebulun ("dwelling"), Asher ("happy"), and Naphtali ("wrestling"). I may simply say the province of Galilee is comprised of "reward," "dwelling," "happy," and "wrestling." I believe that everyone wants to be rewarded for their labor and dwell in blessings with great happiness, but many have to wrestle for it. Does this not explain the lifestyle of many: having to wrestle before getting rewards of their labor? Some find it hard to dwell or be established in anything good; hence, they are not happy.

For these reasons, Jesus became the Man of Galilee by performing His first miracle of turning water into wine in Cana of Galilee (John 2:1–11). He also performed His last miracle at the Sea of Galilee (John 21). He called His first set of disciples in Galilee (Matthew 4:18–20). Searching through the Scriptures, I can recall thirty-three notable miracles in the New Testament performed by Jesus, out of which twenty-five were done within the province of Galilee, equating to 75 percent. Jesus also expressed most kingdom principles in parables; and out of thirty-two parables, nineteen were spoken in Galilee, equating to 59 percent. After being tempted by the devil, "Then Jesus returned in the power of the Spirit to Galilee, and news of Him went out through all the surrounding region" (Luke 4:14). Truly, the right place to go after overcoming the devil and his temptations was to proceed with the "power of the Spirit" into Galilee (the circuit). His fame spread after breaking the circuit. Jesus also predicted His death and what to do thereafter, "But after I have been raised, I will go before you to Galilee" (Mark 14:28). With His power of resurrection, He proceeded to break the circuit.

Even though no prophet arose to prominence in Galilee, Jesus had to become the Man of Galilee to break the circuit. Surely, He rose to prominence; His fame went abroad, even to this day. What held others bound, preventing them from arising and shining, could not hold Him; He prevailed over them. In Galilee, miracles were wrought and the kingdom of God was proclaimed. Contrary to their beliefs, He arose to defile the ancient strongholds and gain victory over all. In like manner, we also can break free from the circuit of never arising and not being rewarded of our labor. Through the "power of the Spirit" we can confront our own Galilee (circuit) and dwell in blessings. The good news is that Jesus had promised to "go before" us into Galilee. Whatever circuit or repeated journey of loss, failure, and defeat, He has gone before us to wrought miracles and establish His kingdom. So Jesus became the man of Galilee as an example for those who are held in circuits and cannot break forth. He did all these that we also might follow His steps: "For to this you were called, because Christ also suffered for us, leaving us an example, that you should follow His steps" (1 Pet. 2:21).

Deliverance of the Head

As hands are to hold, feet are to walk. The head is the seat of the brain, eyes, ears, nose, and jaws. It is not incidental that all the sensory organs are present in the head: eyes for sight, ears for hearing, tongue for tasting, nose for smelling, and skin for touching. No other part of the body consists of all the sense organs as the head does. It is not uncommon to see people whose legs are amputated or hands are cut off, but it is impossible to see a headless human being walking around. A headless being is considered dead. I, therefore, conclude that our head is the symbol of our life.

When David confronted Goliath, he targeted his head by prophesying against it, stoning it, cutting it off, and bringing it to Saul (1 Sam. 17:46–51). When God's judgment came upon the Philistine god Dagon, the head and palms were cut off (2 Sam. 4:12). The children who mocked Elijah spoke against his head, "Go up, you baldhead!" (2 Kings 2:23). The ministry of John the Baptist, the forerunner of Jesus, was terminated as a girl demanded for his head after a seductive dance and an oath by the king to give whatever she asked: "Give me John the Baptist's head here on a platter" (Matt. 14:7).

The Psalmist proclaimed, "You have caused men to ride over our heads; We went through fire and through water; But You brought us out to rich fulfillment" (Ps. 66:12). Truly when people rule over us through oppression and manipulative control, it is like riding over our heads. I will not forget an early morning call I received from a sister in the church to pray for her son. Her son woke her up at about five o'clock in the morning, screaming aloud, "Mummy, wake up and pray for me." This boy, a high school student, had been complaining about a headache for three days, but this time, as he slept, he had a nightmare about someone who fiercely approached him, demanding, "Get me a seat." As he was getting him a seat, the man said, "Never mind, this is good enough," and he sat on his head, taking his head to be a seat. This boy cried, "This is not a seat," and the man replied, "This is a better seat." He struggled to push him away but couldn't until he shouted "Jesus" and he woke up. One thing he remembered while struggling with the man was his remark: "You are trying to put off the load we laid on you." This explained the source of his continuous headache—a load on his head, even though he was carrying no physical load. Why the head? The head wears the crown, and whoever wears the crown reigns.

The human head consists of the braincase and the face. This braincase is the control center of our being and the seat of faculty of intelligence and reason. Within the complexity of the brain is the ability to act purposefully, think rationally, and deal effectively with situations. All that was needed to drive King Nebuchadnezzar from among men and to dwell with beasts of the field and to eat grass as oxen was to withdraw his reasoning. "After this time had passed I, Nebuchadnezzar, looked up to heaven. My sanity returned, and I praised and worshiped the Most High and honored the one who lives forever. His rule is everlasting, and his kingdom is eternal" (Dan. 4:34, ESV). So, God withdrew his sanity—soundness, rationality, and reasonableness—until he learned to honor God. Therefore, we can deduce that a little attack on a human's head can make even kings operate like animals. No wonder the psalmist cried out in protection of his head: "O GOD the Lord, the strength of my salvation, You have covered my head in the day of battle" (Ps. 140:7).

How about the face? For humans, the head and particularly the face are the main distinguishing features between people. The following has a lot to say about faces: a man covering the face of another could be a sign of doom, as if he were dead already. Whereas, turning away the face could be a sign of rejection. Hardening of face could be hardening self against mercy. Being afraid of a face is to be afraid of the person himself. Hiding the face is to withdraw favor. So, different expressions on our faces may reveal the state of our hearts. Don't tears run down our faces when we are emotionally distraught, and we laugh when we are happy? When Moses encountered God, the skin of his face shone, and people could not behold his face (Exod. 34:29–31). As we behold God's glory, it reflects on our faces and transforms our hearts; His presence fills us. In some tradition, they spread their hands to receive blessings when being prayed upon, and they rub their hands on the face after prayers. I am not saying this to establish it as a doctrine or condemn them, but I ask myself, why the face? After all, the power of prayer coupled with your faith can penetrate to the innermost being. Also tribal marks are put mostly on the face for cultural and tribal identity. Such marks cannot be done without contact with blood, "for the life of all flesh is its blood" (Lev. 17:14). Could this be a blood covenant connecting to the foundational power?

> He bowed his head unto death that ours might be raised unto life.

When Jesus was paying the eternal price to redeem mankind, they spat on His face and covered His face (Mark 14:65). They smote Him on the head (Matt. 27:30). Worse still, they put upon Him "a crown of thorns" as mockery (Matt. 27:29). Yet, when man sinned, the ground was cursed for our sakes, and the consequence was to bring "thorns and thistles" (Gen. 3:17–18). So, to break the curse, Jesus had to wear thorns. Surely, blood gushed out, covering His face, dripping down to the ground along with the blood from His hands, feet, and sides, and from multiple beatings. This was for the redemption of our souls. He bowed His head and submitted to death that we might live. Oh! What a love. So, it does not matter the curse on our heads and shame on our faces; Jesus paid the price that we might be free. Jesus wore the crown of thorns that we may wear the crown of glory; His face was marred that ours may reflect His glory. He was rejected and forsaken by the Father as He cried out on the cross saying, "My God my God, why have You forsaken me?" (Matt. 27:46). His hands were stretched out and nailed that we may always be welcomed into the throne room of grace. Can you trust Him? He bowed his head unto death that ours might be raised unto life. We can dedicate our senses, intelligence, and our will unto Him to bring glory to God.

Converting Scars to Stars

I was privileged to attend a leadership seminar in Colorado Spring in 2004; and one of the guest speakers began by saying, "Welcome to the human race! Are you hurting or wounded? Then you're truly human. Hurts are a normal and natural way to know that you're still human." The audience reacted to this differently, but as the teaching progressed, we all agreed that hurts and offenses are mostly unavoidable in life. We are in a world where people are unreasonable, illogical, and self-centered. You are good as long as people are benefiting, but when things change, they turn around. Those whom you help today may rise against you tomorrow. Your success attracts friends that have not been proved, and some may turn out to be false; but the true friends stick with you to go through the rough times together—you are fortunate if you have true friends.

Scars are marks left after the healing of wounds or sores. The trouble with people is that the process of healing of wounds is not complete. A lingering sign of damage or injury, either mentally or physically, could create nightmares, anxieties, and other enduring scars. Some scars can be painful or itchy and most times remain within the original wound site. This may explain why it is hard to forget and forgive the cause of the wounds, especially when scars develop into tumor-like growths which extend beyond the wound's limits.

A lady came to my office weeping with a letter in her hand, asking me to read it. At first I didn't take it from her, but I asked her to tell me what it was all about. She said, "I introduced a friend of mine to my boss for employment; I pressed for her so hard until she got the job. Initially we were both happy working together, until she changed and turned against me. It got worse, and she vowed to get me out of the job, but I didn't take her seriously. Now, she has fulfilled her vow—I'm out of the job." She was fired! I counseled her to forgive her and repent for opening up herself to be offended. This is necessary so that her desire for another job offer will not be hindered through unforgiveness. It took awhile to forgive because she was wounded. Thank God, she got a better job and she was happy. Oftentimes we think we have forgiven, but when an occasion arises to think about those who offended us, or reflect on the trouble they caused us, or having anything to do with them, our feelings toward them stir up. These are scars that we must work on. Seeing scars on our body reminds us of how we got wounded and the pains. So this lady got to meet her friend again on another occasion; guess what? The bitterness toward her friend flooded her to the point of lashing at her. Scars are a constant reminder of the deep agony we have been through, but we can be healed.

I counseled another lady who lost her marriage to her caregiver. On two occasions she had a dream of her caregiver wearing her wedding dress; and she narrated the dreams to her husband, which he tried to despise, counting them as "just dreams." A few months later, she was kicked out, and she discovered that her husband was in love with her caregiver. She was wounded and bitter. Who can heal her wounds and remove her scars? Scars remain when our strength to recovery fails or we feel insufficient. When our search for worth, belonging, and purpose are frustrated and we become insecure, then it becomes evident that scars abound.

The journey of life is full of hills and valleys, mountains and lowlands; sometimes it can be rough or smooth, crooked or plain, and all these may bring pleasant or unpleasant experiences. However, there is cure in God for the healing of wounds and scars. Jesus, the Balm of Gilead, can walk back to the time you were hurt and free you from the effects of the wound. Jesus was wounded that our transgressions might be forgiven, bruised that our iniquities might be purged, and chastised that we might have peace. He received many stripes all for our healing. Oh, what a price!

> He is despised and rejected by men, A Man of sorrows and acquainted with grief. And we hid, as it were, our faces from Him; He was despised, and we did not esteem Him. Surely He has borne our griefs And carried our sorrows; Yet we esteemed Him stricken, Smitten by God, and afflicted. But He was wounded for our transgressions, He was bruised for our iniquities; The chastisement for our peace was upon Him, And by His stripes we are healed.
>
> —ISAIAH 53:3–5

Apostle Paul was a man wounded by friends and fellow countrymen, but he considered the wounds and the scars as outward evidence about his testimony of Jesus. He testified to the Galatian church, "From now on, don't let anyone trouble me with these things. For I bear on my body the scars that show I belong to Jesus" (Gal. 6:17, NLT). I love this other translation, "For I bear on my body the [brand] marks of the Lord Jesus [the wounds, scars, and other outward evidence of persecutions—these testify to His ownership of me]!" (Gal. 6:17, AMP). Evidently, scars can be a "brand," indicating identity or ownership. Aren't we branded for Christ? God's seal is upon the redeemed as a sign of security, approval, and confirmation of ownership that we belong to God, which signifies a finished transaction. So, we can gladly reflect on the wounds and offenses that caused scars in our lives and be grateful to God. Truly, there are lots of things to be grateful for; through this we can walk in victory.

Doing Great Things and Prevailing

It is frustrating to be above average and be exceptionally good, but uncelebrated. It is even more painful when little or no respect is shown to your labor and you are treated without dignity. We can be good and yet be a loser. Be kind and yet be hated. It is, therefore, not about doing, but whom we influence and the effectiveness of our work. We can be skillful, but poor; hardworking but unskillful. However, all depends on excellence and favor.

An elderly woman shared this story with me when I was a teenager: "All the animals in the forest gathered for a conference, and each one had to introduce itself before the meeting. And each boasted of their greatness. 'I am great,' said the lion, 'because I reign as the monarch of the wood and plain!' The elephant replied, 'No quadruped can match my weight! And that makes me great.' The giraffe objected and said, 'I'm great because no animal has half so long a neck as mine.' The kangaroo said, 'See my femoral muscularity! Who can match it?' The possum said, 'Behold, my tail is lithe, bald, and cold, which reveals my greatness.'" Each of them recognized greatness based on their personality make up and what they were capable of doing.

It is a competitive world. Competition arises when two or more parties strive for a goal which cannot be shared. Even when our needs are met, deep rivalries often arise over the pursuit of wealth, prestige, and fame. Notably, competition can be destructive as everyone seems to benefit by damaging and/or eliminating another. It is a "winner takes all" world that we are in—the success of one person is dependent on the failure of the other competing individuals. This tends to promote fear and a "strike-first" mentality. Such was the understanding of King Saul of Israel when he engaged in a deathly pursuit of David after he killed the Philistine giant, Goliath. Saul tried to kill David in every way possible, but God permitted him not. He thought David was competing for the throne, so he must be killed. However, the last encounter David had with Saul before he fled to the land of the Philistines for refuge was notable. It was more of an open confession: "Then Saul said to David, 'May you be blessed, my son David! You shall both do great things and also still prevail.' So David went on his way, and Saul returned to his place" (1 Sam. 26:25).

Saul acknowledged that David had done great things, but the tragedy was he had not prevailed. There is a wall of difference between doing great things and prevailing. David had done great things in the past, but with no lasting joy. He had torn both lion and bear apart with his hands in trying to rescue the sheep but with no reward. I love this other translation: "You will do many heroic deeds and you will surely succeed" (1 Sam. 26:25, NLT). My heart goes out to many people who have done heroic deeds but are considered losers. My prayer for such people is that the wall separating them from being honored be broken down so that recognition and reward may show forth.

Healing at His Feet

Wounds and scars can be totally healed in His presence. Unhealed wounds and damaged emotions can hurt us so deeply as to alter our lives. I will encourage those who are hurting and wounded to cast them at the Master's feet.

> And those who passed by blasphemed Him, wagging their heads and saying, "Aha! You who destroy the temple and build it in three days, save Yourself, and come down from the cross!" Likewise the chief priests also, mocking among themselves with the scribes, said, "He saved others; Himself He cannot save. Let the Christ, the King of Israel, descend now from the cross, that we may see and believe." Even those who were crucified with Him reviled Him.
> —MARK 15:29–31

Jesus went up into a mountain, and sat down there. He is exalted and enthroned, waiting for us to come to Him. He is exalted above our problems and willing to save. You could be part of the multitude that will come to Him: the "lame, blind, dumb, maimed, and many others" (Matt. 15:30, KJV). I believe if you are not physically or spiritually blind, dumb, or maimed, you are part of "many others." Thank God that your situation fits into the category of "many others." The amazing thing about all those who came to Him was that they "cast them down at Jesus' feet" (v. 30, KJV). I would say that they were tired of bearing the burden and the shame, so they abandoned them at His feet. As He is enthroned and exalted above their problems, they cast them at His feet. Why His feet? I would go through Jesus' miraculous ministry in the Bible to see many others getting healed and delivered at His feet. Jairus, a ruler of the Synagogue, "fell at His feet" (Mark 5:22). The Syrophoenician woman: "For a woman whose young daughter had an unclean spirit heard about Him, and she came and fell at His feet" (7:25). The man in which a legion of demons were cast out, after being delivered, sat at His feet, "clothed, and in his right mind" (Luke 8:35). How about the woman with the issue of blood for twelve years, who touched the hem of His garment (Matt. 9:20)? The hem of the garment is, of course, at the feet. I also observed that no one who touched His feet went back to their problems—they were all healed and delivered.

I ask again, why His feet? I trace it back to the first promise about Messiah after the fall: "And I will put enmity Between you and the woman, And between your seed and her Seed; He shall bruise your head, And you shall bruise His heel" (Gen. 3:15). Jesus, being the seed of the woman, crushed the head of every problem cast at His feet. And when the head is broken, the problems are over. The feet are also a type of mobility, freedom, foundation, and conquest; so casting their problems at His feet was for Jesus to bruise the head of the problems even to the foundation, and set the people free that they may advance in victory. At His feet there is freedom and victory. "The LORD said to my Lord, 'Sit at My right hand, Till I make Your enemies Your footstool'" (Ps. 110:1). May we also, by faith, bring all our burdens unto Him, cast them at His feet, and demand that He might crush the head of the problems that we may experience freedom and blessings.

Chapter 7

TERRITORIAL SPIRITUAL WARFARE

I N THE BEGINNING God created the heavens and the earth" (Gen. 1:1). The Almighty God is the Creator, Founder, and the Possessor of heaven and earth; and He reigns over all. "The earth is the LORD's, and all its fullness, The world and those who dwell therein. For He has founded it upon the seas, And established it upon the waters" (Ps. 24:1–2). I love this: "for He has founded it" (v. 2). He created all things for His pleasure (Rev. 4:11). Although sin and rebellion have separated us from Him, He made a redemptive plan to restore us. Ever since the fall of man, the entire creation has been subjected to decay and corruption awaiting the future glory.

"For we know that the whole creation groans and labors with birth pangs together until now" (Rom. 8:22). Believers are not excluded from the pains, even though we have the Holy Spirit who has given us a foretaste of the blissful things to come; yet God has committed the works of reconciliation unto us (2 Cor. 5:18). The creation is a redemptive gift to mankind. God's sovereignty must be revealed over all His works, regardless of the rebellion of His creation.

God gave man dominion over all the works of His hand, but the devil usurped it by exchanging his demoted state with our glorious state, then man became a slave to sin. "You have made him to have dominion over the works of Your hands; You have put all things under his feet" (Ps. 8:6). The dominion given to man reflects on "the field" (land), "the fowl of the air" (air), and "the fish of the sea" (water). I can safely say that the spheres of man's authority include land, air, and water; even "all things under his feet." When Jesus came to restore all things back to God, He was tempted by the usurper, yet He triumphed. Part of the temptation was: "Again, the devil took Him up on an exceedingly high mountain, and showed Him all the kingdoms of the world and their glory. And he said to Him, "All these things I will give You if You will fall down and worship me" (Matt. 4:8–9). Satan is still demanding worship today. Jesus refused, because whomever you worship becomes your Lord. He preferred the agony of death, which is the wages of sin, and through that overcame sin and death, declaring: "All power is given unto me in heaven and in earth" (Matt. 28:18, KJV). Satan showed Him all the kingdoms of the world, and the glory of them, but "the kingdoms of this world are become the kingdoms of our Lord, and of his Christ; and he shall reign for ever and ever" (Rev. 11:15, KJV).

Spiritual Warfare over Our Cities

Satan, though defeated, is still as "a roaring lion, seeking whom he may devour" (1 Pet. 5:8). He wants to control every sphere where man has authority; therefore, our land is defiled through greed, murder, and treachery. Even the sea, the air, and the sky are rebelling against man. There is chaos in our cities, confusion upon our gates, and strife and deceit on our doorposts. Is there any hope for us? Surely, there is! I discovered that the joy of a city or nation may be under serious challenges of wicked forces. "And there was great joy in that city" (Acts 8:8). In the city of Samaria, joy eluded the people because of just one man who through sorcery bewitched the people for a long time, from the least to the greatest. "But there was a certain man, called Simon, which beforetime in the same city used sorcery, and bewitched the people of Samaria, giving out that himself was some great one: To whom they all gave heed, from the least to the greatest, saying, This man is the great power of God. And to him they had regard, because that of long time he had bewitched them with sorceries" (Acts 8:9–11, KJV). If not for the gospel—the good news—the people would have been in bondage forever. The power of God mightily delivered the people. "For unclean spirits, crying with loud voice, came out of many that were possessed with them: and many taken with palsies, and that were lame, were healed (v. 7, KJV). In our city today, there is more than one man practicing sorcery. When the Bible says from the least to the greatest, this implies from slave to king, they were under bewitchment. No wonder the decisions of our rulers are subject to satanic manipulation. And this also explains why people are not always in agreement with leaders. Chaos filled the city because of sorcery and bewitchment. So I ask, who is influencing our cities?

Abraham, the father of faith, was called out from his people by God to dwell in a country which he knew not, but with a guiding principle: "for a city which hath foundations, whose builder and maker is God" (Heb. 11:10, KJV). And when he found the city, he set up an altar to God (Gen. 12:6–7). I asked myself, why didn't he settle anywhere else? His earnest desire was a city with real, eternal foundations, in which God's principles would guide the affairs of men, as God commanded him, saying, "For I have known him, in order that he may command his children and his household after him, that they keep the way of the LORD, to do righteousness and justice, that the LORD may bring to Abraham what He has spoken to him" (18:19). May I ask the reader: What it is the foundation of your city? And upon what was it built upon? Whatever the foundation of the city may be, it will surely be the influencing factor upon the people.

Ezekiel's vision

Ezekiel the prophet had many visions, but I will share just two of them. God opened the secret of nations to him, particularly Israel. He saw the abomination of the people. God revealed unto him what "the house of Israel do in the dark…for they say, the LORD seeth us not; the LORD hath forsaken the earth" (Ezek. 8:12, KJV). To effectively see this, God showed him a hole in the wall (v. 7). He saw people burning incense to idols; women weeping before idols (*tammuz*) (v. 11); turning their backs toward the temple of the Lord; and worshiping the sun (v. 16), which brought the fury of God. It is tragic that the abominations of our time are done openly, in the media, at parks, in malls, and in government offices. Repentance is required for God's mercies to be restored.

Ezekiel the prophet also saw leaders of the nation devising mischief and giving wicked counsel (11:1–2). This revelation was so prophetic that it is an eye-opener to what is happening in nations today. The leaders said, "This city is the caldron, and we be the flesh" (v. 3, KJV). So the people were considered "the flesh" in the caldron? A caldron is a vessel for boiling flesh, for either ceremonial or domestic use. So when a city or nation is consider a cooking pot and the people as flesh put in a pot to cook, the result will be great distress and unrest. According to answers .com, "a more common association in western culture is the cauldron's use in witchcraft. In Wicca, a cauldron can be placed in a sacred circle and used to turn items that will be set alight during a ritual."[1] Symbolically, nations can be put in a cauldron and boiled. This may explain the confusion, pain, and deep agony people go through and also the unrest and frustration that have caused total disorder in the nations of the world. God had to raise up prophet Ezekiel to reverse this situation, so he prophesized: "This city shall not be your caldron, nor shall you be the meat in its midst. I will judge you at the border of Israel" (v. 11). God can miraculously deliver us from the effect of the cauldron. He can pull the people out of boiling situations to experience His peace again. An effective way for a prophetic intercessor to pray for nations of the world would be that God would deliver people from the cauldron and destroy it so that people can be free from agony and frustration.

Daniel's vision

Daniel was an elderly statesman who ruled in a strange land. His book is a book of kings and kingdoms, of thrones and dominions. It embodies prophecies of the sequence of the kingdoms. He had a great understanding of visions. While in the kingdom of Persia in the days of Cyrus the king, he fasted for twenty-one days. He had several divine encounters, one of which was an angel talking to him. "Then he said to me, 'Do not fear, Daniel, for from the first day that you set your heart to understand, and to humble yourself before your God, your words were heard; and I have come because of your words'" (Dan. 10:12). From the first day of his prayer, he was heard, but the angel was delayed by the principalities controlling the region of Persia. "But the prince of the kingdom of Persia withstood me twenty-one days; and behold, Michael, one of the chief princes, came to help me, for I had been left alone there with the kings of Persia" (v. 13). I always wondered if Daniel had not persisted in prayer, what would have happened. His continued prayer released angelic reinforcement to break him free from detaining forces. However, the angel made a remarkable statement about his return; "Then he said, 'Do you know why I have come to you? And now I must return to fight with the prince of Persia; and when I have gone forth, indeed the prince of Greece will come'" (v. 20). After delivering the message, this angel may have had to contend again with the prince of Persia. The angel also perceived that the prince of Persia would network with the prince of Greece. The angel fought through to come and deliver answers to Daniel's prayer and would have to fight again to return.

I believe Daniel's twenty-one-day fasting and prayer was so strategic as to destroy strongholds, cast down thrones, and bring into captivity all opposing forces. He prayed until help and strength came to his angel of blessings. There are princes over nations satanically positioned to blind people's minds and make them rebel against God. "But even if our gospel is veiled, it is veiled to those who are perishing, whose minds the god of this age has blinded, who do not believe, lest the light of the gospel of the glory of Christ, who is the image of God, should shine on them" (2 Cor. 4:3–4). "In which you once walked according to the course of this world, according to the prince of the power of the air, the spirit who now works in the sons of disobedience" (Eph. 2:2). The princes of nations influence rulers and confuse the populace: "Now Satan stood up against Israel, and moved David to number Israel" (1 Chron. 21:1). The prevailing situations over nations of the world are determined by the princes—spiritual forces behind the throne. Therefore, an effective way to pray for our nation is to apply scripturally strategized, prophetic, well-targeted prayers to dethrone the prince and enthrone the lordship of Jesus as the Prince of Peace and the Prince of Glory. Howbeit, there are delayed blessings because of detained angels. The Holy Spirit can quicken us to decree strength to our angels of blessings to break forth unhindered. The good news is that Jesus judged the prince of this world already. "Of judgment, because the ruler of this world is judged" (John 16:11). It was impossible for the god and prince of this world, Satan, to forbid Him from fulfilling His divine assignments (14:30). Though He was tempted and suffered, He triumphed. He conquered and condemned them through His death, burial, resurrection, and accession. He is seated at the right hand of power far above principalities, princes, powers, and dominion. As He is the Head and the church His body, we also are seated together with Him in heavenly places—seated in glory and majesty. We are, therefore, here on earth that His glory may shine through us (Eph. 2:6).

Symbolic identity of nations

There are symbolic representations of nations which may denote animals, trees, inanimate objects, or patriotic symbols that may be national emblems. Canadian national animals are the beaver and the Canadian horse; United States of America's is the bald eagle; South Korea's is the tiger; Mexico's is the golden eagle; Czech Republic's is the double-tailed lion; New Zealand's is the kiwi; Cuba's is the Cuban crocodile; Qatar's is the oryx; Nepal's is the cow; Iceland's is the falcon; Spain's is the bull; Turkey's is the grey wolf; Uganda's is the grey-crowned crane; and Eritrea's is the camel. While the Canadian national tree is the maple; Denmark's is the beech; Greece's is the olive; Vietnam's are bamboo and rice; and United States of America's is the oak. National inanimate objects:

Sweden's is the three crowns; Poland's is the old castle; Germany's is the iron cross; and Denmark's is the round tower. There are patriotic symbols: Switzerland's is the Swiss cross; Chile's is the lonely star; Canada's is the maple leaf; Singapore's is the lion head; and Turkey's is the star and crescent.[2] All these may represent freedom, courage, bravery, and unity.

Why am I sharing this? The Bible also gave some symbolic identities over nations: "Moab is My washpot; Over Edom I will cast My shoe; Over Philistia I will triumph" (Ps. 108:9). Moab's spiritual identity is "washpot," while Edom's spiritual identity is "casting out of shoe." This may suffice to say that the symbolic spiritual identity of nations may determine what controls or influences the people. What does Moab as a wash pot mean? This is a pot or vessel in which anything is washed; it holds the dirty water. Moab, which threatened Israel, was to be so completely subdued and become so utterly contemptible as to be linked to a wash pot. The effect could be shame, low esteem, being devoid of dignity, and being treated disrespectfully. "Over Edom will I cast my shoe." I ask myself what I do as soon as I get home after a hard day's work: I cast off my shoes and relax. This reflects a concluded or accomplished warfare. It is like saying the warfare over Edom is accomplished. There is nothing that can be done; Edom is defeated. I wonder what will be the hope of the Edomites. They may struggle but to no avail. I, therefore, ask, what are the implications of the spiritual identity of our nation? Whatever they are, they determine the nature of the territorial spirit controlling the nation's affairs.

Redeeming the Land

However polluted our land may be, God has a redemptive purpose for it. Jesus shed His blood for this purpose. As blood and water gushed through His side, flowing on the ground, the redemption was perfected. Therefore, those who receive Him are divine representatives here on earth to reconcile all things to Him. I would like to consider some of the people who walked here on earth and engaged in territorial dominion in fulfilling God's eternal purposes. There are lots of things to learn from them. According to Audre Lorde, "Even the smallest victory is never to be taken for granted. Each victory must be applauded."[3]

Moses' strategies

Moses was a man raised by God to lead His people out of Egypt. He contended with the principalities and the gods of Egypt until they bowed to the Holy One of Israel. Moses was a man full of divine strategies; he operated differently at every realm in that the strategies to bring God's people out of Egypt were different from how to operate in the wilderness. In progressing to the Promised Land, he had to trust God to know the right move. At Kadesh-barnea, he sent spies to appraise the land. They were sent with the right strategies to spy so that they may possess the land. The purpose of spying was to prepare them for what was ahead. By the way, these men were leaders of their people, carefully selected because they could be relied upon. So Moses began by giving them a direction to follow, "Go up this way into the South, and go up to the mountains" (Num. 13:17). They could have entered through any direction, but the way we enter into our God-given assignments matters. Divine instructions as to where to start and how to proceed should not be despised. The following are further instructions on how to spy and what to spy for. These could be applied to our lives in redeeming the land:

The kind of land: Good or bad, fat or lean, wooded or barren (vv. 18–20). They were to determine the economic strength, the productivity, and prospect of the land. They fulfilled this first mission by bringing back the fruit of the land (vv. 26–27). They reported that truly the land flowed with milk and honey. If the land was cursed, the people would go through hardship, and if blessed, the people could reap in abundance. Redemptive purpose has to be proclaimed on the land as we dedicate it to God.

The kind of people: They were to see if the people of the land were strong or weak, many or few, small or large (v. 18). The population of the people was necessary to determine the capacity of the land and plan ahead. In returning they reported about the people saying, "Nevertheless the people who dwell in the land are strong; the cities are fortified and very large; moreover we saw the descendants of Anak there. The Amalekites dwell in the land of the South; the Hittites, the Jebusites, and the Amorites dwell in the mountains; and the Canaanites dwell by the sea and along the banks of the Jordan" (vv. 28–29). The good or bad of a land will be determined by the kind of people who live there. If the land is fertile and rich in mineral resources, but the people are weak, they will not be able to get the best out of the land. I do wonder why the spies complained about the giants living in the land. For a land to bring up great fruits and flow in riches, giants are needed to cultivate the land and maintain it. I believe that God needed the giants to keep the land good for His people to inherit. After all, the land cannot be kept empty, someone has to be there to till and dress it. All the people of Israel needed to do was to announce their arrival and take up the land. The healing of the land is connected with the people. If they walk in disobedience and incur the wrath of God, their land becomes unproductive. "If My people who are called by My name will humble themselves, and pray and seek My face, and turn from their wicked ways, then I will hear from heaven, and will forgive their sin and heal their land" (2 Chron. 7:14).

The kind of cities: They were to watch if the cities were walled or opened (Num. 13:19). In returning, they reported that the cities were walled and very great (v. 28). Walls in those days determined the strength of the city. The city shapes the lives and character of many; it determines the use of our time and whom we relate to or associate with. A city may be shut against the gospel, and the people walk in darkness.

While others shrink back in fear, Joshua and Caleb were confident to possess the land. It takes courage to step into God's purposes. Those who gave an evil report never made it to the Promised Land. But those who, through the eyes of God, beheld the land were confident enough to possess it. I reasoned within myself saying, if the spies could go, spend some days, and come back with the fruits of the land without being destroyed by the giants, why would they think it is impossible for the rest of the people to do the same? God who led them, going and coming back, could do even more for the rest of the people. Therefore, in possessing our city for God, we should view it in the light of God. Examining the kind of land, people, and cities will help strategize on how to pray effectively.

Joshua's strategies

Joshua, the servant of Moses, had watched his master wrought exploits and was ready to step in. God used him to conquer many cities and nations. If we adopt the strategies by which Jericho was conquered, the stronghold resisting the gospel of truth in our nation can be pulled down and righteousness prevail. The following were the three steps:

Sending the spies: Spying has always been a great tool in the law of conquest. Moses used it, so did Joshua, and we even use it today. Joshua's spies succeeded when they were hidden by their hostess against the wrath of the king. The true confession of their hostess encouraged them in possessing the land. The spies returned and reported saying: "And they said to Joshua, 'Truly the LORD has delivered all the land into our hands, for indeed all the inhabitants of the country are fainthearted because of us'" (Josh. 2:24). Therefore, believers are in the earth relating back to God our encounters. As the spies had the backing of their nation, so do we also have divine support in our mission on earth. As the spies represented their nation, so are we the ambassadors of Christ. As the spies were sent, so are we on a divine mission to fulfill divine purposes. Before conquering Jericho, there was the Jordan River to cross and reconnecting with the Abrahamic covenant of circumcision, which signified death to the world and cutting off the deeds of the flesh. These proved their readiness to walk with God and possess the land. Then the Captain of the Host appeared to lead them through. When we show readiness to walk with God through the covenant of the blood of Jesus, He will show up.

Appearance of the divine Captain: "The captain of the LORD's host" (5:15, KJV), appeared as Joshua "lifted up his eyes and looked, and, behold" (v. 13, KJV). May our eyes always be lifted up to behold our King in His glory. His eyes were not on the troubles ahead of him but on the Shepherd of Israel. He, therefore, looked and beheld the Captain of the Lord of Hosts who gave the divine plan and formula. Even though Jericho was a stronghold, there was yet a formula to overcome. There is no problem, however great, that cannot be overcome as long as we wait and trust in God for divine direction.

The Captain of the Lord of Hosts revealed the plan for success as Joshua submitted to His lordship and control. The strategy to conquer Jericho might seem foolish, but Joshua trusted God. In winning our cities for God, openness to the Holy Spirit cannot be underestimated. God has always used the weak to confound the strong, and the lowly to make the great foolish.

Carrying out the divine instructions: Obedience to divine will matters in victory. I love it when I read how Joshua commanded the silent march. "Now Joshua had commanded the people, saying, 'You shall not shout or make any noise with your voice, nor shall a word proceed out of your mouth, until the day I say to you, "Shout!" Then you shall shout'" (6:10). I figured out this was the right thing to do because as people encompassed the wall, they would probably murmur, and this would have invoked God's wrath. I see the act of being silent even when there was occasion to talk as discipline needed for victory. There must be a level of discipline for those who want to attain uncommon victory. Rightfully carrying out strategies brings victory. Strategies, however good, if not well executed, may amount to nothing. I have seen people with good plans fail because it lacks right execution. As they shouted the praise of God Almighty, the wall of Jericho responded also in bowing down to worship the God of Israel—it fell flat. The foundation of Jericho quaked at the shout of praise of the almighty God. Even so shall the foundation of our cities respond to our true worship of the Most High God. When this happens, the heart of the people shall open up to the truth of the gospel, and righteousness shall reign in our land.

Apostle Paul's strategies

A persecutor of the church, full of zeal, and rooted in the traditions of his fathers, Paul turned to proclaim what he had persecuted. I pray God will do it again in our time, so we will see hardhearted people turning to Him. After his salvation and miraculous deliverance, God's hand was upon him to proclaim the gospel of truth and advance His kingdom. There is so much to learn from him because of his missionary journey, moving from city to city, and contending with the powers that controlled the land. Through him, the Word of the Lord prevailed, and multitudes turned their hearts to God. He witnessed religious strongholds shattered, human traditions subdued, and rulers bowing to the lordship of Jesus. The sorcerers were no match, neither were the diviners nor the enchanters. Considering his different strategies for different cities as led by the Holy Spirit would also help us to engage in good warfare.

> They did not just depart, but were loosed from the city, free from the confinement and bondages that dominated it.

Loosed from the city: At Paphos, Paul and his companion went through the island and "found a certain sorcerer" (Acts 13:6). It was like a search to discover the power behind the throne. They had to go through the city to prayerfully determine what influenced the city. Truly, they found a sorcerer who had worked himself into the confidence of the governor, Sergius Paulus. I consider how many warlocks are influencing policies and the law of the land to promote ungodliness! Although the governor "desired to hear the word of God" (v. 7, KJV), the sorcerer sought to turn him away from the truth; however, Paul "set his eyes on him" (v. 9, KJV) rather than the sorcerer setting his eyes on Paul.

I think about those in the body of Christ today who fear demons so much as to idolize them. If a witch or wizard sets eye on any believer today, such a one will call prayer lines and run after men or women of God for prayers of deliverance. We seem to major in minor, neglecting the actual work of the kingdom. Apostle Paul was able to do this because he was "filled with the Holy Ghost" (v. 9, KJV). May we not frustrate the grace of God by allowing the wicked to take charge of affairs that may turn around to hinder the gospel.

Apostle Paul rebuked him saying, "'O full of all deceit and all fraud, you son of the devil, you enemy of all righteousness, will you not cease perverting the straight ways of the Lord? And now, indeed, the hand of the Lord is upon you, and you shall be blind, not seeing the sun for a time.' And immediately a dark mist fell on him, and he went around seeking someone to lead him by the hand. Then the proconsul believed, when he saw what had been done, being astonished at the teaching of the Lord" (vv. 10–12).

The demonstration of God's power disgraces the works of darkness and convicts the people. After this wonderful exploit, the apostolic team was aware of the wreckage done to the kingdom of darkness, so the Bible accounted that they were loosed from Phaphos. "Now when Paul and his company loosed from Paphos, they came to Perga in Pamphylia: and John departing from them returned to Jerusalem" (v. 13, KJV). They did not just depart, but were *loosed from the city*, free from the confinement and bondages that dominated it.

It is therefore possible to leave a place bound and damaged, unaware of the trouble. No wonder Jesus commanded His disciples regarding places they were to go: "But whatever house you enter, first say, 'Peace to this house.' And if a son of peace is there, your peace will rest on it; if not, it will return to you" (Luke 10:5–6). So, a house can retain or repel peace. Visiting or living in such a place would require being loosed from the evil dominating the place. "If the household is worthy, let your peace come upon it. But if it is not worthy, let your peace return to you" (Matt. 10:13).

A house may be worthy or unworthy, so is a city or nation. People visit cities picking up the evil in the land which had altered the core of their being. Even in your own city, do you live there bound or loose, free or bound? Why not decree yourself loosed from the evil around you, or else it may rule and ruin your life. I ask you, as you move in and out of cities, does the evil therein easily cleave to you or are you loosed from it?

After the uproar: The economic and political disorders in nations of the world today are making many people confused, but the problem is deeper than we think. No policy or government effort seems to work because they themselves are not in control. There are deeper unresolved issues that determine the fate of the people. In all these things believers have a role to proclaim the gospel of peace as the only antidote to the commotion. Apostle Paul prevailed over the uproar of his days as he contended with idolatrous and corrupt nations.

At Ephesus, the word of God grew mightily and prevailed (Acts 19:20), and special miracles were wrought (v. 11). "So that even handkerchiefs or aprons were brought from his body to the sick, and the diseases left them and the evil spirits went out of them" (v. 12). This brought such a conversion of souls in multitude that they had a bonfire of their magical books, charms, and idols; this was done "before all men" (v. 19, KJV). This was a true conversion—they were sold out to God.

I had an experience of a similar situation in rural evangelism where people brought their fetish and occult materials to be burned publicly. It is an act of no looking back, ready to embrace God and His fullness.

> It is a triumphant life that fears no storm, confronts any tempest, and turns back the floods of the wicked.

Unto the Ephesians, there was a backlash, which is always the case to most kingdom work; how we handle it determines the way forward. Sedition rose up with the intent to change or overthrow the authority of God over the people: "All with one voice about the space of two hours cried out, Great is Diana of the Ephesians" (v. 34, KJV). They exalted their goddess whom they claimed "all Asia and the world worship" (v. 27). Such a cry of unity released an oppressive presence into the environment, causing chaos and invoking evil-spirit trafficking. The long-term effect of this was that the Ephesian church soon lost their first love for Christ (Rev. 2:4). How many such occult voices have we ignored in the land? Those who can hear and see should cry to God that there will be repentance because of the uproar of evil in our time.

The bloodshed, corruption, violence, idolatry, oppression, crave for wealth, immoral acts, cultism, and other vices had polluted the land to the effect that sin was no longer considered evil, and righteousness was seen as a myth. Hope was betrayed and hatred filled the hearts of people.

I am not a pessimist, but I am longing for a revival of our land and people. The whole creation is groaning and awaiting "the sons of God" (Rom. 8:19) to arise to our eternal duty of reconciliation. My deepest heart cry as a prophetic intercessor is: "Will You be angry with us forever? Will You prolong Your anger to all generations? Will You not revive us again, That Your people may rejoice in You? Show us Your mercy, LORD, And grant us Your salvation" (Ps. 85:5–7).

The good news was how the uproar ceased. "After the uproar had ceased, Paul called the disciples to himself, embraced them, and departed to go to Macedonia" (Acts 20:1). It ended. There is no uproar or rage that cannot be stilled by the power of the gospel of peace. The uproar in Ephesus ceased by two positive actions taken by the city clerk—a represented authority. As we also represent the authority of God on earth, we can silence every uproar confusing our age. His first step was to quiet the crowd (19:35). Thereafter, he proceeded to the next step: "he dismissed the assembly" (v. 41).

We can quiet contrary voices and the disorderliness of our age by the Word of God. If we can discern very well, we will know that every evil word is a prescription to pattern our life to wickedness. But we can subdue them by the Word of God, by permitting the Word of God to give direction to lead our lives. The Word of God is powerful to quiet and dismiss evil in our land—mighty to quiet and dismiss any uproar tormenting the people. "Then he dismissed them, and they dispersed" (v. 41, NLT). "After the uproar had ceased, Paul called the disciples to himself, embraced them, and departed to go to Macedonia" (20:1). So there is a life "after the uproar." May we receive grace to enjoy such a life—a life as "more than conquerors" (Rom. 8:37). It is a triumphant life that fears no storm, confronts any tempest, and turns back the floods of the wicked. This should be the lifestyle of every believer—a life *after the uproar.*

Law of Conquest

As there are natural laws, so are spiritual laws. Laws shape our political, economical, and societal lives; so also there are laws for effective spiritual warfare. Victory is no victory at all until we secure control over our lives and gain back all that belongs to us. There are forces claiming superiority over one another, but God rules over all competing claims by establishing boundaries. God is the Man of War (Exod. 15:3), He is the

Lord of the armies of heaven (Ps. 24:10), and He fights the battles of His own (Exod. 14:14). He separated the nation of Israel unto Himself with a set of laws for conquering battles.

> When you go out to battle against your enemies, and see horses and chariots and people more numerous than you, do not be afraid of them; for the LORD your God is with you, who brought you up from the land of Egypt. So it shall be, when you are on the verge of battle, that the priest shall approach and speak to the people. And he shall say to them, "Hear, O Israel: Today you are on the verge of battle with your enemies. Do not let your heart faint, do not be afraid, and do not tremble or be terrified because of them; for the LORD your God is He who goes with you, to fight for you against your enemies, to save you."
> —DEUTERONOMY 20:1–4

"When you go out to battle" —not if, but when. The battle is inevitable. It is part of life, so God gave His people instructions on how to overcome. Applying these to our lives assures us of uncompromising victory.

Be not afraid: God recognizes that our adversaries may be more in number and weapons, but the first law is "be not afraid of them" (v. 1). Why should I not be afraid when I am outnumbered and look inferior? How about when I see destructive weapons and my foes are stronger than I am? I also ask myself why the question about fear is the first law. "Fear has caused proud men to beg; strong men to cry; loving men to hate; and peaceful men to be filled with fury. Like a slave master, fear is controlling."[4] Unless we overcome our fear, the weak enemies will become strong, and noneffective weapons will become mighty. Fearlessly approaching difficult issues of life will not make us doubt what we can overcome. Charles H. Spurgeon said, "He who fears God has nothing else to fear. We should stand in such awe of the living Lord that all the threats that can be used by the proudest persecutor should have no more effect upon us than the whistling on the wind."[5]

"Ask yourself, do I experience sudden fear and panic? Do I go about life feeling insecure or uncertain? Do I feel an oppressive presence around me? It is also important to know that fear can manifest itself in diverse ways, but whichever way, be assured that you can always overcome and prevail over your fears.

"Many people are fearful of death, sicknesses, diseases, evil, wickedness, and danger. Some even dread the future. Imaginative fear and fear of the unknown are twin killers of our time. Fear of man can also be a snare, not just a weakness or a character fault. This can cause you to dwell on things that are not true and live in perpetual ignorance. In your struggle with fear, rest assured that God's eternal Word is the only antidote to overcome your fears."[6]

Fear is a torment, worse than the torment of war. It is like an internal war that weakens and bows before the external war. Without overcoming, it is hard to be declared a champion. I counsel you, therefore, to war against your fear and watch other wars flee before you. It is a divine command to conquer our fear first before engaging in any other battle. God, who commanded them not to fear, also gave them the reason not to fear: "for the Lord your God is with you" (v. 1). An ever assurance of His presence is all that is required to trust Him and possess victory.

Priestly encouragement: "So it shall be, when you are on the verge of battle, that the priest shall approach and speak to the people" (v. 2). This is a deciding factor in victory. Believers are "set apart" and called royal priests (1 Pet. 2:9). What we declare in times of war determines whether we shall be victorious or defeated, captured or free, oppressed or jubilate. God puts His Word in us to declare against any battle such words that are "mighty through God to the pulling down of strong holds" (2 Cor. 10:4, KJV). What are we to declare? "Do not let your heart faint, do not be afraid, and do not tremble or be terrified because of them" (Deut. 20:3). "Faint," "fear," "tremble," and "terrify" are deep issues to deal with before victory is accomplished.

The faint in heart lack conviction of God's power and greatness; they are not bold toward stepping into divine promises. It is a state of loosing God's consciousness, but in tune with the flesh. When we are illuminated by His Word, our spirit comes alive to take a stand for God. The very thought of war is terrifying and makes us tremble. Georgia O'Keeffe said, "I've been absolutely terrified every moment of my life—and I've never let it keep me from doing a single thing I wanted to do."[7] I am confident of victory because God assured me, and His Word is truth: "For the Lord your God is He who goes with you, to fight for you against your enemies, to save you" (v. 4).

Spiritual House Cleansing

By the grace of God as a prophetic intercessor, I travel frequently to attend or minister in conferences, which I enjoy very much. I do travel light so as to avoid delays at the airport. In most cases I have had nothing to declare to customs, except for one day. Although I had nothing to declare, I was pulled aside and directed to a special area of Toronto Airport. In my mind I was thinking, *why is this happening to me*? But I knew all was well. Getting to this huge hall were some other travelers; we were set for thorough searching by the customs authorities. As I queued, I watched others being searched. As I looked at the traveler ahead of me and the customs officer searching his baggage, then I knew why God led me that way. I thought the customs officers knew what they were searching for. As they pulled out things from his bags, I was close to screaming because of what I saw; of course, that was not what they were looking for. What did I see that made me react the way I did? Charms, fetish items, idols, and magical things. They let the man go with all his magical things due to their ignorance or that the law permits it because they look harmless. Then the Spirit of the Lord spoke to me: "This was the reason I made you pass through this way, that you may see the heavy trafficking of idols and demonic materials into nations of the world." When it was my turn to be searched, what do you think happened? Nothing! They let me go within two minutes.

> I have visited homes and saw some of the idols, charms, and demonic objects that people in Africa had renounced and destroyed but are fashionable in America and Europe as furniture or decorative items.

Someone may ask me, how were you able to identify them as being fetish items, charms, idols, and magical things? By the grace of God, I had done missionary works at villages where idol worship dominated the area, and I have been engaged in prophetic intercessory prayers in demon-infested communities. I have visited homes and saw some of the idols, charms, and demonic objects that people in Africa had renounced and destroyed but are fashionable in America and Europe as furniture or decorative items. So many people are ignorant of what they use as decorative items such as furniture, clothing, jewelries, household items, and tools.

I spoke to a group of people in our Prophetic School and asked them if they had been able to visit the city of Ephesus in the days of apostle Paul, when Demetrius the silversmith and other craftsmen were making "silver shrines for Diana" (Acts 19:24), how many would have gotten them as souvenirs. Many said yes; wouldn't you also have brought home a well-finished idol that was well polished to attract travelers? This idol "brought no small gain unto the craftsmen" (v. 24, KJV). "So not only is this trade of ours in danger of falling into disrepute, but also the temple of the great goddess Diana may be despised and her magnificence destroyed, whom all Asia and the world worship" (v. 27). Thank God for the artisans working with stones, ceramics, wood, metals, wax, clay, leather, and many other things; but when those things are fashioned after gods, goddesses, idols, and all demonic works, then God is not honored, neither is He glorified.

The Ephesian church in the days of apostle Paul had true conversion. As they repented of their sins and accepted Jesus as Lord and Savior, the next thing they did was to have a clean search of their homes and environment. As they were cleansed, so also did they cleanse their homes from demonic influences. Magical books, occult materials, and anything fashioned after any god or goddess were not spared. They made a bonfire of them. "Also, many of those who had practiced magic brought their books together and burned them in the sight of all. And they counted up the value of them, and it totaled fifty thousand pieces of silver" (v. 19). This singular step of destroying items with magical influences caused the Word of God to grow mightily and it prevailed (v. 20). Then I thought deeply that in addition to the great teachers and biblical teachings, biblical expositions, conferences, seminars, crusades, and fellowships, is the Word of the Lord growing in people's lives? Do we also talk about mightily growing in the Word of God? How about prevailing? Is the Word of God having dominating control over us and our environment?

They burned whatever could make their houses and city unworthy. I meditated deeply about the sending forth of the disciples of Jesus to declare the gospel of the kingdom. They were sent forth with a special mandate: "Heal the sick, cleanse the lepers, raise the dead, cast out demons. Freely you have received, freely give" (Matt. 10:8). Howbeit, Jesus gave specific instructions about cities they would enter: "Now whatever city or town you enter, inquire who in it is worthy, and stay there till you go out. And when you go into a household, greet it. If the household is worthy, let your peace come upon it. But if it is not worthy, let your peace return to you" (vv. 11–13). So, from Jesus' instructions, a city could be "worthy" and another not. A house could be worthy and another not. Even more so, salutation of peace over a house stays when it is worthy and also, salutation of peace returns when the house is unworthy. This is a very serious thing. I ask myself, what makes the house worthy or unworthy? The best answer would be by finding out if everything about our home honors God. Do all our possessions bring blemish and contempt to God? Someone asked me, "Why can't we pray over them and sanctify them?" I responded by saying, "You can't sanctify demons." The Ephesian church did what was right, then so should we. Demonic objects pollute their environments and render them unworthy.

I pray God to heal the ignorance of our generation, when people of their own accord use their hard-earned money to purchase items that attract demonic presence. I consider toys for children: many are great to develop learning skills and mental state. As a guiding principle for toys, we consider safety, but no safety rule is complete without both physical and spiritual safety. Although parents are concerned with the growing trend toward toys and video games that promote violence, crime, and war, our children are exposed to games practicing how to commit murder and theft to win. They are of different classifications: core games—games across a wide spectrum of genres; casual games—simple-to-understand game play and quick-to-grasp rule sets; and serious games—designed primarily to convey information or learning experience of some sort to the player. However, discernment is necessary to make right choices.

Ask yourself before getting things into your home, if such will bring pollution to the house or if it will stir up an oppressive atmosphere. I witnessed garage sales in the area where I live in Ontario, Canada. I remain thankful to God even today for the privilege because it brought the awareness of my environment to me. I could identify crafted images, paintings, and sculptures fashioned after Asian and African gods. I introduced myself as a neighbor and congratulated the man for getting rid of them. He asked me what I knew about the displayed items. I was gracious enough to tell him some of what I knew; I pointed to one particular item and said, "I know what damage this particular one can do in an environment." I asked him, "Do you see shadows or notice movements of physical objects in your house?" He replied, "How did you know that?" Then, I asked if he still had some more at home. He said a few more. But, he stopped talking to me when the would-be-buyers were approaching. I left with a burdened heart and pity for those who would buy them and put them in their houses. Then I knew what to pray for concerning my neighborhood.

Repentance is required for true purging of our environment. Some people may ask, how do I identify what is good from what is bad for my home? I counsel you by saying, pray over your house and if you feel uneasy about an item, pray again specifically over it. If still concerned, put it away and pray to annul the evil effect. I had a gift item that I kept in my living room. Anytime I engage in fervent prayer, my mind goes to it. After repeated occurrences I put it away. I decreed the evil attached to it be gone, even though the item looked harmless. Two days later, after an evening devotion, I was led to go pray over it again. Before getting there, the revelation flooded my spirit as to reflect on when it was brought into the house. After prayerful consideration, I could recollect extensive continuous damage on our property within the period we had it. For that period of time, either something broke, or was damaged, or needed repairs. I prayed and disposed of it. Now, years have passed, and there have been no more breakages or damages. How about yours? Have you prayed to discern what you put on you or around you? Praying to recognize defiled and forbidden possessions will remove the enemy's ability to access our home. Then we can establish God's power and protection over our family.

I pray the veil be taken off that we may see our house and possessions with the eyes of God. Satan is a trespasser who attempts in subtle ways to invade our homes, but we can live free in Christ by ridding our homes of things that attract and empower spiritual darkness. As we enthrone the lordship of Jesus over our lives, we can do the same over our homes, families, and possessions.

Chapter 8

MARKETPLACE WARFARE

TRUE BUSINESS EXISTS in the physical real world, but success is rooted in the spirit. What we are seeing today in the business world is a display of power, dominion, and control by warlocks and warlords—those who declare war because they have the means and authority to engage in war. Crisis in the business world today is a manipulation rooted in rituals and cults. Regardless of physical connections, education, and training, the spiritual still controls the physical, and the business world is a place of intense spiritual warfare. Any physical preparation that is not rooted in the Spirit may produce an image of success outwardly, but it is slowly dying inside. It is possible to climb the ladder, have the corporate title, financial rewards, and social standing, and yet be rotten inwardly by depression and a cry from being unfulfilled.

Understandably, the market is a public gathering held for buying and selling merchandise and a place where goods are offered for sale. Today, it is a global connection and transaction; consumers research and purchase products and services through i-marketing, web-marketing, online marketing and e-marketing. I love this Italian proverb about the market: "The buyer needs a hundred eyes; the seller but one."[1] This proverb is so true because most buyers are blind about the genuineness of the products and the transaction, but the sellers knows what they are doing or selling. A French proverb says, "There are more fools among buyers than among sellers."[2] This cannot be denied because oftentimes the buyers are not fully aware of the intricacies of the products. Many are being fooled by the commercials and the politics behind the products, which may not have the expected effects.

The Bible prophesies about the fall of Babylon:

> And the merchants of the earth will weep and mourn over her, for no one buys their merchandise anymore: merchandise of gold and silver, precious stones and pearls, fine linen and purple, silk and scarlet,

every kind of citron wood, every kind of object of ivory, every kind of object of most precious wood, bronze, iron, and marble; and cinnamon and incense, fragrant oil and frankincense, wine and oil, fine flour and wheat, cattle and sheep, horses and chariots, and bodies and souls of men.

—REVELATION 18:11–13

The listed merchandise is very common, even to the trafficking of humans as slaves. But how about "and the souls of men" (v. 13)? I asked myself, are human souls sold in markets? I could relate with some of the merchandises like "gold, silver, precious stones, pearls, fine linen, purple, silk, scarlet, wood, brass, iron and marble"; even ointment, fine floors, and slaves. But, how about souls of men as part of the articles of commerce? Surely, the Word of God is true to the letter. We may not literally see souls displaced in markets, but let's be aware that man's soul possesses appetites, feelings, emotions, desires, and passions, and it can exercise mental faculties. So all these can be traded with and exchanged for the inferior. No wonder our appetites, feelings, and emotions have so twisted that we have no desire for God and have lost passion for godly things. This is the spirit behind the business world.

Apostle Paul cast out the spirit of divination from a girl in the name of the Lord. This caused her masters to protest because "the hope of their gains was gone" (Acts 16:19, KJV). The consequence was to arrest Paul and Silas, and they "drew them into the market place unto the rulers" (v. 19, KJV). So the rulers are seated in the marketplace? When the hope of gains is lost, the marketplace is the most likely place to get it back because there are rulers that control the marketplace. Casting out the spirit of divination was the "hope of their gain"—the foretelling of future. Is this not what is controlling the marketplace today by foretelling market prices and standards? One of the controlling influences of hope of gains in the market is the spirit of divination. As Paul and Silas were beaten and imprisoned by rulers in the marketplace, so are people beaten and constrained today through decrees, laws, and divination.

> What we are seeing today in the business world is a display of power, dominion, and control by warlocks and warlords.

Apostle Paul also went to Athens in his missionary journey and "saw the city wholly given to idolatry" (17:16, KJV). He witnessed Jesus to people in the synagogue and "in the market daily" (v. 17, KJV). To a city sold out to idolatry, ministering in the synagogue (church gatherings) will not be enough until daily market ministrations are involved. The marketplace is a place to demonstrate God's power and greatness over idolatrous nations where money, power, and fame are worshiped.

In Africa and Asia, I know that there are some traditions attached to markets, one of which is the location. They are not chosen due to proximity to the people or seaports, but are majorly determined through divination, so also the market days. Another tradition is that markets are considered as altars for ritual purposes and a place where the potency of cultist materials can be tested. Discernment of spirits and watchfulness unto prayers is needed in our daily transactions.

I often wonder why kings, queens, and presidents have to parade from the market square to their palaces during coronation or inauguration. Most African empires practice this. People witness the king in procession from the market square to his palace. We truly understand the implications as the market is the most common gathering place of people; in linking the market square to the palace as the traditional priests perform rituals, people are being subdued under the authority of the king. Through this, fierce ruling kings have been raised up to oppress the people. How about the presidential parade in the United States of America, starting from Capitol Hill and ending at the White House? Part of Capitol Hill includes the U.S. Capitol, the Supreme Court building, the Library of Congress, Marine Barracks, Navy Yard, and Congressional Cemetery; there is a nonresidential corridor: "Pennsylvania Avenue, a lively commercial street with shops, restaurants and bars. Eastern market is an 1873 public market on 7th Street SE, where vendors sell fresh meat and produce indoor stalls and at outdoor farmers' stands. It is also the site of an outdoor flea market every weekend."[3] Even though with a modern outfit, the market is part of the composition. As the president parades after inauguration, authority is being established.

The day money fails: The world economy is deteriorating more quickly than leading economists predicted. Unsold goods are piling up. People losing jobs and investments are multiplying everyday. Great nations are officially in recession. This is a serious shock wave through global financial markets causing the hearts of men to fail.

There was a time in history when the world economy failed, but the solution rested on the shoulders of one man by the name Joseph. He was rejected and abandoned to slavery despite his giftedness. He reigned through the wisdom of God while others fainted by the reason of the famine. It came to pass that they lost all their possessions when money failed (Gen. 47:15). Truly, when money failed and all possessions were gone, they cried out, "Buy us and our land for bread, and we and our land will be servants" (v. 19). And Joseph confirmed, "Behold, I have bought you this day and your land" (v. 23, KJV). We must understand the way the global market runs today: money is failing, possessions are wasting, and bodies are being exchanged not just for pleasure, but as a means of survival. It may get worse soon, but for divine intervention. The good thing about the Egyptians was that there was food to exchange for their resources. In our time, when all things are failing, the exchange might not be possible, because of lack of possession; there is nothing to point to as the gains of labor.

I recognize that in Joseph's days only the priests retained their land, money, and possessions. "Only the land of the priests he did not buy; for the priests had rations allotted to them by Pharaoh, and they ate their rations which Pharaoh gave them; therefore they did not sell their lands...And Joseph made it a law over the land of Egypt to this day, that Pharaoh should have one-fifth, except for the land of the priests only, which did not become Pharaoh's" (vv. 22, 26). If the heathen priests could retain their possessions in the time of recession and were properly fed, how much more the believers in Christ Jesus who have been made the priests of the Most High God through the redemptive blood of Jesus (Rev. 1:6)? We also have our "portion assigned" and need not lose our possessions. We can consecrate our possessions to God and trust Him well

> **The marketplace is a place to demonstrate God's power and greatness over idolatrous nations where money, power, and fame are worshiped.**

enough to preserve us in days of famine. Someone may ask me, "Aren't believers also losing jobs, homes, and careers during this economic crisis?" Of course, so many believers are affected. But the principle of abounding in possession can be applied to our lives. The priests of Egypt

did not lose any of their possessions because they had consecrated them
to their gods. And as watchmen of the land, their portions needed to
be preserved for continuous seeking the favor of their gods. We are of a
better heritage than them because we have been redeemed by the blood
of Jesus and are covenanted to the Creator of the heaven and earth. If we
therefore consecrate all that we have to Him, He becomes our portion
and will always supply all our needs. We need not fear when things are
falling apart; the Almighty watches over all.

The story about the three rich men: Jesus spoke about three rich
men: one was physically and spiritual rich, the second was only physically rich with worldly riches, and the third was poor in real life but
rich toward God (Luke 16:19–31). I ask you, which of these three men
would you live to be? I know most people will never dream or desire
to be the poor man, but the physically and spiritually rich. These three
men were Abraham, Lazarus, and the rich man. While the other two
names were mentioned, the rich man's name was not important because
his riches could not help him in time of trouble. Abraham was righteous and very rich while Lazarus was righteous but poor. The rich man
was far from being righteous. The reason Lazarus remained poor was
that he was "desiring to be fed with the crumbs which fell from the rich
man's table" (v. 21). Our desires when they become so strong can rule us.
Checking our desires with the Word of God helps put our lives under
control. Although Lazarus was "full of sores" lying at the gate of the rich
man, the Bible accounted that "moreover"—beyond what has been stated
or worse still—"the dogs came and licked his sores" (v. 21). After both
died, Lazarus, being righteous, entered into his eternal reward while the
unrighteous rich man entered into eternal perdition.

The rich man in his tormenting state lifted up his eyes and saw father
Abraham and Lazarus in his bosom. He made two major requests: the
first was to "send Lazarus, that he may dip the tip of his finger in water
and cool my tongue; for I am tormented in this flame" (v. 24); and secondly, "send him to my father's house" (v. 27). In both requests he put
demands that Lazarus be sent, because he was used to ordering people
around. Even in hell the spirit that hardened his heart against God while
on earth never departed. He even argued with father Abraham: "And he
said, 'No, father Abraham; but if one goes to them from the dead, they
will repent'" (v. 30). After all, father Abraham was richer than him while
on earth.

Therefore, I counsel those who want to be rich and maintain righteous living at the same time to take this counsel: "Command those who are rich in this present age not to be haughty, nor to trust in uncertain riches but in the living God, who gives us richly all things to enjoy" (1 Tim. 6:17). We need to guard against pride and high mindedness, for these are abominations to God. He referred to riches as "uncertain." This may be because of unforeseeable circumstances that could either destroy the source of wealth or cause the affliction of the rich. So many people have been rich, but have lost it all. Why? Because "riches certainly make themselves wings; they fly away like an eagle toward heaven" (Prov. 23:5). This seems to be inevitable as the word *certainly* is used. It is hard to believe that riches can develop wings to fly. So when somebody is rich, they could be unaware that wings are developing and when strong enough to fly, in a twinkling of an eye, it may disappear. How far can it go? It flies as "an eagle toward heaven." An eagle is a high flyer, implying that once it is lost it may be too hard to get back. I laughed over this at the dinner table as I was discussing with friends this particular verse of the scripture. I said, "The best thing to do with riches is to chain down the wings or cut it off. Do everything you know how to, to prevent it from flying." "In the blink of an eye, wealth disappears, for it will sprout wings and fly away like an eagle" (v. 5, NLT).

> However small or insignificant an opportunity seems, be at your best and do it wholeheartedly. You might not know if this is needed for your next level of greatness.

It is also good to know why Lazarus remained poor apart from his illness of sores and desired it; he was a beggar at the gate (Luke 16:20). The gate implies authority; it is a safe place to beg because it is easy to monitor those going and coming in. At least they can see him and help. The gates can control and subdue to perpetual poverty. Notwithstanding, the "righteous are bold as a lion" (Prov. 28:1). We can arise in the strength of the Lord to possess the gates.

Lacking opportunities: "All the preparation in the world won't matter if there are no opportunities or market. You may be the best at what you do and you may work the hardest and you may be the fastest. But ability alone matters not at all; opportunity and timing also have to converge."[4] "But I rejoiced in the Lord greatly that now at last your care for me has flourished again; though you surely did care, but you lacked opportunity" (Phil. 4:10). The generosity of the Philippian church was greatly commended, but they lacked opportunity. I know many people who are gifted and skilful but are redundant due to lack of opportunity. If given a chance, those whom we feel are useless could do great things with a little encouragement. Should we then see it as a mark of disapproval? Not at all. Unfavorable situations we find ourselves in may be our chance to prove ourselves; though hard and difficult, we can prevail.

Joseph was prosecuted and imprisoned for being lied against. He trusted his colleagues to help him after interpreting their dreams, but he was disappointed. Nonetheless, a day came that his gift made room for him and he was remembered. If he had stayed in Potiphar's house, his interpretation skill would not have been discovered. Consequently, if he had been so sad about his situation as to ignore his friends' dreams in the prison, they would not have discovered who he was. But, however irrelevant and unpleasant the situation, he operated his gifts, which brought him to the bigger audience. "A man's gift makes room for him, And brings him before great men" (Prov. 18:16). I counsel that however small or insignificant an opportunity seems, be at your best and do it wholeheartedly. You might not know if this is needed for your next level of greatness.

How about those who had opportunities but couldn't convert them to blessings? This is disappointing. An athlete who was good in rehearsals but failed in the actual performance is disappointed for losing the chance to proof himself. So also is a student who enrolls for a diploma or degree program, expecting to graduate and pursue his goals but fails—although he had the opportunity, he couldn't achieve success. When we fail to come up to expectations in spite of the opportunities, it becomes frustrated hopes. Oftentimes, what prevents us may not be something hard, but however small, it is still a problem. To the children of Israel, Jericho and Ai were barriers to the Promised Land. Jericho was a strong city, while Ai was small. The victory over Jericho was a one-time victory with intense preparations, but that of Ai had to be repeated with different methods at each attempt.

Our excuses about lack of opportunity and hindrance may be due to the fear of the unknown, ignorance, and most times imaginary hindrance.

Being human we conceive ideas, draw inferences, and make judgments; but if the mind is not transformed by the Holy Spirit, we can become slaves to our thoughts and imaginations. When God called Moses to go to Egypt and deliver His people, he made excuses because he pictured Pharaoh's greatness and fame, the dreadfulness of his gods and army. But Pharaoh was no match to him when he obeyed. Sarah, Abraham's wife, laughed at the saying of the angel that she would give birth by the coming year because she imagined herself being old. The spies to the Promised Land imagined themselves as grasshoppers, considering the enemies as giants and that the land could not be possessed. Gideon doubted his strength to overcome the Midianites because he imagined them too powerful to overcome. Mary and some disciples visited the sepulcher on resurrection morning with an imaginary hindrance: "And they said among themselves, 'Who will roll away the stone from the door of the tomb for us?'" (Mark 16:3). Though the stone was very great and sealed with airtight security, "When they looked up, they saw that the stone had been rolled away—for it was very large" (v. 4). If they had stayed back not advancing toward the sepulcher, they would not have discovered that what they thought was a hindrance, was not. I, therefore, counsel you not to allow the fear of the unknown and hindrances you have imagined to run your opportunities to attain greatness. Learn to seize the moment and be at your best.

Good success: I did a general survey by asking a group of people at different places to write down just one reason why they want to be successful. The survey was for both secular and religious groups; different age groups were also considered. I can sum up my findings into five categories:

1. I want to be successful just for prestige and honor.

2. I believe this will take away reproach.

3. I must be successful to help my family and others.

4. I need to be successful because it's God's will for me.

5. Being successful in life is evidence that I'm free from curses of hardship and failure.

Through the grace of God on my life, I have mingled with both the rich and the poor, high and low, because I believe God's redemptive purposes abound to all. However, in the course of this writing, I tried talking to some people who may be considered successful in their career, social status, marriage, health, and finances. I got various answers when I asked them individually, "What is success to you—what does it really mean?" I'll share some of my findings:

- Success to me is getting ahead.

- Success to me is when things turn out well.

- Success is when I have favorable income in my life's pursuit.

- Success is when I'm free from poverty mentality and possess the right formula to forge ahead in life.

- Success to me is working hard and getting results.

- Success is when I achieve status based on educational attainment and occupational choice.

- Success is my personal effort coupled with the right networking and seeing fruitful results.

- I don't have to work hard because through my family and marriage relationship I'm successful regardless of my ability.

- Success is when I achieve my short- and long-term goals.

In one of my interviews, an elderly friend turned the table around by asking me, "What is success to you?" I tried to avoid answering the question because I wanted to learn from others, but he persisted. So I replied saying, "Success is acting wisely—having the ability to discern what is right, interpreting prosperity signs and symbols, and doing them." After saying this, I applauded myself; the man congratulated me and said, "Go, carry it out." A group of people saw a forest; to many of them, it was just a forest, and only a few saw what could be done, like using the trees to build houses, making furniture, and many more things. We may all be exposed to the same opportunity, but we perceive it differently.

It is so unfortunate that lots of people spend their lives pursuing whatever is counterfeit. The deception about counterfeit is that it may appear real, or even looks better, but it is not authentic. Jesus illustrated how people could cling to the unreal and be so deceived that they lose all opportunities.

> If a son asks for bread from any father among you, will he give him a stone? Or if he asks for a fish, will he give him a serpent instead of a fish? Or if he asks for an egg, will he offer him a scorpion? If you then, being evil, know how to give good gifts to your children, how much more will your heavenly Father give the Holy Spirit to those who ask Him!
>
> —LUKE 11:11–13

A request for bread could either get bread or a stone; so could the request for fish in exchange for a serpent, and an egg for a scorpion. Bread, fish, and eggs have great nutritional values. It was before not a coincidence for Satan to demand Jesus to turn a stone into bread in His first temptation (Matt. 4:3). Jesus also fed the multitude with "bread and fish" on multiple occasions (Mark 6:41–44). Therefore, the bread, the fish, and the egg are likened to blessings due to children: "If a son shall ask…" The devil is still in the business of attacking the bread, the fish, and the egg in exchange for a stone, a serpent, and a scorpion. May I also point out to you that Jesus empowered His disciples: "Behold, I give you the authority to trample on serpents and scorpions, and over all the power of the enemy, and nothing shall by any means hurt you" (Luke 10:19). He empowered them that they may tread on serpents and scorpions. If a serpent is given in place of a fish and a scorpion in place of an egg; think about it! What we are supposed to tread upon is now given as blessings. This is an exchange of superiority with inferiority. No wonder people ask for promotions and they get demoted. Rather than gaining, they are losing. Can we shake this off and get back what belongs to us?

Success is acting wisely—having the ability to discern what is right, interpreting prosperity signs and symbols, and doing them.

Moving to the next level: Success becomes pleasurable when we ascend the ladder regardless of the opposition and retain it. Moses succeeded in taking the Israelites out of Egypt and handed them over to Joshua to complete the work. Joshua aimed at success and was encouraged by God to have good success. What distinguishes real success from common success is an unceasing meditation on and obedience to the Word of God. Because the Word of God is eternally settled, it breaks the wilderness mentality and transforms with peace. I also see success as moving from one level of accomplishment unto another. A measure of success should move us to the next level.

I consider the life of Elijah and how he survived famine after the decree of dryness, "there shall not be dew nor rain" (1 Kings 17:1); yet he needed to survive those dry moments. His first level of success while others were suffering was divine direction as to where to go and how to be revived; he was fed by ravens and drank from the brook (vv. 3–4). The expectation would have been that if God led me to the brook, it must last me throughout the famine period; but contrary to that, "the brook dried up" (v. 7). Elijah did not weep nor mourn over it; rather, he was ready to move to the next level of success. Because of his openness to God, he received another divine direction to be sustained by a widow (v. 9). My expectation is that whosoever will sustain me in time of famine should have enough. Contrary to this, the widow was "gathering two sticks" to prepare food, eat, and die (v. 12). I also ask myself, what made a continuous supply of food possible in time of famine? God could have prevented the brook from drying and also could have kept the raven supplying food, but I believe God wanted him to put his gifts to use. We may get to a level in our walk with God when we step up to maturity—not just being spoon fed, but putting our gifts to use. The gift of God in him through prophesies kept the supply going. This level is also a testing time. The widow's son was attacked to the point of death. God's gifts in him brought the child alive. Therefore, the first level of success is receiving divine direction, while the second level is maturing and testing time.

The third level was the time of showing self after hiding for over three years. Truly he appeared: "Behold, Elijah is here" (18:8, KJV). He had been sought throughout kingdoms and nations with oath (v. 10). At first God told him to hide himself, and now God was saying to show himself. The time of showing forth is the moment of breaking forth. The purpose of hiding before showing forth was so he would be incubated by the power of His presence, that he may break forth in glory. Exposing himself prematurely could cost him a lifetime of unfulfilled dreams. There comes a time after planning and developing our visions that we need to produce results. Planning is good, but at some point you have to produce. God's intentions are wonderful, but intention has to be translated into invention.

The fourth level was obtaining results and maintaining them. Results are good, and they give a lasting joy when retained. Elijah called down fire after mocking the prophets of Baal and the grove. The expectation was that he would have called down rain, since there hadn't been rain for many years, but fire was needed for judgment and purification before rain could refresh. The fire consumed the hindrance that caused drought so as to have a lasting joy.

> A dream is heavenly based when God is the author, executor, and the finisher.

Joseph fulfilled his dream and became successful when he translated his dream from earthly to heavenly. Let's compare his two dreams: "There we were, binding sheaves in the field. Then behold, my sheaf arose and also stood upright; and indeed your sheaves stood all around and bowed down to my sheaf" (Gen. 37:7), and "Then he dreamed still another dream and told it to his brothers, and said, 'Look, I have dreamed another dream. And this time, the sun, the moon, and the eleven stars bowed down to me'" (v. 9). The first dream had to do with the field while the other was about the sun, the moon, and the stars. There was a shift in his dream from the field and the earthly to the heavenly—the sun, the moon, and the stars. He recognized the shining glory of the sun, the moon, and the stars, but he reckoned himself to be of a greater glory. When a dream is earthly based, it can be trampled upon, but when heavenly based, it will be hard to pull down. While his brothers "envied" him, his father "observed" (v. 11).

A dream is heavenly based when God is the author, executor, and the finisher. It is one thing to have a goal but another for God to put one in you and give you grace to execute it. Earthly dreams are the ones engineered by you, orchestrated by circumstances, or initiated through your desires and ambitions. With our ability, we may achieve success in earthly dreams, but the heavenly dreams take God alone to accomplish, as He endows you with gifts and empowers you for success. Oh, for a heavenly dream that no attack can destroy and with God's grace coming to pass regardless of oppositions!

True success, therefore, is turning debt, emptiness, and confusion of mind to peace, favor, and abundance. One day of favor could be worth a lifetime of labor. When doors are shut, opportunities are lost, and the way forward looks unrealistic. What do you do at such times? We can look beyond the impossibilities and press on. "Now Jericho was securely shut up because of the children of Israel; none went out, and none came in. And the LORD said to Joshua: 'See! I have given Jericho into your hand, its king, and the mighty men of valor'" (Josh. 6:1–2). At this point in history, Jericho was a great city with a well fortified wall and gates. It was almost an impossible place to possess. Truly, God's ways are not man's ways. Even though the children of Israel were yet to take over Jericho, God's view was different. He said to Joshua, "See! I have given Jericho into your hand" (v. 2). What we consider as difficult is already captured and delivered to us. God commanded Joshua to see Jericho as already conquered. This is the divine pattern of overcoming what seems impossible. May we also see things in the light of God so that God can commit the solution into our hands. Obeying divine strategies of victory, the children of Israel had an ease of passage and an airtight security; the impossible passage gave way on its own accord.

To attain success in your career, ask yourself if work is a pleasure or pain. We all seek significance in our giftedness, education, and profession; we want to excel regardless of hardship and be successful. It is, therefore, good to know that "our careers are not so much a matter of choice but a matter of calling. We are born with a predisposition toward those skills that will enable us to perform whatever work God has given us to do. This means, of course, that if we're operating in our field (or fields) of giftedness, we'll be more effective than we would be in fields where we have no natural aptitude."[5] Everyone is gifted, but not everyone is gifted equally, even in the same field. Does this seem unfair? One may be more skilled than another, but better skills are not always recognized or rewarded. Some, of course, may rise above their peers because their product or output is exceptional, but others will rise to prominence simply because they have had more opportunity to develop their talent; because they have received training from a prestigious institution; or because their social or political networks have provided them (or their work) with unusual exposure.

After hard work and sowing with the expectation to receive blessings, but with minimal harvesting or success, what do you do? Moreover, what do you do when you are sure this is your passion or what you are called to do? I have seen over the years that many people do not even have what it takes to retain blessings. They have lots of information and work hard, but they can't translate it into wealth. The ideas, education, and skill never profit them. In spiritual warfare terms, this is referred to as "stolen treasures" —when valuables or precious possessions waste away and are not tapped into. Jesus warned His disciples to "provide yourselves money bags which do not grow old, a treasure in the heavens that does not fail, where no thief approaches nor moth destroys" (Luke 12:33). Bags are used for storing valuables or precious possessions of any kind. It is a good thing to ask for blessings, but if there is nothing to keep the blessings, it is like not being blessed at all. So our means of storage can "grow old" or "develop holes" (v. 33, NLT). This explains why blessings slip off because of holes in the bag. "You have sown much, and bring in little; You eat, but do not have enough; You drink, but you are not filled with drink; You clothe yourselves, but no one is warm; And he who earns wages, Earns wages to put into a bag with holes" (Hag. 1:6). The possible attacks on our treasure as warned by Jesus could be because of growing old and developing holes, thieves, or moths. The thief takes what belongs to others without permission and wrongfully deprives the rightful owner. The moth is nocturnal in nature—active at night, which may imply the dark hours when people are tired, weary, and asleep. This reveals that what devours people's wealth is more active when we are asleep and not conscious of what is happening around us. So, people awake to their losses; they have been devoured of wealth. Another thing I know about moths is that they frequently appear to circle artificial lights. I can imagine how difficult it is for many people to arise because their rising and shining attracts a moth-like encirclement. As moths circle light, so are they and so is their success. How we keep our bags— our storage of blessings—will determine how much success we have.

There are different kinds of bags: a merchant uses a bag for carrying weights, and priests and prophets use a girdle as pockets, which is symbol of strength. David the shepherd boy picked up five smooth stones out of the brook and "put them in a shepherd's bag that he had, even in a scrip" (1 Sam. 17:40, KJV); he used one of the stones to bring down the giant. Our possessions, when committed to God, can bring down any giant opposing our well being. This brought David to fame. We carry a lot of things in our bags or purses—keys, identity cards, money, makeup, hair brush, feminine products, and fashion accessories. In like manner, there are lots of virtues and blessings we carry about which when put in proper use can bring us to greatness. I ask, has your treasure carrier been stolen, developed holes or been devoured, to the point that nothing good stays in your life? If so, there is hope for you, no matter how low you have been:

> For there is hope for a tree, If it is cut down, that it will sprout again, And that its tender shoots will not cease. Though its root may grow old in the earth, And its stump may die in the ground, Yet at the scent of water it will bud And bring forth branches like a plant.
>
> —JOB 14:7–9

It is not over with you yet; you can still be hopeful no matter the condition. You might have lost it all, but the remnant can bring great joy to you if well applied. Your little strength can accomplish more success than you think.

Lots of people give up after many attempts without success, forgetting that the formative stage is always complex. I counsel you to know that the beginning is always very difficult. It might seem like a waste of time, but persistently pursuing your passion brings great results. "Though your beginning was small, Yet your latter end would increase abundantly" (8:7). Above all things, ask God for the keys of success, to unlock blessings. For every level of success, keys are needed to go in. This makes it easy to get the required success. There are keys to open people's hearts to favor and help you. At such times communication and transaction flow with ease. The keys also open up the treasure and benefits that determine the success of the business.

Arising out of the ruins: It is easier to destroy than to build; so I ask, why is it difficult to restore to good condition when things go bad? Over the years I have watched people rising up and attaining great things in life. Suddenly they crash, but rising up again becomes an almost impossible task. I am one of the few people who believe ruins can be built again, even more gloriously. However, careful steps, right strategies, and the right approach are essential. Nehemiah was one of my favorites in the Old Testament. This is so for many reasons. He heard about the ruins of Jerusalem and was inspired to raise the ruins. Many people saw the ruins, while others heard about it, but they could not raise it.

Nehemiah ignited the vision and resolved to seek the face of God. He repented, and God gave him favor before the king. Opposition could not stop him, so he prevailed. Likewise, I believe that difficult projects can be accomplished and impossible cases can become possible with God on our side. Following Nehemiah's strategies, whatever good thing that is torn down can be built up again. After Nehemiah got the king's permission, he journeyed to Jerusalem with some people to determine what could be done. His first move was to inspect the ruins, knowing the extent of damage would determine the way forward.

> **Lots of people give up after many attempts without success, forgetting that the formative stage is always complex.**

> And I arose in the night, I and some few men with me; neither told I any man what my God had put in my heart to do at Jerusalem: neither was there any beast with me, save the beast that I rode upon. And I went out by night by the gate of the valley, even before the dragon well, and to the dung port, and viewed the walls of Jerusalem, which were broken down, and the gates thereof were consumed with fire. Then I went on to the gate of the fountain, and to the king's pool: but there was no place for the beast that was under me to pass. Then went I up in the night by the brook, and viewed the wall, and turned back, and entered by the gate of the valley, and so returned. And the rulers knew not whither I went, or what I did; neither had I as yet told it to the Jews, nor to the priests, nor to the nobles, nor to the rulers, nor to the rest that did the work.
>
> —NEHEMIAH 2:12–16, KJV

There are quite a few lessons to learn to help us come out of our own ruins, difficult moments, and disappointing situations.

Arising while yet dark: "And I arose in the night" (v. 12, KJV). Nehemiah got up when it was yet dark. His awakening was in the night when others were sleeping. Nighttime could symbolize our dark and lonely moments. It is the most trying moment when people lose hope, but it is also the right time to arise. So many people wait to see things start picking up or notice significant improvement before working on their ruins. A quick way to build is to arise while it is yet dark and lonely. At such times, no one seems to believe in us or trust the project. Nehemiah did not choose the day when people could see him and ridicule him; these people live among the ruins and are contented with it. It is the same with any goal we are pursuing. Because so many people have tried but failed, they will discourage others. Therefore, to get ahead in life and accomplish the impossible, let it be known to you that it could be lonely and dark; however, it is joyful and fulfilling when the goals are achieved.

When Nehemiah arose at night, he visited strategic places that were relevant to the completion of the project. I also believe that this has significance to how ruins can be built:

- Valley Gate: Just as "Daniel sat in the gate of the King" (Dan. 2:49); and at the gates of cities, courts of justices were frequently held (Deut. 16:18); also Jesus spoke about the "gates of hell" (Matt. 16:18); gates may indicate "authority." Therefore, with Nehemiah's first point of call at the valley gate (Neh. 2:13), it indicates the need to position ourselves to overcome the authority that controls the valley—a lowly, depressive, and rough journey of life. When people are depressed and feel despondent about life, making progress will be difficult. However, if we overcome what brings others down, we can rightly pursue our goals. Therefore in arising out of ruins, the valley state of life must be overcome.

- Dragon Well: From the valley gate to the dragon well (v. 13)—what a journey! Coming out of a valley to discover a well, would have been an exciting experience. A well is an excavation made to extract the treasures buried in the earth. As refreshing as this could be, it was named a dragon well. Although it was a well of treasures, it was hard to get. Those who tried getting the treasure died before they could touch it. So many people give up after going through the valley and rough moments of life, only to discover a treasure that cannot be reached. But Nehemiah pressed on. You also can prevail.

- Dung Port: When things are not working well, goals seem unachievable, and all we have done looks like a mess, what do we do? At such times, life becomes repulsive. It was at that point that Nehemiah "viewed the walls" (v. 13). When things are not working right and hope seems lost, then it is time to view the whole project again. That is, view what can be seen in a range of vision. Get a vision of possible things that can be achieved out of the most difficult situation. Dorothea Brande said, "Envisioning the end is enough to put the means in motion."[6] Having passed through the valley and the dung gates, Nehemiah believed in seeing beyond the ruins. He envisioned the good that can come out of the dung—a possible place of good farm land. Frank Gaines said, "Only he who can see the invisible can do the impossible."[7]

- Fountain Gate—King's Pool: With a right vision and mind-set, good things are bound to spring forth. Nehemiah escaped the initial difficult moments, and through perseverance and steadfastness, he came to the king's pool. "Seest thou a man diligent in his business? he shall stand before kings; he shall not stand before mean men" (Prov. 22:29, kjv). There is a place of influence and attainment for those who tirelessly pursue their goals. However, it is much more laborious to maintain a dignity status than when you are still a crawler. One thing is to press to attain success, another is to retain and abound: "and to the King's pool: but there was no place for the beast that was under me to pass" (Neh. 2:14). That is, the king's pool was blocked. It was as if his journey were to be terminated. Nehemiah found a way forward, "by the brook, and viewed the wall" (v. 15). Even though the king's pool was blocked, he passed by the brook, a small stream. Following the course that brought him to the king's pool, he was disappointed, but he found a narrow path and continued his journey.

So many people pass through similar experiences in life. The path that brought them to success may not continue forever. The opportunity that made them great may not always be there, yet they must not fall short of their goals. At such times when nothing seems to work out, there may be only a little opportunity; however insignificant this may be, success will show up. Nehemiah pursued this little stream and concluded his journey. All he needed to do at this point was to view the ruins again. He deepened his vision. As good as the first vision was, it was not sufficient for the next level of success. Les Brown said, "It takes someone with a vision of the possibilities to attain new levels of experience. Someone with the courage to live his dreams."[8] Thus Nehemiah completed the inspection of the ruins and was determined to build. When he started building, nothing could stop him because he had envisioned the project and was determined to overcome all hindrances. We also can arise out of our difficult situations. The impossibilities can become possible. Starting off may be difficult, but just like the popular saying: "To be a star, you must shine your own light, follow your own path, and don't worry about the darkness, for that is when the stars shine brightest."

Chapter 9

NOT WORTHY TO DIE

L IFE IS PRECIOUS and worth living. It is a gift from God and should be cherished. Even though life is full of trials and heartaches to the point that some wish themselves dead, there are some who are hopeful for a better life. When there is a cessation of all vital functions in the body, one is pronounced dead. Death, whether accidental or medical, sudden or expected, to most human beings is tragic. When it occurs, those left behind mourn, weep, and may not find consolation. People fight, but to no avail; some escape, yet are still fearful and expecting—maybe one day.

I am writing this chapter with the belief that the living God will comfort those who are mourning their loved ones and deliver those "who through fear of death were all their lifetime subject to bondage" (Heb. 2:15). The thought of death is scary to many people. Oh, dreams about the dead will set many panicking all day long. Any strange feeling in the body will set many confused, and they will think about the worst-case scenario. It is scary to see some people doubting themselves, their doctors, medication, and worse still, doubting prayers. They are afraid to travel by air or by road. Sleep becomes a terror; they are afraid of the dark and frightened by news either through media or by any means of communication. My counsel to the fainting in heart is, "Why should you die before your time?" (Eccles. 7:17).

Job was a man who suffered afflictions; it was like passing through the shadow of death, but he was redeemed to live and see many days. The phrase "shadow of death" was mentioned in the book of Job nine times. When God decided to help him out of his troubles, He interrogated him: "Have the gates of death been revealed to you? Or have you seen the doors of the shadow of death?" (Job 38:17). So there are gates and the shadow of death? If not for God's mercy, Job would have been swallowed up by death.

The curse of infirmity: The curse of infirmity is a ravaging force that has brought death to many. It is the spirit that produces weaknesses— physical, mental, emotional, and spiritual. It is noteworthy that not all sicknesses and diseases are spiritual. However, if spiritual attacks are involved, the simplest condition may defy solutions and be hard to diagnose, not responding to treatments and full of medical errors. I have seen experts, consultants, specialists, and gifted people who are good at what they are doing, but they become confused and disoriented, not knowing what to do. They may be good on other patients but helpless before those marked with the curse of infirmity. When the curses are taken away, things work out much better. I have visited the sick in the hospital to pray, and the Spirit of God will lead me to pray for the equipment, sanctify the room, and pray for the hospital staff. I have been led a few times to pray against bewitchment so that the attack on the patient will not make them operate in error.

It is scary to know how tragic and sudden death can wreck homes and how untimely death can cut short the lives of many people. Breakouts of sicknesses and diseases sometimes spare no one. Researchers do not always catch up with casualties. Sad still, so many people are being drawn to death: "If you faint in the day of adversity, Your strength is small. Deliver those who are drawn toward death, And hold back those stumbling to the slaughter" (Prov. 24:10–11). Why should people be cut short before their time and live unfulfilled lives? I truly believe that God still hears the groaning of His people: "For He looked down from the height of His sanctuary; From heaven the LORD viewed the earth, To hear the groaning of the prisoner, To release those appointed to death" (Ps. 102:19–20). With joy we can fulfill the number of our days.

At the time of the creation of the World Health Organization (WHO) in 1948, health was defined as being "a state of complete physical, mental and social well-being and not merely the absence of disease or infirmity."[1] Achieving and maintaining health should be an ongoing process. Staying healthy is the key to achieving goals and values. Just like a safe environment, enhanced immunity, good nutrition, stress reduction, good sleep, and exercise help maintain good health; right balancing of all these with the creative Word of God and prayer ensure total well being. A quote from Peace Pilgrim: "I don't eat junk food and I don't think junk thoughts."[2] We are what we think, and what we think controls us because "for as he thinks in his heart, so is he" (Prov. 23:7).

Instruments of death: While death manifests suddenly, it gives signs and warnings to others. If worked upon, it can be averted. Even the sudden attacks of death sometimes have flashes as signals before the actual death. When the means by which something is achieved is dealt with, the possibility of occurrence is limited. I'll consider some verses of the Word of God to see some implements facilitating death and how to overcome them. "He also prepares for Himself instruments of death; He makes His arrows into fiery shafts" (Ps. 7:13).

- Sleep of Death: Sleep is a natural periodic state of rest for the mind and body. At such a time, man is withdrawn from his activities and is in a state of unconsciousness. This could positively or negatively affect our soul. As much as our body needs rest, God will also grant us sweet sleep. "When you lie down, you will not be afraid; Yes, you will lie down and your sleep will be sweet" (Prov. 3:24). But the wicked ones take advantage. "But while men slept, his enemy came and sowed tares among the wheat and went his way" (Matt. 13:25). Nightmares and terrible attacks have plagued many people, and they are desperately crying out for help. It is unfortunate that many people have slept never to wake up; they had the sleep of death. "Consider and hear me, O LORD my God; Enlighten my eyes, Lest I sleep the sleep of death" (Ps. 13:3).

- Shadow of Death: A shadow shows that the real image is close by. This is when death hovers around someone. King David was in this situation, but he prevailed. He was in "the valley of the shadow of death" (Ps. 23:4), but God led him through and brought him out. The same God is still alive to save and deliver you.

- Gates of Death: "Have the gates of death been revealed to you? Or have you seen the doors of the shadow of death?" (Job 38:17). This was God's question to Job. No matter what the level of sickness is, if the gates of death are not opened, the person may not die; but if opened, it would be difficult to help such a person. You can, therefore, decree against the gates of hell and death never to swallow you up and your loved ones. "Have mercy on me, O Lord! Consider my trouble from those who hate me, You who lift me up from the gates of death" (Ps. 9:13).

- Snares of Death: Death can be a trap, which when fallen into may be hard to escape. Traps usually may be things we ignore, but they are deadly. Many people are trapped by their choices. What ought to give joy can stir up discouragement and heaviness of heart, leading to health problems. We are often led into situations in which escape is difficult, but we can trust God to make an escape route for us. "The sorrows of Sheol surrounded me; The snares of death confronted me" (Ps. 18:5).

- Sorrows of Death: Cycle of pains, suffering, and misfortune can break our heart. This is when death flashes its terror to break our defenses, causing us to yield to its threats. "The pangs of death surrounded me, And the floods of ungodliness made me afraid" (Ps. 18:4).

- Dust of Death: The Messiah in His deepest state of humanity cried out saying, "My strength is dried up like a potsherd, And My tongue clings to My jaws; You have brought Me to the dust of death" (Ps. 22:15). Since we are made from dust, and the breath of the Almighty gave us life, the flesh, when subjected to affliction, can give way to death.

- Terrors of Death: "My heart is severely pained within me, And the terrors of death have fallen upon me. Fearfulness and trembling have come upon me, And horror has overwhelmed me. So I said, 'Oh, that I had wings like a dove! I would fly away and be at rest'" (Ps. 55:4–6). Death is a terror that produces fear and trembling, but we can be protected from its horrors, just like the psalmist prayed for the wings of a dove to fly away and rest from the horror of death. Truly, the Holy Spirit (dove) can make us escape the overwhelming terror of death.

- Appointed to Death: We live in a strange world in which the spiritual dictates to the physical. When there is a witchcraft designation over an environment or a family line, chaos and calamity can break forth. An increase of demonic activities in an environment can result in a breakout of evil. "To hear the groaning of the prisoner, To release those appointed to death" (Ps. 102:20). We can pray to cancel an appointment with death and establish an appointment with life by the covenant of the blood of Jesus.

- Chambers of Death: "Her house is the way to hell, Descending to the chambers of death" (Prov. 7:27). The spirit of death summons the souls of men to its chambers, thus resulting in a breakdown of health. You can decree against it and refuse the invitation to death's chamber by the blood of Jesus and command the rescue of your soul.

- Ways of Death: "There is a way that seems right to a man, But its end is the way of death" (Prov. 14:12). This is when our decisions and behaviors are life threatening, yet we refuse to yield to warnings. It could be pleasurable initially, but it comes with lots of health hazards. An obsession to wrongdoing without the retrieving of steps could cut life short.

- Messengers of Death: A messenger carries messages or performs errands. Messengers of death prepare the ground for the spirit of death to operate. The individual concerned is fully aware of the invading danger ahead through torments in dreams and chains in unexpected occurrences. This could be averted by prayerfully binding both the messenger and his message.

- Pains of Death: When the attack of death has a grip on any soul, such an individual could be afflicted with pain causing slow death. "Whom God raised up, having loosed the pains of death, because it was not possible that He should be held by it" (Acts 2:24).

- Sting of Death: "O Death, where is your sting? O Hades, where is your victory?" (1 Cor. 15:55–56). Death is a torturer, especially when it injects its venom, causing complications and a sudden collapse of bodily organs. Only the blood of Jesus can flush it out and restore one to health.

- Sentence of Death: The enemy of our soul always seeks for faults to establish attacks. When found guilty, forgiveness is out of the way. He sees death as the only possible thing that can settle the matter, so he condemns his victim to death. "For we do not want you to be ignorant, brethren, of our trouble which came to us in Asia: that we were burdened beyond measure, above strength, so that we despaired even of life. Yes, we had the sentence of death in ourselves, that we should not trust in ourselves but in God who raises the dead" (2 Cor. 1:8–9). Thanks be to God because He only has the final say to our lives. His throne of grace and mercy can annul such sentences. "Having wiped out the handwriting of requirements that was against us, which was contrary to us. And He has taken it out of the way, having nailed it to the cross. Having disarmed principalities and powers, He made a public spectacle of them, triumphing over them in it" (Col. 2:14–15).

- Suffering of Death: This is when people are going through the lifestyle of sorrow, grief, and lamentation. The pressures of life can bring so much suffering as to cause someone to desire death. "But we see Jesus, who was made a little lower than the angels, for the suffering of death crowned with glory and honor, that He, by the grace of God, might taste death for everyone" (Heb. 2:9).

- Fear of Death: A couple came to me for counseling some time ago, and the husband got up from his seat, pointing to the wife and requesting special deliverance for the wife: "This woman needs special deliverance." I asked why. He said, "We have four children, and my wife gets up in the middle of the night when everybody is sleeping and puts her ear close enough to each of the children to check if

they're still breathing. She does this everyday. While, I
believe it's good to check on the children, her motive is
to check if they're still breathing. I believe she needs to
break free from the fear of death." The fear of death can
make people become a slave to death. "And release those
who through fear of death were all their lifetime subject to
bondage" (Heb. 2:15).

No matter how the instruments of death manifest, Jesus swallowed
up death in victory (1 Cor. 15:54). He has the keys of death (Rev. 1:18).
He abolishes death and brought life and immortality to light (2 Tim.
1:10). He tasted death for our sakes, that we might live (Heb. 2:9); and He
destroyed him that had the power of death (v. 14).

With this understanding, I can boldly say, "For You have delivered my
soul from death. Have You not kept my feet from falling, That I may walk
before God In the light of the living?" (Ps. 56:13). "I said, 'O my God, Do
not take me away in the midst of my days; Your years are throughout all
generations'" (102:24).

Death threat: We stand at great risk and grave harm when our health
is challenged or we are inflicted with pains. Such cannot be ignored,
but the ways in which we seek a solution determines how life goes.
Continuous threats can surely jeopardize our health, and the long-term
effects may make us cave in to the consequence of death. It is fearful to
see so many hardworking people, diligent in their ways, whose health is
threatened by sickness and unexpected disease. Some try to fight it but
have become weak after a long trial. My heart goes to the people who
are hopeful about life, but they soon received bad reports about their
health. It is like a death sentence without remedy. Withdrawal of friends
or companions at such times can worsen the matter.

I read with interest about how the prophet Jeremiah was threatened
with death by the priests, prophets, and all the people. He was arrested
for declaring the Word of the Lord. This was what he was called to do—to
turn people's hearts back to God. They all agreed that he must surely die.

Now it happened, when Jeremiah had made an end of speaking all
that the LORD had commanded him to speak to all the people that the
priests and the prophets and all the people seized him, saying, "You
will surely die! Why have you prophesied in the name of the LORD,
saying, 'This house shall be like Shiloh, and this city shall be desolate,

without an inhabitant'?" And all the people were gathered against Jeremiah in the house of the LORD.

                                                        —JEREMIAH 26:8–9

Those involved were the priests, the prophets, and all the people. I see the implications of this as what is happening to many people today. While the prophets prophesy, the priests perform the rituals, and the people wait to see it happen. In spiritual warfare, there are priests before the altars performing elaborate rituals in carrying out what the prophets declare. The outcome of this to the individual can result in serious damages. Jesus Christ has become our High Priest to bring to pass the sayings of the prophets. He offered Himself as an eternal sacrifice that people may be reconciled to God. He did all this to set free those who are under the yoke of sin and death, and to break free from the arrests.

After Jeremiah's arrest, the princes left the royal palace to go to the gate of the Lord's house to plead for him. They contended against the death sentence and declared that "this man is not worthy to die" (v. 16, KJV). My earnest prayer is that as many whose souls are being arrested and threatened with death, the Prince of Glory, Jesus Christ, will arise from His royal throne to go to the gates of our arresters and contend against them and declare, "You are not worthy to die." So the priests, prophets, and all the people could not execute their purpose because Jeremiah was not handed over to them to be put to death (v. 24). In like manner, I pray for every reader of this book never to be handed over to those who will destroy you. May you be protected and preserved in the presence of the Lord. Jeremiah also gave his reason why he should not be killed: "The LORD sent me" (v. 12). We also can boldly proclaim that the Lord sent us on a mission, appointed us for His glory, and separated us for His purpose so as to reverse the verdict of destruction.

Apostle Paul also had several death threats, but none could catch up with him until his mission was fulfilled. He finished his course and ran a good race. He was arrested, beaten up, and bound with chains, and he faced the council. He was under the vow of death. "And when it was day, some of the Jews banded together and bound themselves under an oath, saying that they would neither eat nor drink till they had killed Paul" (Acts 23:12). Thank God for the intervention of the chief captain. The demand on his life was that he was worthy to die. "And Festus said: 'King Agrippa and all the men who are here present with us, you see this man about whom the whole assembly of the Jews petitioned me, both at Jerusalem and here, crying out that he was not fit to live any longer. But when I found that he had committed nothing deserving of death, and that he himself had appealed to Augustus, I decided to send him'" (25:24–25). People condemned him to death, but after careful examination he was found not guilty. Yet his accusers wouldn't give up. "And when they had gone aside, they talked among themselves, saying, 'This man is doing nothing deserving of death or chains'" (26:31). When they would not give up on their pursuit, he was constrained to appeal to Caesar (28:19). He transferred his case to the highest court in the land. May we also learn how to appeal our case unto the heavenly court where Jehovah rules over all as the eternal Judge and Jesus is our Advocate (1 John 2:1). The earthly realm has committed several errors in judging and condemning us, which was sufficiently serious to invalidate the outcome of life. If the Julian law condemned any magistrate who condemned, tortured, imprisoned, or put to death anyone who would appeal to Caesar, how much more the divine law. God's law supersedes any law that held us bound. "For the law of the Spirit of life in Christ Jesus has made me free from the law of sin and death" (Rom. 8:2). Could you petition the heavenly court that you are not worthy to die? The Lord God is more willing to save than we are. Present your case to Him and He will vindicate you.

Death to vultures: I lived briefly in an area of eastern Nigeria where vultures are in large number. I carefully studied them and can relate my observations to spiritual warfare. They are scavenging birds that feed on dead or decaying matter. They seldom attack healthy animals, but they may kill the wounded or the sick. That is why weakness and being wounded in spirit can be to our disadvantage if not worked upon. There are spiritual vultures waiting to attack and kill. We may get weak and weary, but remaining in this state for too long may jeopardize our souls. Trusting God and relying on Him for strength and grace to rise up again pushes back the vultures waiting our destruction.

Many people aim high but get nowhere. Just like the eagles, we want to move swiftly unhindered to achieve our desired goals. I also discovered that eagles and the old-world vultures are in the same family, *Accipitridae*. This implies a family tie. As an eagle, you want to fly high, but there could be a family tie with a vulture. No wonder people of great vision who are hard working and goal getters fall short and never get their desired objectives. When we have good ideas but are in the company of those who desire to see the death of our ideas, never reaching fulfillment, then it is a great trouble. It is unfortunate that we associate with those who are not interested in our vision, neither are they attracted to our success, nor are they excited about our desired goals; they are indifferent and bored when we share our goals. There are vulture-like people waiting to see us become feeble and get wasted away. However, you can break off to a higher height, mounting your wings as eagles, never giving up until you reach your goal.

Vultures mostly have a bald head, devoid of feathers, which is an indication of no glory. A tie with people void of peace, love, and glory has brought many people down. Vulture-like people desire nothing but death: death of visions, plans, virtues, and values. Awake, therefore, and look up to God to release His glory upon you.

In observing vultures, two things give me concern. The first is how they can adapt to feeding on carcasses, and secondly is how they walk over decaying places. My finding is that they adapt to feeding on the dead because they have an exceptionally corrosive and highly acidic stomach to safely digest whatever is harmful and deadly to other animals. They can safely walk over decaying places because they "urinate straight down their legs; the uric acid kills bacteria accumulated from walking through carcasses, and also acts as evaporative cooling."[3] I, therefore, figured out that it is natural with vultures to do what they are doing; just like it can be natural for the enemy of our soul to do wickedness, so is it natural with God to show compassion. May we connect with His enduring mercies to enjoy freedom in all things.

> **Death to the vultures manifesting sicknesses, diseases, weariness, and confusion in your life, in Jesus Christ's name. They shall wait, but in vain, because you are coming alive to the glory of God.**

I walked into a hospital to pray for someone who had been admitted for four and a half weeks. The moment I stepped into the hospital complex, the Holy Spirit opened my eyes to see vultures hovering over the place. And I heard the voice of the Lord saying, "I have souls in this hospital that I want to heal and deliver from the pit of death today; therefore, decree death to vultures, and my people shall be healed." In obedience to the Word of God, I stood outside the hospital complex with my hands lifted up and decreed against the vultures that were waiting to devour the carcasses of God's people. I commanded them to let go and flee to desolation. Immediately after the prayer, I headed up to see the woman I came to visit. Arriving at the room was the medical team just getting in a few seconds before me. She was examined as I stepped aside listening, and I heard very pleasant comments: "If you continue this way, you'll be discharged within few days." Another said, "What happened? Why the sudden positive turnaround?" When they left the room, I stepped in saying, "The vultures are dead; you shall live." The vultures assigned to devour her failed, and she was set free. So also I pray for the readers of this book: Death to the vultures manifesting sicknesses, diseases, weariness, and confusion in your life, in Jesus Christ's name. They shall wait, but in vain, because you are coming alive to the glory of God.

Job declared, "There is a path which no fowl knoweth, and which the vulture's eye hath not seen" (Job 28:7, KJV). It is unsafe for the vultures to discover the great treasures of our lives and to know our path to greatness. Job was righteous and very wealthy, but he lost it all because while celebrating his greatness, unknown to him, the vultures were waiting to devour his health, wealth, and family. Surely they devoured, but thank God for His divine restoration. In the end Job possessed much more than he lost. There are vulture-like spirits waiting to devour many people, but God is greater and more powerful to deliver.

There is hope for the wounded and the sick regardless of the hovering of the vultures. A desperate cry to God can fix the problem. "God, pick up the pieces. Put me back together again. You are my praise!" (Jer. 17:14, THE MESSAGE). When God heals, He gives soundness of both body and mind, and freedom from abnormality; He restores to health. Truly, He makes people whole. Jesus healed many and gave them a quality of life full of joy and abundance, which is the state of being healthy, happy, and prosperous. We also can trust Him to move from sickness to wholeness and from the fear of death to life, even life in abundance.

Chapter 10

STRATEGIES FOR THE OVERCOMERS

T HE ARMS RACE has continued into the current era and remains a drain on the resources of most nations of the world. For effective warfare, proper handling of weapons is necessary. With a weapon you can gain advantage over an adversary or place them at a disadvantage. Apart from the harm or damage done by the weapon, it also reduces the morale of the enemies. However good weapons are, confidence and discipline are needed for a weapon to work.

From the first murderer, Cain who slew his brother (Gen. 4:8), weapons have been put to use in combat. There are variations of weapons which have been improved for effective combating: from wooden clubs, slings, and unshaped stone bows to arrows, swords, spears, shields, armors, battering rams, horse-drawn chariots, and pikes (pole weapons). Then we move to the age of gunpowder, guns, rockets, machine guns, warships, and space warfare. Advancement has led to the atomic bomb, nuclear weapons, ballistic missiles, and weapons of mass destruction such as nuclear, chemical, and biological weapons. There are more accurate, well-targeted weapons today that are computer-guided weaponry. If in physical warfare, weapons are improved upon for swift, effective, and well-targeted defensive and offensive operations, how much more spiritual weapons that are so vast and highly advanced that many cannot comprehend.

There came a time when Israel as a nation was under the reign of Saul, and it became helpless before the Philistines. The spoilers came from different directions when they knew that there was "no blacksmith found throughout all the land of Israel, for the Philistines said, 'Lest the Hebrews make swords or spears'" (1 Sam. 13:19). So, when weapons were not being produced, "All the Israelites would go down to the Philistines to sharpen each man's plowshare, his mattock, his ax, and his sickle; and the charge for a sharpening was a pim for the plowshares, the mattocks, the forks, and the axes, and to set the points of the goads. So it came about, on the day of battle, that there was neither sword nor spear found in the hand of any of the people who were with Saul and Jonathan. But they were found with Saul and Jonathan his son" (vv. 20–22). Only the king and his son had the right weapons for war. What a tragedy! Consequently, considering the body of Christ today, how many people are well equipped for kingdom warfare? Except for those who have passed through rigorous and intense discipleship, which is not common today, this is a generation that is only seeking what they can get from God and not what they can do for Him. Are we not like the Israelites "going down" to the Philistines (the heathen) to sharpen our weapons? Don't we depend on the New Age doctrine to train ourselves? How about using occult means, thinking the Bible is not enough? We have gone so far down that the world doesn't value us, neither do we know how superior we are. Those who seem to be doing well among us are just carrying a file for smoothing.

Believers in Christ are of a better covenant and are well fortified by the Holy Spirit for exploits. I love the way apostle Paul regarded anything short of the saving grace as "weak and beggarly elements" (Gal. 4:9). I was working closely with an elderly friend in ministry, who after casting out demons and seeing demonic manifestations, would say, "You weak and beggarly elements." Demonic people begged Jesus in His days not to cast them out. As they recognized Him as Lord over all, so they should recognize us. The true nature of demons is that they are weak, but through deceit they enslave many. However, if they are beggarly and weak, how are they able to afflict so many people with bondages?

> If in physical warfare, weapons are improved upon for swift, effective, and well-targeted defensive and offensive operations, how much more spiritual weapons that are so vast and highly advanced that many cannot comprehend.

Can we reflect on where and how beggars operate? Beggars operate where they know they can receive something. You can find them mostly at the automated banking machine area, stores, and restaurants because they think you have no business going to those places if you don't have money. How about during rush hour when traffic is heavy? You see them by the traffic lights hoping to get something from you. They are often very persistent; they run after you when they notice a chance of getting something. So are demons; because of what we possess and the heritage laid before us, they run after us with the hope of getting something from us. Some beggars will annoy you to the point of provocation, and some can rob you. You have a heritage to protect; defend it. I would, therefore, like to run you through some biblical strategies profitable for kingdom warfare. Applying this to your life is a proof of victory.

Developing a Champion's Mind-set

Life is full of challenges; you don't have to aim high before the unimaginable side of life shows up. So many people find themselves in situations that are hard to endure and hard to comprehend, and they have to deal with people who are hard to please. However, as Napoleon Bonaparte said, "Victory belongs to the most persevering."[1] We often face difficult tasks that may determine the blessings ahead. Henry Ward Beecher said, "Victories that are easy are cheap. Those only are worth having which come as the result of hard fighting."[2] A lot of people struggle through life and see life as competition; some see it as war zone, while others see it as playground or a marketplace where we exchange virtues and relate with one another. Whichever way our outlook on life is, we don't have to go through life as losers.

> A true champion is one who, having become a champion, raises up the champion in others.

Our responses and interpretations of situations will determine if we are champions or losers. Twelve men were sent to view the Promised Land ahead of the others. They were representatives of their tribes. They spent forty days in the land, and they came with the fruits of the land. They saw giants inhabiting the land, and they reported saying, "It truly flows with milk and honey, and this is its fruit" (Num. 13:27). I often imagine that if they saw giants and plucked from the fruits they did not sow, but were not destroyed, wouldn't the same God who protected the twelve do same to the entire congregation? Their trouble was their mental attitude: "We were like grasshoppers in our own sight, and so we were in their sight" (v. 33). Their problem began by seeing themselves as no match for the giants, and the people of the land as "stronger than we" (v. 31). People see you as you consider yourself to be. You are what you think yourself to be. It is all about the mind-set.

To the contrary, Joshua and Caleb, who also visited the land with them, perceived it differently. Although "the men who had gone up with him said, 'We are not able to go up against the people, for they are stronger than we'" (v. 31), Joshua and Caleb both believed that "their defence is departed from them, and the LORD is with us: fear them not" (14:9, KJV). While Joshua and Caleb made it to the Promised Land, others couldn't; they perished because of their negative and unbelieving mind-set. David confronted Goliath. Although he was a giant, David came against him, "in the name of the LORD of hosts, the God of the armies of Israel" (1 Sam. 17:45). If we see what is difficult for us in the light of God, we will gain victory over it.

David was a man who can be considered a champion, not just because he killed the champion of the Philistines, Goliath, but also because he rose up champions. A true champion is one who, having become a champion, raises up the champion in others.

There came a time in David's life when he had to run from cave to cave because of Saul's vow to destroy him. At the beginning of his life, people who were not good were attracted to him, such as "losers and vagrants and misfits of all sorts. David became their leader. There were about four hundred in all" (22:2, THE MESSAGE). There came a time when their camp was invaded, and they were so grieved as to think of stoning David, "but David encouraged himself in the LORD his God" (30:6, KJV).

"Then David and the people who were with him lifted up their voices and wept, until they had no more power to weep" (v. 4). They became so discouraged as to cause David to also lose courage. How easy it is for our environment to affect us if we don't stand out and reveal our unique identity. No one was strong enough to comfort him; he had to encourage himself especially in the Lord. When our environment becomes hostile and life's situations turn sour, it is only in God that we can get comfort and strength.

I can't imagine having to be the leader of losers, debtors, and misfits of all sorts. Truly speaking, it wouldn't be an easy job. I can envisage daily murmuring, complaints, arguments, fighting, and insubordination of all sorts. I have been to pastors' prayer meetings where the pastors pray for people with good minds who are kind hearted, loving, and getting people to attend their church. Oftentimes, these kinds of prayers are not denied, but to the contrary, hard and difficult people show up. I often ask myself, why would God do so? I simply believe that God allows it to use these people to bring out the best in us. Although in the midst of losers, David refused to be a loser. Their negative attitudes could not make him lose his identity. He permitted God to shine through him until he raised a champion in them. May we also permit God to shine through us and stand strong in every situation that we may live as champions and not losers.

I read the Bible with amazement on how David later had "mighty men" around him (23:8). The same man whose life attracted losers now had a team of champions to help him fulfill his dreams. I would like to consider what made them "mighty," so as to use the principles that made them great to pattern our way to being champions.

One-time repeated victory

"These are the names of the mighty men whom David had: Josheb-Basshebeth the Tachmonite, chief among the captains. He was called Adino the Eznite, because he had killed eight hundred men at one time" (v. 8).

Adino, one of David's men, had a one-time victory over many foes. He was never afraid of the size of the multitude, neither was he afraid of being alone. It may be hard to accomplish victory, but someone with a champion's mind-set confronts the hardest situation and settles in victory. Winston Churchill said, "Victory at all costs, victory in spite of all terror; victory however long and hard the road may be."[3] A one-time victory involves subduing and achieving control over what was supposed to destroy us.

Wearied yet victorious

"And after him was Eleazar the son of Dodo, the Ahohite, one of the three mighty men with David when they defied the Philistines who were gathered there for battle, and the men of Israel had retreated. He arose and attacked the Philistines until his hand was weary, and his hand stuck to the sword. The LORD brought about a great victory that day; and the people returned after him only to plunder" (vv. 9–10).

Eleazar was another mighty man in David's army. He became a champion because of his mighty deeds. When he was left alone in battle after the "men of Israel were gone away" (v. 9, KJV). I ask myself, if people abandoned me to do the difficult task, how would I react? If support and help are withdrawn from me, what will be my response? When people give up on me and never respond to the love I show them, will I still pursue my goal? The fear of being deserted or rejected is a nightmare to many people. Eleazar's approach when abandoned was different: "He arose and attacked" (v. 10). He didn't give in to fear; rather, he drew strength from the champion in him and confronted the host of the Philistines.

Although his hand got wearied, he "stuck to the sword" (v. 10). May our hands and life stick to the sword of the Word of God. However weary we become when we cling to the Word of God—holding fast and remaining close in our relationship with God—victory will surely be accomplished. After the great victory, the people returned "only to spoil," that is, help carry the good of the defeated, even though they were not involved in the battle. Eleazer did not complain about being left alone to do the hard part, neither did he murmur at their returning to the spoil. Rather, he

> A champion having obtained victory presses on to greater achievements. No failure is strong enough to stop him or her until he or she reaches a flourishing finish.

considered that it was through the help of God, just as in the interpretation of his name, "God is Helper." Truly, when we see God as our helper, we can overcome any battle.

Defending your heritage

"And after him was Shammah the son of Agee the Hararite. The Philistines had gathered together into a troop where there was a piece of ground full of lentils. So the people fled from the Philistines. But he stationed himself in the middle of the field, defended it, and killed the Philistines. So the LORD brought about a great victory" (vv. 11–12)

Shammah "stood in the midst of the ground, and defended it" (KJV) while others fled. He was never intimidated by the host of the Philistines, neither did he allow the cowardliness of his fellow Israelites to weaken him. He saw it as a reproach for God's heritage to be turned into the hands of the heathen. He had the mind of a champion. Such are the people God is looking for in our day—those who will stand their ground to proclaim God's greatness as they defend the kingdom of God.

Pressing on until you reach your goal

A champion having obtained victory presses on to greater achievements. No failure is strong enough to stop him or her until he or she reaches a flourishing finish. Such was Abishai, the captain of David's army. "Now Abishai the brother of Joab, the son of Zeruiah, was chief of another three. He lifted his spear against three hundred men, killed them, and won a name among these three. Was he not the most honored of three? Therefore, he became their captain. However, he did not attain to the first three: (vv. 18–19). He pressed through until he gained recognition among the army. It is so unfortunate that so many people stop at the salvation experience and never aspire for more of God, being saved but seeing no need for salvation of others. When some people are brought out of the pit of iniquity and affliction, they stay too close to the pit where they were delivered, until they slip into it again. We should go an extra mile in our walk with God so as not to be trapped back to the bondage we have escaped. One victory should encourage us to aim higher to better days ahead; such is the champion's mind-set.

Prevailing over the lion-like and the lion

A true champion refuses to be devoured by a lion, neither would he be terrified by the roaring of the lion. He does not see himself as prey, but as prevailing over all oppositions. Such was Benaiah of David's army. "Benaiah was the son of Jehoiada, the son of a valiant man from Kabzeel, who had done many deeds. He had killed two lion-like heroes of Moab. He also had gone down and killed a lion in the midst of a pit on a snowy day" (v. 20). He slew two lion-like men and a lion. Yes, they were brave as lions, but they were not lions; a champion defeats both. The lion-like men first appeared then the lion. We often struggle with what may appear real while the real shows up later. So many people devote their lives pursuing whatever is false and so become unreal. A champion is not distracted by whatever is false but faces reality with an assurance of victory.

Prevailing over unfavorable conditions

"And he killed an Egyptian, a spectacular man. The Egyptian had a spear in his hand; so he went down to him with a staff, wrested the spear out of the Egyptian's hand, and killed him with his own spear" (v. 21).

Benaiah slew the lion in the midst of the pit on a snowy day. The pit couldn't trap him, neither could the harsh weather stopped him from killing the lion. No matter the bad conditions, a champion cannot be trapped. Age and time cannot be hindrances to achieving the desired goals. Oh, for a people who look beyond their unfavorable conditions and reach out to God until victory is attained!

Never see yourself as inferior

Benaiah truly did many acts. "And he killed an Egyptian, a spectacular man. The Egyptian had a spear in his hand; so he went down to him with a staff, wrested the spear out of the Egyptian's hand, and killed him with his own spear" (v. 21). There came a time when he confronted an Egyptian warrior who had a spear, but he had a staff. Who can compare a spear and a staff (a wooden rod) when both are used as weapons? Being a champion, he never looked on his foe as being superior, neither did he consider himself as inferior. He "plucked the spear out of the Egyptian's hand, and slew him with his own spear" (v. 21, KJV). A champion sees whatever he has as being good enough for victory. I, therefore, counsel you not to look down on yourself, but give thanks and reflect on how you can use whatever you have to obtain great results.

Faith is the language of a champion

Communication of thoughts and feelings can reflect who we are and what we stand for. We all communicate something with our life that others can perceive however hard we try to hide it. As a loser's language is defeat and failure, a champion's language is faith. "But without faith it is impossible to please Him, for he who comes to God must believe that He is, and that He is a rewarder of those who diligently seek Him" (Heb. 11:6). The Bible is full of lists of heroes of faith, who were champions indeed. In their weaknesses they became strong until they obtained promised blessings. Faith was their language, as they called "those things which be not as though they were" (Rom. 4:17, KJV). May we also drop our doubts and shake off our unbelief to lay hold of God, just like father Abraham: "He didn't tiptoe around God's promise asking cautiously skeptical questions. He lunged into the promise and came up strong, ready for God, sure that God would make good on what he had said" (vv. 20–21, The Message).

Not on their terms

Demons love to give conditions as to when to live, where to go, and how to live. Victory is effective when you determine the terms and are not confined to their conditions. The devil tempted Jesus, and on each occasion he dictated the terms, but Jesus refused them all. The first was "when the tempter came to Him, he said, 'If You are the Son of God, command that these stones become bread'" (Matt. 4:3). Second was when he "said to Him, 'If You are the Son of God, throw Yourself down. For it is written: "He shall give His angels charge over you," and, "In their hands they shall bear you up, Lest you dash your foot against a stone"'" (v. 6). The third happened when "again, the devil took Him up on an exceedingly high mountain, and showed Him all the kingdoms of the world and their glory" (v. 8). In all these, Jesus did not agree to his terms.

When Elijah confronted the Baal prophets and the prophets of the groves, he was in charge. He gave them the conditions and what will determine the true God: "Then you call on the name of your gods, and I will call on the name of the Lord; and the God who answers by fire, He is God" (1 Kings 18:24). He did not permit them to prescribe the manner of sacrifice.

Joseph was hated by his brethren because of his dreams. Although the hatred was fierce, it could not stop him from dreaming. They hated him, he dreamed, "and they hated him yet the more…And they hated him yet the more for his dreams and for his words" (Gen. 37:5, 8, kjv). After that "he dreamed yet another dream" (v. 9, kjv). Even in prison, he interpreted dreams because he was a man sold out to fulfill his dreams and asked that he might be remembered because he was persuaded of the accuracy of his interpretation. "But remember me when it is well with you, and please show kindness to me; make mention of me to Pharaoh, and get me out of this house" (40:14). He was not subjected to the conditions of his brothers to stop him from dreaming, neither did he subscribe to the seduction of Potiphar's wife. He developed principles around his dream and was not willing to go by the terms of others who might ruin his dream.

Elisha was a man with a double portion of anointing; nothing could stop him from receiving Elijah's double portion, not even the "sons of the prophets"—the fellow students in the prophetic school. As he followed Elijah from Bethel to Jericho, and on to Jordan, there were the sons of the prophets in each of these cities, telling him of the vision they had that his master would be taken away, and they were certain that it would be the same day. What was Elisha's response? "Yea, I know it; hold ye your peace" (2 Kings 2:3, KJV). They watched both Elijah and Elisha pass through Jordan on dry ground. Finally when the mantle rested on Elisha, these sons of the prophets "came to meet him, and bowed themselves to the ground before him" (v. 15, KJV). Did not Joseph's brothers who hated him and tried stopping him from dreaming bow before Joseph? When you refuse their terms, you may be hated, but when you persevere and fulfill your dreams, they will bow.

May I ask, why would the term of the wicked prevail against the righteous? It is because we give them the consent. Consent has to do with approval and agreement. That gives the enemy the control to violate our rights, which opens us to unceasing conflict and a repeated cycle of clashes, confrontations, and difficulties. We have been authorized and commissioned by God through the Holy Spirit to operate solely on God's terms that we may manifest His glory. Consenting to their terms subjects us to their manipulations—unlawful authority with intent to rule over us.

Therefore, you can announce your victory before the battle, just like David did before Goliath. "This day the LORD will deliver you into my hand, and I will strike you and take your head from you. And this day I will give the carcasses of the camp of the Philistines to the birds of the air and the wild beasts of the earth, that all the earth may know that there is a God in Israel" (1 Sam. 17:46). Your real life emerges when you command deliverance upon yourself and your situation. Consent not to their terms; rather, command possibilities out of your impossibilities, peace out of chaos, light out of darkness, and favor out of disgrace. Develop principles rooted in the Word of God around your dreams and goals in life for easy accomplishment in overcoming obstacles. Set the terms by which your dream should follow, which will be a pattern for your life; otherwise, others will set their terms to rule and control you, which may cause aborted vision.

Devour their palaces and their thrones

Palace and throne are the seats of rulers in order to enforce their dominion. Effective warfare can be established by capturing the palace, dethroning the king, and taking charge. Jesus, the Captain of the Lord's Host, gave the marching order on how we can walk in victory. "When a strong man, fully armed, guards his own palace, his goods are in peace. But when a stronger than he comes upon him and overcomes him, he takes from him all his armor in which he trusted, and divides his spoils" (Luke 11:21–22). So, the strongman has a palace full of stolen goods and is at peace because he is unchallenged. His palaces are well fortified; but if we must possess our blessings, then we must overcome his palaces.

Amos the prophet gave some significant insight on how to deal with palaces as he pronounced God's judgment upon cities and nations: Damascus, Gaza, Tyrus, Edom, Ammon, Moab, and Judah. One thing was common in all these judgments—palaces. "But I will send a fire into the house of Hazael, Which shall devour the palaces of Ben-Hadad...But I will send a fire upon the wall of Gaza, Which shall devour its palaces...But I will send a fire upon the wall of Tyre, Which shall devour its palaces...I will send a fire upon Teman, Which shall devour the palaces of Bozrah...But I will kindle a fire in the wall of Rabbah, And it shall devour its palaces" (Amos 1:4, 7, 10, 12, 14). "But I will send a fire upon Moab, And it shall devour the palaces of Kerioth; Moab shall die with tumult, With shouting and trumpet sound. But I will send a fire upon Judah, And it shall devour the palaces of Jerusalem" (2:2, 5).

Considering some physical palaces as a type to spiritual

The largest palace in Europe is the Royal Palace of Madrid in Spain, also referred to as the Palacio Real. "When you look at the design and style of the Palace you would notice no room is similar...The palace is the largest palace in Europe with over 2,800 rooms."[4] I found this very interesting because it reveals deep meaning. Also considering a spiritual palace with each room as a stronghold and no room the same is a type of problem with different battles, so the strategy for victory differs. No battle is the same, though manifesting the same problem.

How about thrones? Thrones are for kings and sovereigns. With a crown and a scepter, a staff held by a sovereign as an emblem of authority, the ruler confers his authority. "In Greek history, thrones were identified as

> That is why in missions to Africa, believers are advised to enthrone Jesus as Lord over their homes, jobs, even their finances and health.

seats of the gods…In ancient times the Indian throne was a combined throne-altar, serving both a royal and a religious purpose."[5] Whatever is enthroned reigns. No wonder Lucifer coveted a throne to reign, "For you have said in your heart: 'I will ascend into heaven, I will exalt my throne above the stars of God; I will also sit on the mount of the congregation on the farthest sides of the north'" (Isa. 14:13). But the Almighty God cast him down: "Yet thou shalt be brought down to hell, to the sides of the pit" (v. 15, KJV).

Fetish priests in Africa use stool as a throne after invoking demons into it. They give it to people who consult them to help bring down those whom they want to frustrate out of position so they can take over. That is why in missions to Africa, believers are advised to enthrone Jesus as Lord over their homes, jobs, even their finances and health. With this stool as thrones, so many lives have been brought down, plundered, and become a byword among people.

A lady came to me for prayers after sharing her dream of seeing herself being escorted into a palace by military officers and standing before a huge throne. An unrecognized person on the throne lifted up a scepter and started decreeing evil over her. The echo of the voice woke her up trembling. Right after, she had feverish feelings for three days. Then, she knew the dream was not to be taken lightly. This is an act of summoning the soul to lay judgment against her. Her prayers were well targeted and strategic: dethrone the king, terminate his reign over her, and scatter the throne. The second step was to decree the angels of God to arrest the military escorts and everyone in that palace and chain them down for destruction. The third step was to ask for the angelic withdrawal of the scepter and the crown, and break them asunder, while the fourth step was to pray for the release of the blood of Jesus to annul the evil decrees and command that they shall not be executed upon her life. The fifth step was to pray to blast asunder the palace and the thrones decreeing after the order of Joshua that it shall not be built again, nor its gates raised up. The sixth step was to command the fire of separation between her and whatever caused her to be attracted to such a throne and palace, and finally to enthrone the lordship of Jesus and ask Him to reign. Her life was never the same after this prayer. She was truly delivered. The prayers were very strategic. It takes a strategic approach to undo the wickedness of the wicked.

Issues that have to do with thrones and palaces require well-targeted biblical prayers to obtain results. In another case, it was a person finding himself in a courtroom, facing the judge in judgment; as the gavel was about to be applied, he woke up. This is also an evil summoning of his soul, because there were no pending court cases for him. This could be an evil prescription by which such a life would be patterned. A better approach in prayer would be to prayerfully recall this dream and nullify it by the blood of Jesus. For a better result I counseled him to subject everyone in the courtroom to divine arrest, declaring the Almighty God as the Judge of all to execute judgment, and to get disconnected from the evil judgment and command that it shall not be executed. Also he should ask for an angelic escape from the evil arrest of his soul and that the blood of Jesus should blast asunder the judgment seat and palace (courtroom) in Jesus' name, concluding by decreeing God's blessings upon himself. It is, therefore, a kingdom strategy to know that there are raging palaces and thrones at war with us, and they are determined to rule over us. Permit them not! Rather let God's throne, His power, and His presence rule over you.

Taking off their chariots' wheels

A chariot is a type of vehicle used either for warlike or peaceful purposes, but most commonly the former. Warfare chariots are swift, and their wheels are like a whirlwind as the warriors roar like lions. With the chariot wheels in place, the warriors are ready to plunder. So were the Egyptians against the Israelites. They pursued the Israelites at the command of Pharaoh with the determination to slay them. They were unstoppable in their mission, but God prevented them. How? "And He took off their chariot wheels, so that they drove them with difficulty; and the Egyptians said, 'Let us flee from the face of Israel, for the LORD fights for them against the Egyptians'" (Exod. 14:25).

I cannot imagine driving a car without wheels. If I moved at all, how fast would I go? No matter how hard I tried, it would be an unrealistic venture. So were the Egyptian warriors. The Bible accounted that they drove with difficulty. I imagine the Israelites on the other side watching the Egyptian warriors driving their chariots hard, roaring like lions with the noise of loosened chariots and hard driving. The noise terrified the Israelites, but they were unaware of the difficulties their adversaries were facing.

This applies to us today: God opens the door of escape from trouble to get blessed, and we are joyful; but soon after the enemy of our soul pursues us with the intent to "steal, and to kill and to destroy" (John 10:10). In their pursuit, we hear their roaring sound of rage and we are terrified. Many times we are unaware of the fact that their chariots' wheels have been taken off; so we cry, weep, and mourn because of the terrible noise of the oppressors. The noise is about the loosened chariot wheels; they are more in distress that we realize. "They cried there, 'Pharaoh, king of Egypt, is but a noise. He has passed by the appointed time!'" (Jer. 46:17). Therefore, let not the cries of the oppressors intimidate you, neither let the chariots or weapons make you afraid. It is an effective prayer to pray that God should take off the chariot wheels of your oppressors. It is always a kingdom strategy to advance regardless of the raging noise of the enemy of your soul.

Egypt against Egypt

Egypt as a nation has a longstanding history, both in the secular and religious worlds. The patriarchs had a lot to do with Egypt. Abraham went down into Egypt (Gen. 12:10). God commanded Isaac not to go down to Egypt. "Then the LORD appeared to him and said: 'Do not go down to Egypt; live in the land of which I shall tell you. Dwell in this land, and I will be with you and bless you; for to you and your descendants I give all these lands, and I will perform the oath which I swore to Abraham your father. And I will make your descendants multiply as the stars of heaven; I will give to your descendants all these lands; and in your seed all the nations of the earth shall be blessed'" (26:2–4).

Jacob, his children, and grandchildren went down to Egypt (46:7). Joseph was sold into slavery, served in Egypt, and was imprisoned until God sought him out to rule over the land. The descendants of Jacob grew mighty in Egypt, but the powers of Egypt rose against them, afflicted them, and enslaved them. If it had not been for divine intervention, they would have perished in Egypt. God's plagues and wrath came upon Egypt until the Israelites were set free, but Egypt would not let go. They pursued the Israelites, but they perished at the Red Sea. However, some Egyptians were part of the congregation of Israelites that left Egypt. While the pursuing Egyptians failed, the Egyptians in their midst succeeded. They were like thorns in the flesh until they made them sin against God and were wasted in the wilderness.

So the spirit of Egypt is a pursuing spirit, persistent in oppressing God's people. Prophet Isaiah prophesied about the spirit of Egypt: "The spirit of Egypt will fail in its midst; I will destroy their counsel, And they will consult the idols and the charmers, The mediums and the sorcerers" (Isa. 19:3). Why did he say, "The spirit of Egypt shall fail"? Because it is the same spirit the patriarchs contended with, and it is still a strong spirit we must overcome today. To many people it is the spirit of bondage, affliction, oppression, and slavery. In defending His people, God had to raise Egypt against Egypt:

> The burden against Egypt. Behold, the LORD rides on a swift cloud, And will come into Egypt; The idols of Egypt will totter at His presence, And the heart of Egypt will melt in its midst. "I will set Egyptians against Egyptians; Everyone will fight against his brother, And everyone against his neighbor, City against city, kingdom against kingdom. The spirit of Egypt will fail in its midst; I will destroy their counsel, And they will consult the idols and the charmers, The mediums and the sorcerers."
>
> —ISAIAH 19:1–3

This prophesy points to Messiah's reign. The third verse reveals the spirit of Egypt—idols, charmers, familiar spirits, and wizards. So the spirit of Egypt is a servant spirit that lives with, travels with, and assists magicians, sorcerers, and witches. They serve their owners as spies and companions to bewitch others.

A lot of people will never stop wondering why there is so much encompassing evil and overwhelming sorrow. The manipulation of people's minds and the fear of constant danger are the compelling forces of the spirit of Egypt. I enjoy listening to national anthems of nations of the world; as a prophetic intercessor, it enables me to discern the heart of the nation. The ninth line of the modern Egypt national anthem reads: "No evil hand can harm or do you wrong."[6] This reveals the awareness of harm and wrongdoing and the readiness to resist them. So, the world system will surely hurt us because of the wrongdoing, but God will help His people. The lust and the wickedness in the world could be a prey to our soul, but God rides on a swift cloud to deliver His people.

Egypt against Egypt is a type of confusion in the world system to ensnare those who are in the world, but not of the world: "I do not pray that You should take them out of the world, but that You should keep them from the evil one. They are not of the world, just as I am not of the world. Sanctify them by Your truth. Your word is truth" (John 17:15–17). So, when God set Egypt against Egypt, it is similar to when oppression arises against you. It will be to the oppressor of your soul when affliction is set against you; it will be to the afflicters and even destruction to the destroyer, because God rides on a swift cloud to defend you.

Joseph ruled over Egypt, but Simeon was detained in Egypt. When Joseph's brothers made their visit to Egypt during famine and Joseph had not yet revealed himself to them, before letting them go back to Canaan, he held back one of them to ensure their returning back to Egypt. He detained Simeon in Egypt. "And he turned himself away from them and wept. Then he returned to them again, and talked with them. And he took Simeon from them and bound him before their eyes" (Gen. 42:24). Why Simeon? Why not any other person? Joseph, being a wise man and full of the Spirit of God, knew the right person to pick and the right thing to do. By interpretation, *Simeon* means "heard": "The LORD has heard" (29:33). Before the eyes of his brothers, he bound Simeon but allowed the rest of them to go. So they left Egypt without Simeon.

Even though they had plenty of goods, abundant food and their money returned back to them, without Simeon (God has heard—answered prayers) they would soon return to Egypt. Whatever they had with their answered prayer detained in Egypt, it was just a matter of time; all would soon be gone. Joseph detained Simeon—"God has heard" —and bound him before their eyes. It was like saying, this is all I need, even in Egypt; I need to hold on to an assured answered prayer. Joseph needed such an encouragement to assure him that God had heard him. Ruling in Egypt without the guarantee of answered prayer would have been vanity. So, he held on to answered prayers while his other brothers returned without Simeon. Leaving Egypt with Simeon was like embarking in the journey of life without the certainty of answered prayers.

I ask you, where is your Simeon—your answered prayer? Is he held in Egypt? The forces of Egypt have detained the manifestation of answered prayers of many. The spirit of Egypt is contending with the fulfillment of the prayers of many people. As Egypt contended with Moses and challenged God's power in letting His people go, so is the refusal of freedom of many today. If Egypt succeeds in detaining our prayers, the same spirit will want to direct and supervise our labors. How far can we go in life without the guarantee of answered prayers? May we, like Joseph, bind our answered prayer before our accusers. When prayers are withheld, frustration, reproach, and lack set in. Life becomes harder than we can imagine. I, therefore, challenge you to win back your Simeon. Through repentance and rededication, we can get God's attention. His mercy shall return our Simeon detained in Egypt. It is, therefore, a kingdom warfare strategy to set Egypt against Egypt.

The ancient war cry—raze it!

War is not a game for the cowardly; it is for the brave. It involves taking risks and rising to the challenge with a focus for victory. In ancient times, when nations or cities went to war against each other and as the armies were set in an array, well equipped for battle, the commander of the host would charge his people with a dreadful look and a roaring voice, pointing his weapon against the opposing army and saying, "Raze it! Raze it!" The host would go on the offensive, determined to achieve nothing but victory. Such was the cry of the Edomites as they watched Jerusalem being destroyed. "Remember, O LORD, against the sons of Edom The day of Jerusalem, Who said, 'Raze it, raze it, To its very foundation!'" (Ps. 137:7). The soldiers understood this command; this was the energy and strength needed for the battle. With this declaration, the warring soldiers understood it to mean "level it to the ground; demolish, so that reconstruction is impossible; and tear down and destroy completely."[7]

This is still the war cry against many people today. The enemy of our soul desires nothing but to bring us down and demolish us so that reconstruction will be hard and almost impossible. When we look back at the ruins, it can only take the grace of God to repair and restore. Is this not what we witness every time we are trying to get back our life in order—when we feel we should put our lives together for a better future, regardless of the troubles of the past? The goals for the future seems unrealizable to many because of the deep damages done. This has caused vexation of the spirit—painful experiences due to offenses. The same people who have had pleasurable moments together, after stepping on each others' toes, feel insulted and hurt; they attack each other without leaving any trace of reconciliation.

The Edomites who cried, "Raze it!" against Jerusalem were descended from the children of Esau, the twin brother of Jacob. Jacob and Esau's contention had been from the womb (Gen. 25:22). The fight for superiority and claim of inheritance were the unresolved crisis between them. Even though Jacob and Esau tried reconciling (Gen. 33), the deep wounds were not healed, and it continued through to their descendants. When the opportunity for vengeance came for the Edomites, seeing Jacob's heritage being destroyed, they cried aloud to support the ruin, "Raze it, raze it, to its very foundation!"

Such is the war cry being pronounced against us. It is the enemy's intention to bring people to the ground. Why has the reconstruction of your life been so difficult? Why is it almost impossible for you to rise up after you fall? Perhaps a war cry to raze it to the foundation is gone forth against you. So Jacob's descendents in captivity put God in remembrance of the cry of total destruction proclaimed over them. May we also put God in remembrance of desolation over our godly heritage. We can come boldly before His throne of grace and freely recall before Him the cry of our adversary and his destructive work. "Put me in remembrance: let us plead together: declare thou, that thou mayest be justified" (Isa. 43:26, KJV). God is more than willing to justify us. He delights to see nothing short of peace and freedom in us. Can we trust Him? He only can restore and rebuild our wasted heritage. In a human's eye, reconstruction may be totally impossible. The destruction may be so vast that we are wondering if it is possible to come out of it. Let it be known to you, that no ruin, however devastating, is impossible for God to rebuild. Through His favor, we can regain all that we have lost. He is abundantly able!

We also can turn this strategy of war against the adversary of our soul. When dealing with strongholds of curses, spells, enchantments, bewitchments, incantations, and all forms of evil, victory is assured as you decree to God's angels to raze it! Raze it! Nothing about such strongholds should be left without total demolition; otherwise they will come back strong, even stronger than before. Tearing down of altars, destruction of strongholds, and binding the strongman assure us of victory through the blood of Jesus.

Devouring their gates

Gates may prevent or control entry or exit, or may be merely decorative. In ancient times, they were places of public deliberation and administration of justice (Josh. 20:4; Judg. 9:35). At the gates of cities, courts of justice were frequently held; hence, "judges of the gate" are spoken of (Deut. 16:18). Prophets delivered messages at the gate (Prov. 1:21; Jer. 17:19–20). Criminals were punished outside the gates (1 Kings 21:13; Acts 7:59). No wonder Jesus declared against gates of hell, the powers of hell: "And I also say to you that you are Peter, and on this rock I will build My church, and the gates of Hades shall not prevail against it" (Matt. 16:18). He also broke the gates and took authority over it to set mankind free from captivity. Gates were lifted up and possessed to rescue us from the captivity of sin and darkness (Ps. 24:7, 9; 107:16).

The Bible spoke about Daniel who sat in the gate of the king (Dan. 2:49). Obviously he was a man of authority. Patriarchic blessings always include "possessing of gates" (Gen. 22:17; 24:60). Whoever possesses the gates rules over all. Moses stood in the gate of the camp to instruct the people: "Then Moses stood in the entrance of the camp, and said, 'Whoever is on the LORD's side—come to me!' And all the sons of Levi gathered themselves together to him" (Exod. 32:26). The battle is toughest at the gate, and more strength is needed because justice, victory, and control are determined at the gates. "For a spirit of justice to him who sits in judgment, And for strength to those who turn back the battle at the gate" (Isa. 28:6). With the strength of the Lord, we can possess the gates of our adversaries; otherwise, they rule over us, control us, and subject us to their evil reign.

Prophet Zechariah prophesied: "Open thy doors, O Lebanon, that the fire may devour thy cedars. Howl, fir tree; for the cedar is fallen; because the mighty are spoiled: howl, O ye oaks of Bashan; for the forest of the vintage is come down" (Zech. 11:1-2, KJV). He ordered the gates and doors of Lebanon to open that the fire may devour. If fire is set forth as a weapon of destruction without the gates opening, the purpose of attack may be ineffective. But when gates are opened, authority and control are shifted and dethroned; the destruction can be accomplished. The warfare strategy, therefore, is to order the gates (authority) to open so that your weapons of war might have an effect. When Zechariah ordered the gates opened, cedar trees fell, which is a type of stronghold fallen apart; "the mighty are spoiled" and the oaks of Bashan cried as the forest came down (v. 2). Jesus possessed the gates of hell and death; death could not hold Him captive. He rose from the death and is alive forevermore. My earnest prayer, therefore, for the readers of this book, is for the gates to open that they may possess their blessings, "Open the gates, That the righteous nation which keeps the truth may enter in" (Isa. 26:2). Territories are the redemptive plans of God in advancing His kingdom, and it is a divine strategy to possess the gates—authority resisting God's glory.

Possessing the wall

In recent years, especially during this economic crisis when so many people are in a hard-pressed situation, I have heard people say, "My back is against the wall, but I'm fighting hard." A mother brought her son for counseling and prayer, saying, "I have tried many times to convince him to stop smoking, but I'm beating my head against a brick wall." People use the word *wall* to express their frustration, blockage, and helplessness. In ancient times, cities were often walled with gates and watchtowers strategically placed. The watchmen ascended into the watchtower—an elevated position to view the city inside out—and watched out for the approaching armies. Communication was often kept strong to reinforce and warn the garrisons of the enemy's movements (Isa. 62:6). So, a wall defines and sometimes protects an area. Even in our personal lives, we have to deal with walls.

King David was a man who had several obstacles to the throne. Troops were assigned against him, but he ran them down. "For by You I can run against a troop, By my God I can leap over a wall" (Ps. 18:29). In all the conquest of the Promised Land, Jericho was exceptional. It took the "captain of the host of the LORD" (Josh. 5:14, KJV) to appear to give the right strategy. Issues with walls need the right approach. I consider with deep interest how the children of Israel encompassed the city once for six days and seven times on the seventh day without the people of Jericho fighting back. Can you imagine a group of strangers trespassing on your property, walking around your house for seven days, and you not doing something? At least you would cry for help or do something, and even more so if you know they have come to take over. Yes, the terror of God filled the land and the people's hearts melted for fear (2:9). Consequently, the strength of Jericho was in their wall; it was well built and highly fortified. As long as they shut their gates, they felt secure.

Part of the strategy was for the people of Israel to engage in a silent march. "Now Joshua had commanded the people, saying, 'You shall not shout or make any noise with your voice, nor shall a word proceed out of your mouth, until the day I say to you, "Shout!" Then you shall shout'" (6:10). I asked myself why there was no talking as they marched along. I suppose they would have murmured and complained to provoke God and incur His wrath; they also could have perished at the gates of their enemies. Can you imagine someone stepping on you and you cannot talk, complain, or fight back? This is true discipline—mortifying the flesh so that the spirit man may be strengthened. No wonder, when they were to shout, power was released and the presence of God was strong. It was a march of possessing the land (1:3).

As they shouted, "the wall fell down flat" (6:20). There was the blasting of the trumpets and a command to shout: "Shout, for the LORD has given you the city!" (v. 16). It was a shout to the Lord, proclaiming His greatness. At the declaration of His name every knee bows, and every tongue confesses (Phil. 2:10–11)—just as Dagon, the god of the Philistines, bowed before the ark of the Lord (1 Sam. 5:4). So, the wall of Jericho bowed before the ark and the shout to the Lord. The wall of Jericho responded to the shout of praise and fell down to worship.

Wall has lots of spiritual implications

Jezebel influenced the people through witchcraft, but Elijah prophesied her end: "And concerning Jezebel the LORD also spoke, saying, 'The dogs shall eat Jezebel by the wall of Jezreel'" (1 Kings 21:23). And truly this word came to pass. "Then he said, 'Throw her down.' So they threw her down, and some of her blood spattered on the wall and on the horses; and he trampled her underfoot" (2 Kings 9:33). The splash of her blood on the wall was licked up by dogs. She fell at her strength. The prophecy involved the wall as a witness. Walls can also serve as screens where things can be inscribed. Whatever is inscribed on the wall rules our lives. The handwriting on the wall determined the judgment against Belshazzar: "In the same hour the fingers of a man's hand appeared and wrote opposite the lampstand on the plaster of the wall of the king's palace; and the king saw the part of the hand that wrote" (Dan. 5:5). Walls can also serve as altars.

> So He brought me to the door of the court; and when I looked, there was a hole in the wall. Then He said to me, "Son of man, dig into the wall"; and when I dug into the wall, there was a door. And He said to me, "Go in, and see the wicked abominations which they are doing there." So I went in and saw, and there—every sort of creeping thing, abominable beasts, and all the idols of the house of Israel, portrayed all around on the walls. And there stood before them seventy men of the elders of the house of Israel, and in their midst stood Jaazaniah the son of Shaphan. Each man had a censer in his hand, and a thick cloud of incense went up. Then He said to me, "Son of man, have you seen what the elders of the house of Israel do in the dark, every man in the room of his idols? For they say, 'The LORD does not see us, the LORD has forsaken the land.'" And He said to me, "Turn again, and you will see greater abominations that they are doing." So He brought me to the door of the north gate of the LORD's house; and to my dismay,

women were sitting there weeping for Tammuz. Then He said to me, "Have you seen this, O son of man? Turn again, you will see greater abominations than these." So He brought me into the inner court of the Lord's house; and there, at the door of the temple of the Lord, between the porch and the altar, were about twenty-five men with their backs toward the temple of the Lord and their faces toward the east, and they were worshiping the sun toward the east. And He said to me, "Have you seen this, O son of man? Is it a trivial thing to the house of Judah to commit the abominations which they commit here? For they have filled the land with violence; then they have returned to provoke Me to anger. Indeed they put the branch to their nose."

—Ezekiel 8:7–17

"A hole in the wall" (v. 7), and within was "a door" (v. 8); he turned "yet again" (v. 13), and there was yet another turn within the wall (v. 15). All forms of wickedness and abomination were within the wall, so walls can serve as altars.

In praying for people, on some occasions the Holy Spirit will say to me, "Pull down the walls in the mind." This bounces back the idea that would have profited. This makes it hard to reach out to others and hard to touch their hearts. Walls limit us and cage us. No wonder Jacob blessed Joseph saying, "Joseph is a fruitful bough, even a fruitful bough by a well; whose branches run over the wall" (Gen. 49:22, kjv). I also pray for you that "your branches shall run over the wall." This is when God increases your glorious influence, going beyond your limit. Another great prayer for Jerusalem is: "Pray for the peace of Jerusalem: 'May they prosper who love you. Peace be within your walls, Prosperity within your palaces'" (Ps. 122:6–7). When peace abounds within your walls, wars are kept away from you. Your territory will not be invaded, neither will it be destroyed.

We also can dedicate the walls of our lives to God through the blood of Jesus and be fortified by the power of the Holy Spirit, just like Nehemiah raising the ruins of Jerusalem and setting up the walls. We can apply the blood of Jesus to break asunder the walls of partition preventing help from coming to us: "For He Himself is our peace, who has made both one, and has broken down the middle wall of separation" (Eph. 2:14). The blood of Jesus can also blot out handwritings on the walls of our lives, "having wiped out the handwriting of requirements that was against us, which was contrary to us. And He has taken it out of the way, having nailed it to the cross. Having disarmed principalities and powers,

He made a public spectacle of them, triumphing over them in it" (Col. 2:14–15). Another strategic way of prevailing in prayer is to command our adversaries to fall at their strength after the order of Jezebel. We can also command walls as altars and screens to collapse. You need not be caged or limited further; the Holy Spirit can quicken you to leap over the walls. As walls are immovably hard, so are some situations in our lives; they refuse to give up. If anyone kicks the wall, he or she feels the pain; so do we feel the pain of some problems. As the walls of Jericho fell, even so will such problems fall. But the strategy is, don't complain about the size or height of the wall, rather shout about the greatness of the Lord Your God and watch the walls collapse.

Forbidden mad spirit

It takes some level of madness to engage in wickedness and to persistently do evil. Is it not madness to be bitter and enraged over someone because you are envious of his or her success? Isn't it madness to be filled with jealousy and devise ways to pull down someone whom you feel is better than you? Isn't it madness to set up your friends and watch their downfall? Isn't it madness to despise goodness shown to you and reward with evil? The psalmist when afflicted and overwhelmed by troubles poured out his heart to God as he considered his oppressors as being mad against him. "Mine enemies reproach me all the day; and they that are mad against me are sworn against me" (Ps. 102:8). *Madness* is a term for somebody who is mentally ill, dangerous, foolish, and unpredictable. Such a person can be considered as suffering from disorder of mind or insane. Such a one exhibits irrationality and mental unsoundness.

> It is, therefore, a kingdom strategy to know that the persistent rage of our adversaries is simply madness of the spirit— being sold out to wickedness without reasoning the consequences.

It is expected that a normal person will consider the basis or motive for an action or decision, even though not all people do, but they suffer the consequences thereafter. With a spirit of madness, there is a cycle of confusion, uproar, and disorderliness. Anyone under the manipulation of such spirit is unrestrained and reasoning is withdrawn. Oftentimes when people complain and are bitter about what people did to them, the damages and pains, we are be moved with compassion. Apostle Peter referred to what Balaam did to the Israelites as "madness of the prophet" (2 Pet. 2:16). "But Balaam was stopped from his mad course when his donkey rebuked him with a human voice" (v. 16, NLT). It is unnatural for donkeys to talk. Any other person would have been scared, but he was conversing with the donkey. The donkey saw the angelic appearance before God opened Balaam's eyes. He was so drawn to evil and drunken by it that even the voice of a donkey didn't scare him. When we refuse to be sensible, reasonable, and thoughtful, but we allow a negative mindset to control us to the degree of foolishness, it is like pursuing a mad course. At such a time the fear of God is totally forgotten.

I have seen a pastor of a church physically fighting his wife during a worship service and the congregation trying to settle them. I was shocked when the pastor returned to the pulpit and said, "Praise God, the presence of God is here." I have also seen the congregants setting up their pastor and being ready to tear down the meeting, not minding if souls would be lost through this. It is foolishness and lack of fear of God for couples to be fighting and exchanging words, even worse when it is done before their children. It is madness of the spirit to damn the consequences of disobeying God's law, risking the joy of eternity with momentary pleasure. Can we ask God for forgiveness and obtain mercy that we might be filled with His Holy Spirit?

It is, therefore, a kingdom strategy to know that the persistent rage of our adversaries is simply madness of the spirit—being sold out to wickedness without reasoning the consequences. Is it not madness to kill a fellow man, either as a game or vengeance? Is it not madness to be filled with suicidal thoughts in killing yourself? As the angel of the Lord withstood the "madness" of Balaam, so should we ask God to forbid the pursuit of those who are mad toward us. "Then God's anger was aroused because he went, and the Angel of the LORD took His stand in the way as an adversary against him. And he was riding on his donkey, and his two servants were with him" (Num. 22:22). Just like it is normal for a mad person to fight privately or publicly without being ashamed, so it is with anyone who is obsessed with wickedness. Such a one can unleash trouble anywhere and at anytime. The danger is that we look at the wicked with a normal eye, but they have lost their reasoning in their unwavering aggression to do evil. Applying the ministry of angels can restrain them.

Alternate prayer

Lack and a desperate search to meet needs have made many people request for what would cause deeper problems in their lives. When answers to prayers are delayed, what we ask for or think negates the things we assuredly desire. Steadfastness and persistence of faith are needed in receiving answered prayers. When Rachel, the wife of Jacob, couldn't bear children, she approached her husband demanding children at all cost; but she wasn't steadfast enough with her request because she provided an option, an alternate request. "Now when Rachel saw that she bore Jacob no children, Rachel envied her sister, and said to Jacob, 'Give me children, or else I die!' And Jacob's anger was aroused against Rachel, and he said, 'Am I in the place of God, who has withheld from you the fruit of the womb?'" (Gen. 30:1–2). Her demand for children was mingled with a request to die.

I consider those who are pushed to their wit's end, but were single-minded in their belief of what they needed. After all, the man Jabez, acquainted with sorrow, was named and called sorrow. He was specific in his demand, "And Jabez called on the God of Israel saying, 'Oh, that You would bless me indeed, and enlarge my territory, that Your hand would be with me, and that You would keep me from evil, that I may not cause pain!' So God granted him what he requested" (1 Chron. 4:10). He asked to be blessed indeed, not making occasion for eventuality. How about Jacob as he wrestled with the God in the form of a man? "And He said, 'Let Me go, for the day breaks.' But he said, 'I will not let You go unless You bless me!'" (Gen. 32:26). He never gave an option to choose from; it is like saying, "Bless me or bless me." He was not ready to give up until he was blessed. Hannah was a woman who was provoked relentlessly because she had no child. Her prayer was specific without providing an alternative.

The unfortunate thing about making an alternate request is that it confuses the angel of blessing. After requesting what we need from God, angels are released to bring them to pass. Now, consider a situation of someone praying, "O God, provide a husband for me." However, soon after, because of a troubled heart and weariness of soul, she murmurs saying, "I'm even tired about everything in life; there are no good men around. I prefer to stay single." Peradventure, an angel was standing by to release the package; what a confusion it would be on hearing, "I prefer to stay single." The alternate request encourages demons to lay hold of those words and war with them to oppose the actual request.

Another thing that happens when we make an alternate prayer is that we conceive both requests. So we carry about two requests in our womb of miracle, one contending with another. The one that we feed constantly with words, thoughts, and actions gets stronger. The stronger may prevail over the weaker. And whoever or whatsoever prevails manifests. If it is the negative, that is what we see happening to us. The substitute provided oftentimes is what the enemy of our soul uses against us to contend with the angel of blessings. The devil, being the accuser of the brethren, stands in opposition, using our own words, thoughts, and actions against us. I imagine telling my daughter, "Go get me a cup of water." As she goes, I say, "I don't even like water, it makes me sick." What would be her reaction? I guess she would stop for awhile and watch me or ask me if I truly meant what I was saying. However, I truly needed the water. So with an alternate prayer, what we mean is either/or, one or the other. "Now to Him Who, by (in consequence of) the [action of His] power that is at work within us, is able to [carry out His purpose and] do superabundantly, far over and above all that we [dare] ask or think [infinitely beyond our highest prayers, desires, thoughts, hopes, or dreams]" (Eph. 3:20, AMP).

So prayers can be in form of desired thoughts, hopes, or dreams. It is more than just talking. Even when we ask, is it not the same tongue we use in asking that we also use in condemning, complaining, and blaspheming against God? "But no man can tame the tongue. It is an unruly evil, full of deadly poison. With it we bless our God and Father, and with it we curse men, who have been made in the similitude of God. Out of the same mouth proceed blessing and cursing. My brethren, these things ought not to be so. Does a spring send forth fresh water and bitter from the same opening? Can a fig tree, my brethren, bear olives, or a grapevine bear figs? Thus no spring yields both salt water and fresh" (James 3:8–12). "But let your 'Yes' be 'Yes,' and your 'No,' 'No.' For whatever is more than these is from the evil one" (Matt. 5:37).

How about Rachel's request to "give me children, or else I die" (Gen. 30:1)? Through God's mercies, her womb was opened and she conceived and had a child named Joseph. After awhile she conceived again. "Then they journeyed from Bethel. And when there was but a little distance to go to Ephrath, Rachel labored in childbirth, and she had hard labor. Now it came to pass, when she was in hard labor, that the midwife said to her, 'Do not fear; you will have this son also.' And so it was, as her soul was departing (for she died), that she called his name Ben-Oni; but his father called him Benjamin. So Rachel died and was buried on the way to Ephrath (that is, Bethlehem)" (35:16–19). Remember that her request was "give me children" and not "give me a child." When she had the first, Joseph, that was a child, but from the second going, that became children. That was the time her desperate request manifested. Her alternate request came strong against her, "or else I die." As they journeyed from Bethel to Ephrath (Bethlehem)—that is, from Bethel, the House of God, to Bethlehem, the house of bread—her other request warred against her. So also, as we rise from the house of God, even in His presence, where we have made our request known and head toward the house of provision (bread) where needs are met, our other negative request or desire comes into remembrance to oppose the manifestations. Rachel got the children she demanded, but she lost her life. While going through the sorrow of death, she named her miracle baby Ben-Oni (son of my sorrow); but the father, Jacob, objected and named him Benjamin (son of my right hand).

A group of us were invited to pray for a man who was terribly sick. We all prayed one after the other. I was the last person to pray, and I was led to pray against the spirit of poverty. I struggled with myself because that may not sound right. Anyhow, I prayed as I was led by the Holy Spirit against the spirit of poverty. I observed the reactions of the people around me weren't pleasant, so I stopped and everyone was staring at me. Then the Holy Spirit gave me a word of knowledge; and I asked the man, "Did you at anytime say, 'I'd rather die than to be poor?'" The man responded, "I say that everyday." Then I had the boldness to talk to the brethren around me. I said, "This man had requested that he would rather die than to be poor. So the enemy attacked him with the spirit of poverty. Now that he is poor, death is inevitable. Therefore, for this sickness not to lead to death, repentance and withdrawal of those words are required. Then we can cast out the spirit of poverty. Because, if that is gone out of him, he will live and blessing will come." Everyone around now joined me in prayers. Within a few weeks, he was discharged from the hospital and was healed and delivered.

There was another lady who always said, "I'd rather be sick than my children." This was when her children were always sick. Her prayers were answered as the children got better, but she became very sick, until she renounced her contradicting request. How about a friend of mine who loves nice cars? He usually says, "I prefer a good car than a house." After he got married, his wife encouraged him that they should get a house. He agreed and they got a beautiful huge house in Mississauga, Ontario. This was a brand new house, and they were the first owners. The first two and a half years were terrible moments for them in that every week a major repair had to be done on the house. They asked the neighbors if they had experienced the same, but even the builders confirmed everything was in order. If it was not electrical, it was plumbing or utensils that would be broken. I was invited to pray over the house, which I did. The wife called me the following day about the revelation she had: "My husband drove in his car, parked in our driveway, but refused to come out from the car. I saw myself trying to see what was happening as I moved closer to the car, and lo and behold, my husband had just finished eating in the car and was ready to sleep inside the car. I tried pulling him out, but he refused to enter the house." Then the vision cleared. I explained to her that her husband preferred his car to the house. That was the reason he refused coming out of the car, and he preferred to eat, sleep, and do everything in the car. They both repented and annulled the effect, declaring, "We want both the car and the house together, and not either house or car." Then things started getting better.

How about you? What other requests have you made alternate to your real desire? What have you thought, desired, or said that is struggling with your original heart's desire? Samson was a man anointed by God for his generation. He fell into the traps of the Philistines, and they plucked out his eyes, "bound him with fetters of brass and he did grind in the prison house" (Judg. 16:21, KJV). He repented and consecrated his life to God again, and his hair began growing. His time of vengeance came as the Philistines gathered. "Then Samson called to the LORD, saying, 'O Lord GOD, remember me, I pray! Strengthen me, I pray, just this once, O God, that I may with one blow take vengeance on the Philistines for my two eyes!'" (v. 28). His prayer was answered, and as the pillars were about to collapse, he added another request; "Let me die with the Philistines!" (v. 30). This other prayer was answered, and he died with his enemies. I strongly believe that if Samson had not requested that he might die with his enemies, he would have escaped, and his enemies would have died alone.

When tempted into an alternate prayer, you can declare like Job, "For I know that my Redeemer lives, And He shall stand at last on the earth" (Job 19:25). Or like the apostle Paul, "For this reason I also suffer these things; nevertheless I am not ashamed, for I know whom I have believed and am persuaded that He is able to keep what I have committed to Him until that Day" (2 Tim. 1:12).

The birth of miracles

Miracles are precious and wonderful, gladdening the heart of those who receive them. I take counsel from Eliphaz, one of Job's friends, in using his words to define a miracle: miracles are "great things, and unsearchable, Marvelous things without number" (Job 5:9). Though he was talking about God, yet truly God is the Author of miracles, and He alone works miracles. When something is great, beyond us, and is so marvelous that we can only trace the source to God Almighty, then it is a miracle. God does "great things past finding out; yea, and wonders without number" (9:10, KJV).

We often conceive visions, goals, and dreams, and reflect on how our lives should be. It is so sad that oftentimes these visions are aborted at the embryonic state and never come to light. Some people even taste good things, but it doesn't last before they lose it and never regain it. I sincerely believe that miracles are children's bread (Matt. 15:26). It is God's earnest plea that we experience His miraculous power daily. How can we as God's people enjoy the miraculous, dwell in it, and let it be part of our lives?

The children of Israel in Egypt are a wonderful case study. They were oppressed and subjected to taskmasters who "made their lives bitter with hard bondage" (Exod. 1:14, KJV); yet they "multiplied, and waxed very mighty" (v. 20, KJV). This stirred up the wrath of the king of Egypt, a type of the rulership spirit of the world system, who made decrees regarding the birth of Hebrew children. The first has to do with the killing of the male child and sparing the female (v. 16), while the second was to drown the male child and spare the female (v. 22). The target of both decrees was the male child. I reason why the male child? Perhaps to destroy the seed of the woman, the Messiah, so that no deliverer would arise to rescue them. The other reason for the male child is that the male symbolizes strength; their strength for war was cut off so that they could not raise up an army to fight and take over the kingdom. I reasoned further that if all the males were killed at birth and the female children were spared, who would marry the women? Of course, the Egyptians, thus polluting their heritage. Why? It was forbidden for a Hebrew to marry an Egyptian. The children of such a union would be dedicated to the Egyptian gods and goddesses.

So as the birth of babies brings joy, so do miracles. Just as we conceive babies, so we conceive miracles. When we conceive goals and visions, nurtured until they are well developed and bringing forth, then our joy is fulfilled. It takes the miracle of God to see what we have believed and trusted God for coming to pass. Many people fail and fall along the way, while others can't even hold vision or retain their dreams for a day. The rulership spirit of the world has set us up to kill or drown our miracles, but such shall not prosper.

As the male child signifies strength, so is strength needed to conceive, to retain and bring forth our goals, dreams, and visions. I love the saying of King Hezekiah when threatened by his enemies: "Thus says Hezekiah: 'This day is a day of trouble, and rebuke, and blasphemy; for the children have come to birth, but there is no strength to bring them forth'" (2 Kings 19:3). It is indeed a day of trouble when we can't fulfill our dreams. It is also a day of rebuke when dreams are shattered. Friends and everyone whom we have shared our dreams with will rebuke us and ask why we fail. There are emotional and heartbreaking moments that cause us to blaspheme. It is even worse when we have labored extensively to the point of reaping the fruit of our labor, but because of failing strength, we fail to deliver. Stillbirth is so deadly and painful that no one prays to experience it twice; how much worse for the birth of miracles? The enemy tries to kill our strength in bringing forth miracles—no strength to conceive, retain, and bring forth. This is a grave problem that has caused so many people to faint and give up. "For by strength shall no man prevail" (1 Sam. 2:9) because "a horse is a vain hope for safety; Neither shall it deliver any by its great strength" (Ps. 33:17). When we receive strength from God, through Him we will subdue all oppositions to blessings. Nonetheless, we can cry out to God for strength to bring forth all His purposes for our lives.

The other decree given by the king of Egypt was to "cast into the river" every male child; that is to sink, submerge, and suffocate. Let them go below the surface. May I ask, hasn't the rulership spirit of this world succeeded in keeping many gifted people below the surface? No matter how hard people try, they are submerged and kept below average. People are suffocating and gasping for breath because of stress and the pressure of surviving at all cost. The first decree of killing the male children was given to the midwives who through the fear of God refused to carry out the assignments. The fear of God was reflected in their names, Shiprah (beauty) and Puah (splendor). Having a correctly appointed midwife could help in a safe delivery. My wife used to practice as a midwife; she would come back home telling stories of complicated deliveries, but with the help of God and her experience, she helped many people. So also, many visions have died and many dreams have perished in the hands of poor and inexperienced helpers. Many people are not aware of the complexity of the dreams we have conceived and the trouble of developing them. They appear to be helping, but end up destroying. May God raise up the right midwives to help carry to fulfillment our dreams and visions. With "beauty" and "splendor" we are guaranteed of safe delivery. Miracles will survive or perish in the hand of the midwives—those who are associated with our visions and dreams.

When the midwives were asked why they spared the male children, they made a true confession: "And the midwives said to Pharaoh, 'Because the Hebrew women are not like the Egyptian women; for they are lively and give birth before the midwives come to them'" (Exod. 1:19). What a true confession, that we are not like the people of the world; we are lively and bring forth miracles without assistance but with God's help. With God on your side, you can conceive dreams, and develop and bring forth only with God's help and favor. But the king of Egypt withdrew the assignment from the midwives and "charged all his people" (v. 22). The Hebrews were now under a wide network of monitors—"all his people." So, nowhere was safe, and everyone was involved in executing evil decrees. How could anyone escape? It became much more difficult to get dreams fulfilled under such a network.

In the midst of these decrees, there was a woman who considered her child "a goodly child" (2:2). Because she believed in what she was carrying in her womb, she refused to give up her child for casting into the river. I still can't fathom how she made it, when all the people were charged to execute the decree. How could somebody be pregnant and deliver without people noticing? I perceive she did not only hide but was also protected by God against the destroyers because she was carrying a proper child. Through the wisdom of God, her child floated while others were drowned. Her child was raised in the king's palace while others had no life. Her child lived to reign, while others perished. The same people who issued decrees to kill and cast into the river gave him a name, Moses, "because I drew him out of the water" (2:10). So, the child was considered drowned in the water, but divine interception halted the act.

Who are those who will cry out to God, saying come what may, their glory will not sink and they will not be put under the surface? More importantly, they should pray for strength to carry out divine assignments that shall not fail. Our dreams need not die, neither should they be submerged. We can connect back to God, the Miracle Giver, for strength until His glory fills our hearts for miraculous exploits.

The Ministry of Angels

Angels are heavenly beings, God's messengers to execute His will and purposes.

Some of their duties

They are exceedingly innumerable, but not to be worshiped: "Now I, John, saw and heard these things. And when I heard and saw, I fell down to worship before the feet of the angel who showed me these things. Then he said to me, 'See that you do not do that. For I am your fellow servant, and of your brethren the prophets, and of those who keep the words of this book. Worship God'" (Rev. 22:8–9).

They are assigned to protect: "For He shall give His angels charge over you, To keep you in all your ways. In their hands they shall bear you up, Lest you dash your foot against a stone" (Ps. 91:11–12).

They watch over us: "The angel of the LORD encamps all around those who fear Him, And delivers them" (Ps. 34:7).

They provide physical necessities: "And God heard the voice of the lad. Then the angel of God called to Hagar out of heaven, and said to her, 'What ails you, Hagar? Fear not, for God has heard the voice of the lad where he is. Arise, lift up the lad and hold him with your hand, for I will make him a great nation.' Then God opened her eyes, and she saw a well of water. And she went and filled the skin with water, and gave the lad a drink" (Gen. 21:17–19). "But he himself went a day's journey into the wilderness, and came and sat down under a broom tree. And he prayed that he might die, and said, 'It is enough! Now, LORD, take my life, for I am no better than my fathers!' Then as he lay and slept under a broom tree, suddenly an angel touched him, and said to him, 'Arise and eat.' Then he looked, and there by his head was a cake baked on coals, and a jar of water. So he ate and drank, and lay down again" (1 Kings 19:4–6).

They strengthen and encourage us: "So he answered, 'Do not fear, for those who are with us are more than those who are with them.' And Elisha prayed, and said, 'LORD, I pray, open his eyes that he may see.' Then the LORD opened the eyes of the young man, and he saw. And behold, the mountain was full of horses and chariots of fire all around Elisha" (2 Kings 6:16–17). "Then an angel appeared to Him from heaven, strengthening Him" (Luke 22:43).

They serve as messengers: "Are they not all ministering spirits sent forth to minister for those who will inherit salvation?" (Heb. 1:14).

They minister healing: "For an angel went down at a certain time into the pool and stirred up the water; then whoever stepped in first, after the stirring of the water, was made well of whatever disease he had" (John 5:4).

They are great warriors: "'For I will defend this city, to save it For My own sake and for My servant David's sake.' And it came to pass on a certain night that the angel of the LORD went out, and killed in the camp of the Assyrians one hundred and eighty-five thousand; and when people arose early in the morning, there were the corpses—all dead" (2 Kings 19:34–35).

They execute God's judgment: "So on a set day Herod, arrayed in royal apparel, sat on his throne and gave an oration to them. And the people kept shouting, 'The voice of a god and not of a man!' Then immediately an angel of the Lord struck him, because he did not give glory to God. And he was eaten by worms and died" (Acts 12:21–23).

They rejoice in salvation; angels of the Lord rejoice to see sinners turn back to God, even as they love to celebrate God's goodness always with the righteous (Luke 15:10).

And most importantly, they worship the Most High God: "Above it stood seraphim; each one had six wings: with two he covered his face, with two he covered his feet, and with two he flew. And one cried to another and said: 'Holy, holy, holy is the LORD of hosts; The whole earth is full of His glory!' And the posts of the door were shaken by the voice of him who cried out, and the house was filled with smoke" (Isa. 6:2–4). "The twenty-four elders fall down before Him who sits on the throne and worship Him who lives forever and ever, and cast their crowns before the throne" (Rev. 4:10).

Angelic/divine visitations

Going through the Word of God, I find that many people had angelic visitations.

Abraham entertained angels and had fellowship with them, which resulted in announcing the birth of his promised child, despite the old age of his wife, Sarah (Gen. 18:1).

Joshua got the right formula to defeat Jericho and the marching order to conquer the rest of the Promised Land (Josh. 5:13–14).

Gideon had an angelic visitation that made him discover who he was and what God can do through him (Judg. 6).

Manoah and his wife, the parents of Samson, had an angelic visitation resulting into the birth of Samson (Judg. 13).

David "lifted his eyes and saw the angel of the Lord standing between earth and heaven, having in his hand a drawn sword stretched out over Jerusalem. So David and the elders, clothed in sackcloth, fell on their faces" (1 Chron. 21:16).

The shepherd at the birth of Jesus witnessed an angelic visitation (Luke 2:9–15).

The imprisoned disciples were set free by the angel of the Lord (Acts 5:18–20).

Peter was miraculously rescued by angel from the prison (Acts 12:7–16).

Many saw angels in their dreams like Cornelius (Acts 10), and others were spoken to by the angel of the Lord. Jacob even wrestled with one and also saw them ascending and descending (Gen 32:22; 28:12).

Daniel, when cast into the lions' den, was not devoured by lions. He acknowledged: "My God sent His angel and shut the lions' mouths, so that they have not hurt me, because I was found innocent before Him; and also, O king, I have done no wrong before you" (Dan. 6:22). Truly, if it had not been for God's angelic intervention, he would have been torn into pieces. Contrary to that, when his adversaries and their families were thrown into the same lions' den, "the lions had the mastery of them, and broke all their bones into pieces or ever they came at the bottom of the den" (Dan. 6:24).

Angels in Jesus' ministry

How about Jesus' ministry? Angels announced His birth (Matt. 1:20–21); protected Him as a baby (Matt. 2:13); strengthened Him when tempted (Matt. 4:11); ministered to Him at the garden of Gethsemane (Luke 22:43); defended Him in ministry (Matt. 26:53); rolled away the stone at His tomb (Matt. 28:2–4); announced His resurrection (Matt. 28:5–6); they were at His ascension (Acts 1:10–11); and will even be at His return: "When the

Son of Man comes in His glory, and all the holy angels with Him, then He will sit on the throne of His glory" (Matt. 25:31).

Ministry of angels today

How about today? Can we still have an angelic encounter? Yes, I do believe so! The problem is that we have been programmed to believe that angels are always with wings, so even if we do see one without wings we may not be aware. I have a feeling that if we saw an angel bodily with wings, many people would be scared to death. Wouldn't you? However, they often relate to us with simplicity in order to fulfill their mission. "Do not forget to entertain strangers, for by so doing some have unwittingly entertained angels" (Heb. 13:2). We are often confronted with an unexpected opportunity to reach out with the love of God, and without proper discernment we may miss out and forfeit an opportunity to be blessed. Even if we do not see an angel physically or in dreams and visions, we can still ask God to give charge to His angels to assist us in our daily endeavors. The angels of God can serve as harvesters to reap our hidden and scattered blessings known and unknown to us because "the reapers are the angels" (Matt. 13:39). They can reach out on our behalf to war and to minister. Even though we were made a little lower than angels, yet God has given us dominion over all the works of His hands. "For You have made him a little lower than the angels, And You have crowned him with glory and honor. You have made him to have dominion over the works of Your hands; You have put all things under his feet" (Ps. 8:5–6).

Therefore, we can profit in the ministry of angels because they see what we don't see and cannot be confined to time and space; they can ascend and descend and reach where we cannot reach. So, when we ask God to "give charge to His angels" to help us, we should ask in faith. We may not see angels physically, but we can believe, acknowledge, and welcome them. This will stir them into action. Because they are messengers of God sent to fulfill His intent for our lives, we should receive them with an open heart, and with gratitude to God. "Are not the angels all ministering spirits (servants) sent out in the service [of God for the assistance] of those who are to inherit salvation?" (Heb. 1:14, AMP). As God's people, we should expect them while we worship God, either privately or corporately. They show up to minister deliverance and healing, even to deep wounds that no one understands; because they can see the invisible, they get right to the root of the problem, disengage the wicked forces, and administer healing.

I ask, why do we take for granted the ministry of angels? Why do we feel we can go through life alone with all the loads and pressure? When the weight of sin of the world became too heavy for our Lord Jesus, even though He knew no sin, it was placed in Him (2 Cor. 5:21), and an angel of the Lord came forth "strengthening Him" (Luke 22:42) in order for Him to do the will of God the Father. In like manner, we also can trust God for angelic release to strengthen us and shake off the burdens and the dust that have almost wrecked our lives. I have done that several times when I felt burdened. I just ask God's angels to carry the burden as I cast them onto God. This is how I go through tough times without being crushed. The angels are more willing to serve us than we expect. May we allow them to do what our human strength cannot accomplish. Because they are spirits, distance is no barrier to them. They can break through the most difficult blockage. I pray you start profiting in the ministry of angels henceforth! All you need do is to ask God to give charge to them to execute His will in your life.

We also can trust God to receive angelic rescue in order to escape troubles. Those men and women who had angelic encounters were men and women like us, more so, with the redeeming love and grace we receive through the shed blood of Jesus. More importantly, God who did it for them, is still the same (Heb. 13:8), and He can do much more abundantly today. As we journey through this world under these perilous circumstances, never before has the ministry of angels been required more than today. How great will it be, when we come to the consciousness of angelic guards accompanying us everywhere with the indwelling Holy Spirit, that we shall walk courageously and victoriously over every foe.

The Power of His Blood

I searched with interest when the word *blood* first appeared in the Word of God. I am quite aware that when Adam and Eve sinned and became naked, before they were cast out of the garden of Eden, "the LORD God make coats of skins, and clothed them" (Gen. 3:21, KJV). Understand that animal skin cannot be used without the shedding of the animal's blood. Even though they had made aprons of leaves, without proper atonement for sin, redemption was impossible. So, God made the atonement on their behalf and clothed them. God has always made the first move to reconcile man to Himself. However, the shedding of blood first occurred in the Bible when Cain slew his brother. "And He said, 'What have you done? The voice of your brother's blood cries out to Me from the ground. So now you are cursed from the earth, which has opened its mouth to receive your brother's blood from your hand'" (4:10–11). "The voice of your brother's blood cries out" means blood is a living entity; although it is dead, yet it speaks.

How about the New Testament? The word *blood* first appeared in connection with the woman with the issue of blood. "And suddenly, a woman who had a flow of blood for twelve years came from behind and touched the hem of His garment" (Matt. 9:20). This does not happen by chance, being cured of a hemorrhage. What good news for those plagued with blood diseases. Even though Jesus had turned water to wine (John 2)—His first miracle and a type of His blood—this woman "came from behind." Yea, iniquity has pushed us behind, but like this woman, we can resolve to touch our Savior and be healed. How about when the word *blood* appeared last in the Bible? "He was clothed with a robe dipped in blood, and His name is called The Word of God" (Rev. 19:13). It has to do with the Savior on the white horse. He was referred to as "Faithful and True, and in righteousness He judges and makes war. His eyes were like a flame of fire and on His head were many crowns" (Rev. 19:11–12). He has conquered and is still conquering, having crushed the satanic rebellion and bruised the head of the serpent (Gen. 3:15). His "robe dipped in blood" refers to his shedding of His own blood to redeem mankind. This blood-dipped robe is still dripping blood today for our redemption. We can be washed, cleansed, and purged by it.

At the overthrow of Satan's rebellion, victory was only proclaimed through the blood of the Lamb. "And they overcame him by the blood of the Lamb and by the word of their testimony, and they did not love their lives to the death" (Rev. 12:11). Our utterances and bold witnessing of the power of His blood establishes unquestionable victory. What power are we to proclaim about His blood? What are the blessings we can receive through His blood?

His blood saves from wrath: "Much more then, having now been justified by His blood, we shall be saved from wrath through Him" (Rom. 5:9).

His blood cleanses: "But if we walk in the light as He is in the light, we have fellowship with one another, and the blood of Jesus Christ His Son cleanses us from all sin" (1 John 1:7).

His blood redeems: "Not with the blood of goats and calves, but with His own blood He entered the Most Holy Place once for all, having obtained eternal redemption" (Heb. 9:12). "In Him we have redemption through His blood, the forgiveness of sins, according to the riches of His grace" (Eph. 1:7).

His blood remits and purges: "And according to the law almost all things are purified with blood, and without shedding of blood there is no remission" (Heb. 9:22).

His blood made peace: "And by Him to reconcile all things to Himself, by Him, whether things on earth or things in heaven, having made peace through the blood of His cross" (Col. 1:20).

His blood justifies: "Much more then, having now been justified by His blood, we shall be saved from wrath through Him" (Rom. 5:9).

His blood destroys the power of death: His blood destroys him that has the power of death, that is, the devil, "inasmuch then as the children have partaken of flesh and blood, He Himself likewise shared in the same, that through death He might destroy him who had the power of death, that is, the devil" (Heb. 2:14).

His blood purges: His blood purges our conscience from dead works. "How much more shall the blood of Christ, who through the eternal Spirit offered Himself without spot to God, cleanse your conscience from dead works to serve the living God?" (Heb. 9:14).

His blood gives us boldness into the holiest: "Therefore, brethren, having boldness to enter the Holiest by the blood of Jesus" (Heb. 10:19)

His blood heals: "But He was wounded for our transgressions, He was bruised for our iniquities; The chastisement for our peace was upon Him, And by His stripes we are healed" (Isa. 53:5).

He is the Mediator of the New Covenant: "To Jesus the Mediator of the new covenant, and to the blood of sprinkling that speaks better things than that of Abel" (Heb. 12:24).

Oh, what a blessing in the blood that liberates, protects, secures, pardons, delivers from condemnation, grants access into the heavenly court, and guarantees a better life!

As he interceded for mankind because of the agony of the ransom price, He prayed until "His sweat became like great drops of blood falling down to the ground" (Luke 22:44). He shed His blood through brutal scourging, wearing the crown of thorns, nails on his hands and legs, and a spear piercing His side. He did all these to spoil principalities and powers, "having wiped out the handwriting of requirements that was against us, which was contrary to us. And He has taken it out of the way, having nailed it to the cross. Having disarmed principalities and powers, He made a public spectacle of them, triumphing over them in it" (Col. 2:14–15). I tell people that if the devil had known that crucifying Jesus would bring his total destruction, he would have spared Him to live longer than Methuselah. The greatest regret of the devil was to crucify the Lord of glory, "for had they known, they would not have crucified the Lord of glory" (1 Cor. 2:8).

Of a truth, there is life in His blood, "for the life of all flesh is its blood" (Lev. 17:14). So, His flesh was broken that His life might flow into us. As many that are purged by His blood are partakers of His life, even eternal life. We can apply the power of His blood upon our lives, homes, and all that concerns us, as a guarantee of His presence and power. His blood repels evil and attracts blessings and God's glory. Apply His efficacious blood by faith and enjoy peace.

The Ministry of the Holy Spirit

A weary mind is confused, living without hope, discouraged, and despondent. How else can we be justified and walk in freedom without the same Spirit that convicted us unto salvation—the Holy Spirit. As the Holy Spirit reveals Jesus to us, He convinces us to repent, and after true confession and repentance, we are filled and empowered to start fellowshiping with God. He became the true Witness of our eternal covenant with God, even as He teaches us all things (John 14:26). He quickens us, gives us life every day, and grants strength to mortify the flesh (Rom. 8:12–13). He imparts the character of God that we may work in liberty and not in bondage.

This is the same Spirit that raised Jesus from death and moved in the miraculous. Jesus was conceived by the Holy Spirit (Luke 1:35), filled with the Holy Spirit (Matt. 3:16), led by the Holy Spirit (Mark 1:12), and resurrected by the Holy Spirit (Rom. 8:11; 1 Pet. 3:18). This same Holy Spirit dwells in those who have accepted Jesus as Lord and Savior. What makes a believer powerful? The Holy Spirit! His power is immeasurable, unlimited, surpassingly great, and mighty. Such an eternal excellent power gives great grace and joy to every believer to experience great wonders and miracles. He flows through our innermost being to cleanse and refresh. Through Him we can discern the mind of God to pray correctly:

> Likewise the Spirit also helps in our weaknesses. For we do not know what we should pray for as we ought, but the Spirit Himself makes intercession for us with groanings which cannot be uttered. Now He who searches the hearts knows what the mind of the Spirit is, because He makes intercession for the saints according to the will of God.
>
> —ROMANS 8:26–27

This is the Spirit of grace and supplication that we might flow in wisdom and the counsel of God. Through Him we are full of power and anointing that destroys yoke and bondages. Even at the time of unceasing flooding of evil, He quenches their rage and grants victory.

How then can we enjoy the presence of the Holy Spirit to the fullest? "But I say, walk and live [habitually] in the [Holy] Spirit [responsive to and controlled and guided by the Spirit]; then you will certainly not gratify the carvings and desires of the flesh (of human nature without God)" (Gal. 5:16, AMP). The personality of the Holy Spirit can be grieved when we suppress and deny His dealings in our lives. "And do not grieve the Holy Spirit of God [do not offend or vex or sadden Him], by whom you were sealed (marked, branded as God's own, secured) for the day of redemption (for final deliverance through Christ from evil and the consequences of sin)" (Eph. 4:30, AMP).

Power Praise

Praise is the sure overcoming strategy in spiritual warfare. It is the most powerful force that reckons heaven with the earth. Heaven cannot despise the shout of praise from a broken and contrite heart. It is our surety of victory and possessing possession (Gen. 43:9). Praise rules over all (49:10), subdues the enemy of our soul (v. 8), and devours like a mighty lion (v. 9). What makes it more glorious is that God is enthroned in our praises (Ps. 22:3).

Judah means "praise" (29:35). I discovered a prophecy about Judah relating to Egypt—a type of the world of sin, slavery, and affliction. Relating this to the power of praise fires up my spirit. "And the land of Judah will be a terror

> Let praise be your lifestyle as you are wrapped up in the praise of Him that is above all.

to Egypt; everyone who makes mention of it will be afraid in himself, because of the counsel of the LORD of hosts which He has determined against it (Isa. 19:17). So, praise terrifies affliction and all bondages. What a power we have through praises. I challenge you into the praise of God to shatter all opposing forces to miracles asunder. Let praise be your lifestyle as you are wrapped up in the praise of Him that is above all.

> Let the high praises of God be in their mouth, And a two-edged sword in their hand, To execute vengeance on the nations, And punishments on the peoples; To bind their kings with chains, And their nobles with fetters of iron; To execute on them the written judgment—This honor have all His saints. Praise the LORD!
>
> —PSALM 149:6–9

Through our praise and proclaiming the truth of the Word of God, we can execute vengeance and punishments, and bind kings and nobles. The power of praise makes us stronger than the strongman in possessing possessions.

The Power of Love

Love is a strong spiritual warfare weapon. Hatred bows at its feet, so do the enemies submit their weapons at the gate of love. Because of our sinful nature, it is easier to hate than to love. The power of love is rooted in God because "God is love" (1 John 4:8, 16). To determine how great love is, consider this passage, "And now abide faith, hope, love, these three; but the greatest of these is love" (1 Cor. 13:13). Compare the three foundational principles of our relationship with God: faith, hope, and love.

By faith we can move mountains (Mark 11:23); we are justified by faith (Rom. 5:1) and "without faith it is impossible to please Him, for he who comes to God must believe that He is, and that He is a rewarder of those who diligently seek Him" (Heb. 11:6). How about hope? Hope is a joyful and confident expectation of eternal salvation. "Now hope does not disappoint, because the love of God has been poured out in our hearts by the Holy Spirit who was given to us" (Rom. 5:5). As great as faith and hope are, love is the greatest (1 Cor. 13:13). If "faith without works is dead" (James 2:26), then love without

> **So when you say, "I love (charity) you," all you are saying is I have all it takes to help, bless, and improve you.**

expression is dead and buried. Expressing love through appreciation, service, and spending quality time with one another in fellowship heal wounds and refresh us. "But if we walk in the light as He is in the light, we have fellowship with one another, and the blood of Jesus Christ His Son cleanses us from all sin" (1 John 1:7). Jesus often said to those who looked unto Him, "Your faith has made you whole" (Luke 8:48). Then, I say to myself, if faith makes me whole and love is greater, it is safe to say that love makes perfect.

> Love has been perfected among us in this: that we may have boldness in the Day of Judgment; because as He is, so are we in this world. There is no fear in love; but perfect love casts out fear, because fear involves torment. But he who fears has not been made perfect in love.
> —1 JOHN 1:17–18

How about hope? If "hope makes not ashamed" (Rom. 5:5), and love is greater, then love brings honor and respect. If faith and hope are required for a victorious life, completing the cycle by adding love makes our foes flee without looking back. Our love for God makes us stand in His will and counsel.

Love is sacrificing: "For God so loved the world that He gave His only begotten Son, that whoever believes in Him should not perish but have everlasting life" (John 3:16). Love made God love us while we were still sinners and enemies of righteousness. "But God demonstrates His own love toward us, in that while we were still sinners, Christ died for us" (Rom. 5:8).

I love the old English word for love—*charity*. It is derived from the Latin word for affection. Charity as used in the Holy Scriptures refers to love and benevolence. I consider what it takes to run a charitable organization. It is doing with the intention to help the needy and the poor. To be able to do this, all you are saying is, "I have all it takes to help and improve others, even though there may not be anything for me to profit." That is why it is called a nonprofit organization. So when you say, "I love (charity) you," all you are saying is I have all it takes to help, bless, and improve you. Our profit lies in seeing people blessed with an improved condition of life; this is our joy. Even if your partner or the person you are showering love (charity) on may not give anything in return for your help, you are glad to continue. If this is truly how we love others, then the love of God is perfected in us. I, therefore, challenge you to apply the weapons of love and watch God for miracles.

The wickedness of the end of the age shall be measured by love. "And because lawlessness will abound, the love of many will grow cold" (Matt. 24:12). When our love to God, His kingdom, and one another grows cold, lawlessness and all forms of evil abound. Love determines the potency of every other thing. When love is fervent, peace abounds because love covers, shields, and protects. "Above all things have intense and unfailing love for one another, for love covers a multitude of sins [forgives and disregards the offenses of others]" (1 Pet. 4:8, AMP). I encourage you to discover the power of love rooted in God.

Rewards of Victories

The continent of Africa has gone through tribal war with devastating consequences, destroying communities and wrecking families. The traumatic effect on the people is yet to be healed. In some of the tribal wars, as the warriors got ready for battle, the fetish priest would stand before them with a mandate for the battle saying, "Go fight, invade, conquer, spoil, and bring slaves." Under this mandate, the warriors would fight out their hearts and would be victory conscious. I strongly believe that this has lots of spiritual implications because the fetish priest would have invoked the realm of the spirit before his declaration. Consequently, the devil has given his hosts warfare mandates to steal, kill, and destroy, which they carry out daily. Believers in Christ are also under divine mandate: "Go therefore and make disciples of all the nations, baptizing them in the name of the Father and of the Son and of the Holy Spirit, teaching them to observe all things that I have commanded you; and lo, I am with you always, even to the end of the age" (Matt. 28:19–20).

Every battle won has a reward, and every race won has a trophy. Thank God for our eternal rewards: God is a "rewarder of them that diligently seek him" (Heb. 11:6). There are rewards for our labors, for our labor in Christ is not in vain. Unto the seven churches addressed by Christ in the Book of Revelation, the common declaration, "he that overcomes," was said to all the churches. So, there are rewards for the overcomers. God even commanded Moses on how the spoils should be shared (Num. 31:21–54).

David, before battling with Goliath, demanded to know the rewards at stake: "Then David spoke to the men who stood by him, saying, 'What shall be done for the man who kills this Philistine and takes away the reproach from Israel? For who is this uncircumcised Philistine, that he should defy the armies of the living God?'" (1 Sam. 17:26). He was certain of victory and the rewards. Hannah, who was mocked because she was childless, prayed to God and was rewarded with three sons and two daughters (1 Sam. 2:21). She even gave birth to the last judge of Israel. Hannah's offspring judged and ruled over all those who ridiculed her. I pray for readers of this book that you will bring forth that which shall reign over your oppressors, in Jesus' name. Jehoshaphat reaped abundance of rewards beyond what he and his people could carry; even three days were not sufficient for total possession (2 Chron. 20:25).

The tragic situation I see today in the body of Christ as a prophetic intercessor is that we engage in spiritual warfare, prayer, praise, and worship with donations and offerings, but we never wait on the Lord to reap the reward. You engage in battle, then where are your rewards? You are a worshiper, then where are your rewards? You are a giver, then where are your rewards? You love and care for others, then where are your rewards? You have been laboring for the advancement of God's kingdom, then where are your rewards?

David knew his right to demand for the reward of slaying Goliath (1 Sam. 17:26), and "Jehoshaphat and his people came to take away their spoil" (2 Chron. 20:25). Would you also arise in the strength of the Lord to take over your spoil? They are waiting for you; God reserved them for you, so pick them up. Jesus overcame Satan and possessed the spoil. "And having spoiled principalities and powers, he made a show of them openly, triumphing over them in it" (Col. 2:15, KJV). He charged His disciples to do the same: "When a strong man, fully armed, guards his own palace, his goods are in peace. But

> Every battle won has a reward, and every race won has a trophy. Thank God for our eternal rewards: God is a "rewarder of them that diligently seek him."

when a stronger than he comes upon him and overcomes him, he takes from him all his armor in which he trusted, and divides his spoils" (Luke 11:21–22). Is it your kingdom strategy to possess your reward? May God honor His word in your life as you abound in blessings.

Chapter 11

WHO IS ON THE LORD'S SIDE?

A S A SPORTS lover, I watch supporter groups and fan clubs that are renowned for their fanatical vocal support create an atmosphere that intimidates opposing players and supporters, as well as encouraging their own team. They never stop singing or chanting during a match, no matter the result of the game. In like manner, there is a huge campaign over mankind to win us either to God's side or the devil's side. It is so unfortunate that no one person can be on both sides; you either belong to one or the other. This was the cry of Moses after encountering God in the mount: "Then Moses stood in the entrance of the camp, and said, 'Whoever is on the LORD's side—come to me!' And all the sons of Levi gathered themselves together to him" (Exod. 32:26). I wonder why this call was necessary since all of them were God's children. Yes, they were, but not all had a personal encounter with God. This was a call to repentance; but not every one of them was willing to take a stand for God, except for the sons of Levi. Why? Others had been so bound to their idols that they could not abandon them. They were so blind and excessively devoted to the idols that serving God was no longer relevant.

> **Whatever we surrender our will to, controls us.**

Idols kept them back from responding to God's call. It is very easy for people today to say, "I have no idol, neither do I serve any." We may all profess to be on the Lord's side, but how about the idols in our hearts?

> Therefore speak to them, and say to them, "Thus says the Lord GOD: 'Everyone of the house of Israel who sets up his idols in his heart, and puts before him what causes him to stumble into iniquity, and then comes to the prophet, I the LORD will answer him who comes, according to the multitude of his idols.'"
>
> —EZEKIEL 14:4

There are lots of things competing for God's place in our lives and demanding worship. When we come before God in prayer or worship and our heart is clouded or overwhelmed with issues that completely shift our focus from God, we dwell on them until we are deprived of the joy of His presence. This is an idol. I ask you, can you identify what replaces your devotion and worship time? How is your attitude when you come before His presence? "I was glad when they said to me, 'Let us go into the house of the LORD'" (Ps. 122:1). "Not forsaking the assembling of ourselves together, as is the manner of some, but exhorting one another, and so much the more as you see the Day approaching" (Heb. 10:25). How about your thought life? Is it clouded with lust, revenge, and unholy desires? So many people are lost in thought to the point of being robbed of prayer time. How you handle your life's struggles and difficulties will reflect what controls your life. Your fears and insecurity expose the idols in your heart because of doubt and loss of confidence in God's power to deliver. The idols in our hearts prevent us from maturing, consume our desire for God's Word, compete with God's love, and suppress the truth. Whatever we surrender our will to, controls us.

In one of the prayer seminars I conducted, I asked the congregation to make a prayer list of their crucial needs. I gave them some time to do that. This was in effect to probe their hearts' desire. Then I asked them which of their requests are motivated by the flesh to gratify their lustful desires? And which of them will promote God's kingdom and His eternal purposes? I saw some people cancelling, tearing their list, and others making a new list. Thank God, I didn't ask them to hand them over to me. Our needs show where our hearts are and to what we are devoted. How about the search for happiness and pleasure? As good as they are, are we so sold out to them that we forgot God? Even in pleasure, God should still be the center of our joy.

Jesus, in the parable of the sower, gave different types of soils which represent different ways we respond to God's Word. So, while some have a wayside attitude, others are stonyhearted, some have a thorny heart, and others have a good heart.

> The sower sows the word. And these are the ones by the wayside where the word is sown. When they hear, Satan comes immediately and takes away the word that was sown in their hearts. These likewise are the ones sown on stony ground who, when they hear the word, immediately receive it with gladness; and they have no root in themselves, and

so endure only for a time. Afterward, when tribulation or persecution arises for the word's sake, immediately they stumble. Now these are the ones sown among thorns; they are the ones who hear the word, and the cares of this world, the deceitfulness of riches, and the desires for other things entering in choke the word, and it becomes unfruitful. But these are the ones sown on good ground, those who hear the word, accept it, and bear fruit: some thirtyfold, some sixty and some a hundred.

—MARK 4:14–20

What kind of a heart do you have? Forsake the idols and turn to God that He might fill you with His presence. May we take counsel from the prayer of Jonah, "Those who cling to worthless idols forfeit the grace that could be theirs" (Jon. 2:8, NIV). May we cry out to God to give us the heart to know and serve Him. "Then I will give them a heart to know Me, that I am the LORD; and they shall be My people, and I will be their God, for they shall return to Me with their whole heart" (Jer. 24:7).

Awake out of slumber! There seems to be an irresistible urge on human lives to slumber when tired. At such times, even the mightiest man is at a state of surrender. It permits the enemy to terrorize us. It makes the champion lose grip of his weapons. Saul with his chosen men went after David to kill him, but he was stricken with slumber and unable to wake up until his spear and jug of water were taken away (1 Sam. 26:11). So the spirit of slumber results in the crippling of one's ability to function. Have you ever been in a conversation with someone, thinking he was tracking with you, when suddenly the person says something totally irrelevant? You are thinking you are tuned in to each other, but he had just lost focus and missed you all together because he slumbers. The spirit of slumber causes the inability to communicate intimately and to sustain a close relationship. Many relationships problems today are slumber problems because one who slumbers cannot see your need or show concern. Such a one cannot hear you clearly, will miss out some, and then try joining together, which makes no sense.

To awake out of slumber, we must determine the degree of slumber. To some people, a little tap or distraction wakes them up. Simply calling can awake others. Some may need to be shaken up. Those who sleepwalk are much more difficult to wake. They can get up, open the door, and walk down the street until there is a major interruption to bring them to consciousness. So are many who have slumbered in their walk with God.

May we not slumber to the point we can no longer heed God's warning and ignore the danger signs on our eternal walk.

> And do this, knowing the time, that now it is high time to awake out of sleep; for now our salvation is nearer than when we first believed. The night is far spent, the day is at hand. Therefore let us cast off the works of darkness, and let us put on the armor of light. Let us walk properly, as in the day, not in revelry and drunkenness; not in lewdness and lust, not in strife and envy. But put on the Lord Jesus Christ, and make no provision for the flesh, to fulfill its lusts.
>
> —ROMANS 13:11–14

An introspective consideration of one's own thought or emotions could be a check to prevent sinking further. Self-examination, not condemnation, but with intention to correct our ways may restore us to the right path. "Test yourselves to make sure you are solid in the faith. Don't drift along taking everything for granted. Give yourselves regular checkups. You need firsthand evidence, not mere hearsay that Jesus Christ is in you. Test it out. If you fail the test, do something about it. I hope the test won't show that we have failed" (2 Cor. 13:5–6, THE MESSAGE).

Many relationships problems today are slumber problems because one who slumbers cannot see your need or show concern.

I grew up with a boy whose parents could neither read nor write. We attended the same elementary school. When we got our report cards at the end of the term, usually he failed all the subjects, so he would get his pen and change all his marks to excellent. He would present the report card to his parents who would ask his elder brother to read and interpret. His elder brother would reveal what he had done, but he would deny it and sometimes lie that the teacher made the mistakes but later changed the marks. He may have deceived everyone, but the truth of the matter is when school resumed, he repeated the class. So with many people today, if we give the wrong assessment of ourselves, God determines the outcome. But if we put ourselves under the divine searchlight, God reveals our shortcomings, and if we are willing He releases grace to be converted.

True conversion is having the mind of Christ, which is gentle, persevering, and liberating. We become loving and forgiven because we appreciate the price for our redemption. This makes us zealous in our service for God and His kingdom. This is proof of an awakened spirit and one who is on the Lord's side.

Advancing or Withdrawing

One grave danger I see eating deep into the body of Christ is to retrogress in our walk with God, but to think we are progressing. We are declining in our relationship with the Holy Spirit but deceiving ourselves that we are improving; we are deteriorating in understanding the word of God but feeling we are gaining ground. The church is "called out" and separated unto God as divine representatives on earth. It is God's intent to reign through us as invading armies subduing strongholds and as flaming fire (Ps. 104:4) devouring unrighteousness; we are reconciling souls even as we advance His kingdom by revealing His love and mercies.

We are a mighty host united in purpose, supporting one another, and disciplined in achieving our eternal goal. Being under the blood of His covenant, we shall never retreat nor surrender to the enemy of our soul, because we are under mandate from Him who has made us more than conquerors. Like King David of old, we can say, "For by You, I can run against a troop, by my God I can leap over a wall" (Ps. 18:29). Samuel the judge and priest said, "It is the LORD that advanced Moses and Aaron, and that brought your fathers up out of the land of Egypt" (1 Sam. 12:6). So the advancement of Moses was the help the people of Israel needed to escape captivity. He could boldly tell the people the commandment of the Lord was "that they go forward" (Exod. 14:15). When we advance, others profit. May God advance you and bring you up and out of whatever has limited you!

Who Shall Order the Battle?

We need not go downhill and lose hope when battered by opposing forces. The intent is to break us down and force us to surrender. However, breakthrough is determined by who has authoritative command over us. Whoever orders the battle has the right to enforce obedience and determine how the battle will go. King Ahab asked the prophet, "Who shall order the battle?" (1 Kings 20:14). So also, I ask you, who is ordering the battle of your life? Who is determining the affairs and is in charge of your daily struggles? David defeated Goliath because he understood that "the battle is the LORD's, and He will give you into our hands" (1 Sam. 17:47). Jehoshaphat, the king of Judah, was encouraged by hearing this, "Thus says the LORD to you: 'Do not be afraid nor dismayed because of this great multitude, for the battle is not yours, but God's'" (2 Chron. 20:15). And God gave him and his people victory. Hezekiah, the king of Judah recognized when confronted by the enemy: "'With him is an arm of flesh; but with us is the LORD our God, to help us and to fight our battles.' And the people were strengthened by the words of Hezekiah king of Judah" (2 Chron. 32:8). Multitudes may gather against you, but when you consciously hand over all your struggles to God and ask Him to fight for you, you are assured of victory no matter what.

When you trust God to take charge of your battles, you will conquer and keep conquering. The wicked may do everything possible to sabotage a divine assignment, but you will march forward in victory nonetheless and recover lost ground. It is a daily battle as we struggle between belief and unbelief, faith and fear, love and hate, life and death, obedience and disobedience.

I ask again, who orders your battle? There came a time when the Canaanites harshly oppressed the Israelites for twenty years. Victory was determined by who led their battle. The Canaanites' army was under Sisera as the commander (Judg. 4:2), while the Israelites were under Deborah as the judge and prophetess, and Barak as the commander. This war was so significant that the psalmist referred to it regarding how the portion of the enemies should be. "Deal with them as with Midian, As with Sisera, As with Jabin at the Brook Kishon, Who perished at En Dor, Who became as refuse on the earth" (Ps. 83:9–10). The victory over Sisera was so resounding that it was worth being a reference point for other battles. Why? As we consider those who ordered the battle, deeper issues are revealed. The Canaanite commander was Sisera, whose name means "binding in chain." Truly, the enemy of our soul loves to fasten us to captivity, and he does that continuously. The commander of the enemy's army derives joy in tying people down. Those who try to break off are constantly pursued and tied back. This explains why the Israelites were oppressed by them for twenty years until God raised up a deliverer for His people.

How about the Israelites' army? Their commander was Barak, which means "thunderbolt," a discharge of lightning accompanied by thunder. Liken this to the battle we face daily; while the enemy wants to tie us down continuously, the Commander of our host breaks forth with lightning and thunder. While the lightning consumes the tie, the thunder scatters them. Also, Israel had Deborah as their judge, who also commanded the battle. Deborah's name means "bee," which reflects a multifunction and a symbol of diligence as a pollinator and honey producer. Bees sting. So she went forth into the battle to sting those who tied them down. What confusion there was in the enemy's camp when they were stung! This is used defensively as well as to kill or paralyze prey. So God stirred up a deliverer as a bee to set His people free. God had used this against the enemies before: "And I will send hornets before you, which shall drive out the Hivite, the Canaanite, and the Hittite from before you" (Exod. 23:28). Bees are pollinators; no wonder Israel prospered in the midst of oppression. There are honey-producing bees, so God could bring honey out of the battle. We can be joyful in the midst of battle and be sweetened when oppressed because the Captain of our host causes joy to flow over us as He stings the invading army. He makes us strong and multiplies to overthrow oppression and destroy the domination of evil over us.

With Barak and Deborah leading Israel, "the LORD routed Sisera and all his chariots and all his army with the edge of the sword before Barak; and Sisera alighted from his chariot and fled away on foot" (Judg. 4:15). When "thunderbolt" and "bee" appeared in the battle, Sisera ("binding in chain") jumped out from his chariot and fled away on foot. I ask, which way is easier to escape an invading army? To escape by chariots or run on foot? Chariots, of course. Sisera was so confused and disoriented at the sound of thunder with the striking of lightning, along with the stinging of the bee, that he had to abandon his weapons of war and fled for his life. What is the Spirit of God saying to the church? No matter what the harsh oppression is that continuously ties us down, God orders our battles and releases lightning to chase off the darkness surrounding us, along with the accomplishment of thunder

> **When God orders the battle of your life, it becomes a reference point for other people.**

that strikes down the stronghold of oppression. Even as we keep holding onto God, the bees of His presence will sting all our adversaries. We need not be oppressed further; neither should we be afraid of their strength, nor their deadly weapons, because God has appointed a Deliverer for us to break us free from oppression.

No wonder the psalmist referred to such a battle as a type of what God will do to their encompassing enemies. When God orders the battle of your life, it becomes a reference point for other people. The terribleness by which God sets His people free can be an unforgettable encounter that keeps alarming for generations. I pray that your victory over the oppressors of your soul will be so profound and resounding that everyone will desire such a victory over the battles of their lives. Will you allow God to order your battles? You can consciously talk to God, mentioning the difficult areas of your life, what you groan about daily, your heart pains, unceasing tears, and anguish of spirit. Ask God to take over, fight for you, and give you victory. As you do that in faith, He will answer and will truly fight for you.

The God Factor

God Almighty is all powerful and all knowing; He orders the affairs of men. Things that are and yet to be are subject to Him. Hopelessness and failure can go through the process of time and turn to pleasant surprises when God's hand comes upon them.

What is supposed to work to the contrary may turn out to be a blessing when God steps into it. When God's power is at work, the oppressed shall shout for joy, the captives are loosed, the wearied rejoice, the afflicted are delivered, and the hopeless are full of hope. His unsearchable greatness makes waste places a fortress; even the defeated turn out to be champions. Then will the conquered become conquerors. How about the emptied? They will not be forgotten, so also the lonely and the rejected will have joyful company. Unaccomplished dreams will be fulfilled, and the lowly will be exalted. The outcast will be restored to honor. Even the crooked places will be straightened. At such times, flood and storms are quieted because "The LORD has His way in the whirlwind and in the storm, and the clouds are the dust of His feet" (Nah. 1:3).

No wonder He laughs to scorn and ridicule those who rage against the righteous. For the sake of the righteous, God can do the unusual. He does not ignore the desperate heart cry of His people. His love is unsearchable, and His mercy knows no end. Through His loving kindness, He delivers those who are at their wit's end and sets the prisoners free. He empowers the weak against the mighty and subdues the invading armies because He rules over all. When there seems to be no way forward, He is both the Way and the Door. When weapons are thrown at you, He is your shield. He exposes the lies that entrap your soul and reveals truth to you as He enlightens your mind and your ways. No wonder apostle Paul could boldly declare:

> What is supposed to work to the contrary may turn out to be a blessing when God steps into it.

> Who shall separate us from the love of Christ? Shall tribulation, or distress, or persecution, or famine, or nakedness, or peril, or sword?... Yet in all these things we are more than conquerors through Him who loved us. For I am persuaded that neither death nor life, nor angels nor principalities nor powers, nor things present nor things to come, nor height nor depth, nor any other created thing, shall be able to separate us from the love of God which is in Christ Jesus our Lord.
>
> —Romans 8:35, 37–39

The greatness of God is unimaginable because He can do the opposite effect from what has been stated, said, or thought, just to favor His righteous course. When He determines to bless, nothing stands in His way; whatever opposition there is works for His good to bring to pass what He has purposed.

> The Lord of hosts has sworn, saying, "Surely, as I have thought, so it shall come to pass, And as I have purposed, so it shall stand. For the Lord of hosts has purposed, And who will annul it? His hand is stretched out, And who will turn it back?"
>
> —Isaiah 14:24, 27

Joseph declared before his brothers, "But as for you, you meant evil against me; but God meant it for good, in order to bring it about as it is this day, to save many people alive" (Gen. 50:20).

Saul pursued David to kill him, "but God did not deliver him into his hand" (1 Sam. 23:14). I ask you, are you victimized, taken advantage of, defrauded, and treated unjustly? Be it known to you that God is the Judge (Ps. 75:7). Trust Him and He will reveal His power in you. Is there a situation that is too strong that you cannot overcome? For this purpose Jesus suffered, was crucified, died, and was buried, but God raised Him up. Therefore, arise and declare like the psalmist, "My flesh and my heart fail; But God is the strength of my heart and my portion forever" (Ps. 73:26). You may be mightily oppressed, but you shall be mightily delivered.

Soul Winning

"O Lord, give me souls or take my soul": this was the desperate heart cry of George Whitefield.[1] He was a leading evangelist who helped spread the Great Awakening. Oh, that God would raise up men and women, old and young, who will know the worth of a soul. "For what will it profit a man if he gains the whole world, and loses his own soul? Or what will a man give in exchange for his soul?" (Mark 8:36–37). Souls are of eternal value and are precious to God. That is why the devil will contend over a soul to ruin it. This explains the reasons why the angels of God rejoice over a repentant soul that turns to God (Luke 15:10).

Jesus devoted time to share His burden for souls with His disciples as He illustrated the parables of the lost sheep, the lost coin, and the lost son (Luke 15). No creature strays more easily than a lost sheep; none is more heedless and helpless in finding its way home, and none is more defenseless and exposed to destruction by other animals than a lost sheep. The coin is also a symbol of a lost sinner. But the difference between the sheep and the coin is that at least the sheep can bleat, but the coin, depending on where it falls, may roll away beyond reach. The lost son, of his own accord, fled and returned after "he came to himself." Recovery of the sheep, the coin, and the son is worth celebrating.

Souls are lost, but we care not; they are perishing, but we show less concern; and they are eternally doomed, but who cares, as long as we are saved. If we truly know the eternal worth of a soul and that the whole world put together is not worth the value of a soul, then we will be sold out to God in reaching the lost. Jesus gave the parable of the hidden treasure and the great pearl: "Again, the kingdom of heaven is like treasure hidden in a field, which a man found and hid; and for joy over it he goes and sells all that he has and buys that field. Again, the kingdom of heaven is like a merchant seeking beautiful pearls, who, when he had found one pearl of great price, went and sold all that he had and bought it" (Matt. 13:44–46).

Both treasure and pearls were so valuable that whoever discovered them would sell all that he had. This probably is a field despised by all, counted as nothing, but with buried treasure. I perceive the neighbors would have scorned the man when selling all his goods to buy the so-called worthless field. Anyway, he got it and started profiting in the treasure. Every one of them would blame themselves for their lifetime for failure to get the field. So Jesus forsook all His glory to purchase us back to God. In the same manner, we should forsake all to reconcile all to God. Even until today, so many people have not discovered the treasure and the pearl of souls.

I ask myself, if people truly valued the salvation of their soul and all that it took God to rescue us from the shackle of sin, we would not give rest until we reached out to the lost, even the hardened ones? Man is separated from God, but God took the first step in winning us back. God is more willing to save the lost than we are ever willing. Contrary to this, the devil wants man to be eternally lost, so as to despise Christ's redemptive purposes.

There is an ungodly self-satisfaction that has made the body of Christ be at ease. People are becoming less concerned about the lost. Gone are those days when believers were weeping and crying in deep agony for the lost. So many people profess to be born again, but have never reached out to souls or testified to others about their salvation. If we understand what it means to be lost, we will repent and obey. A lost person is guilty of sin, is dead in sin, and is condemned already (John 3:18). They are without hope and at jeopardy of eternal fire. Unless God opens up their eyes and hearts, they may not perceive. There is danger in being complacent. God does not take it lightly with fruitless trees. He labored to see us come into understanding of Him and expects us to do the same to others. Jesus cursed the fruitless fig tree (Matt. 21:18–19). He also gave a parable of a fig tree:

> A certain man had a fig tree planted in his vineyard, and he came seeking fruit on it and found none. Then he said to the keeper of his vineyard, "Look, for three years I have come seeking fruit on this fig tree and find none. Cut it down; why does it use up the ground?" But

he answered and said to him, "Sir, let it alone this year also, until I dig around it and fertilize it. And if it bears fruit, well. But if not, after that you can cut it down."

—LUKE 13:6–9

Although this referred to the Jews, it may also be a warning to the church that is grafted in. The Lord is seeking fruits, and if He finds none, He will cut it down. It is a waste of space to abound in God's vineyard without producing fruit.

Refusing to witness is like a doctor mocking his patient or a lifeguard watching a swimmer drowning. The major obstacles I have seen in soul winning are no excuse to God at all. Some people say they are scared, and others say they don't understand the Bible. Some procrastinate, while others put before them an imaginary hindrance—judging who to be saved or not, and who is of hardened heart or difficult to reach. I visited Chicago in the spring of 1999 to minister the gospel to a group of people. In one of my free moments, I decided to visit the mall. As I was coming out of the mall, I saw a man smoking marijuana, and the Spirit of the Lord said to me, "Go minister salvation to him." I hesitated and tried to ignore the voice of the Spirit, but this became strong in me, saying, "You're here for the lost and to encourage the saved one." I approached the man and said, "God bless you." He replied in a deep, terrifying voice, "How can I help you?" I was frightened and did not know what to say any further. I grabbed his left hand and started praying for salvation of his soul. He tried stopping me, but I continued. He tried loosing his hand, but I became firm, continuing praying. At this point an unusual boldness came upon me. I noticed that he started softening and became unresisting. Suddenly, he broke down into tears, dropped his marijuana, and hugged me. Then Satan whispered to me, "The police will arrest both of you for taking marijuana." But I ignored such a voice, for it was the voice of a stranger; I listen more closely to my Shepherd's voice. Then this man began to say, "I was in church, but I was disappointed by people, and I turned away and never got back. Lately, I thought of getting back to God, but it was hard. All I did was to tell God that if He truly loves me, He should save me." I was his answered prayer. Would you be an answered prayer to someone today?

Your major problem to soul winning could be the fear of men. However rich or poor, highly or lowly placed any individual is, he or she is lost without God. "So we may boldly say: 'The LORD is my helper; I will not fear. What can man do to me?'" (Heb. 13:6). I figured out two major hindrances to soul winning in our age: lightly esteeming the eternal judgment and losing a sense of urgency (Heb. 2:3). Soul winning is a command, not an option or suggestion: "And He said to them, 'Go into all the world and preach the gospel to every creature'" (Mark 16:15). It is the greatest concern of hell (Luke 16:27–31) and the greatest joy of heaven (15:7, 10). It is also the greatest responsibility on earth (Mark 5:19). Therefore, passion for the lost should be our priority and should be presented through the love of God and in light of eternity. "And on some have compassion, making a distinction; but others save with fear, pulling them out of the fire, hating even the garment defiled by the flesh" (Jude 22–23).

Who is a soul winner? A soul winner is a carrier of the divine message, sacrificing personal rights and privileges even as he awaits his crown of rejoicing (1 Thess. 2:19–20). Such a person is wise. "The fruit of the righteous is a tree of life, And he who wins souls is wise" (Prov. 11:30). Believers in Christ are called many names in the word of God: Ambassadors (2 Cor. 5:20); laborers (1 Thess. 3:2); messengers (2 Cor. 8:23); soldiers (2 Tim. 2:3); watchmen (Isa. 62:6); stewards (Titus 1:7); light (Matt. 5:14); workers (2 Cor. 6:1); stars (Rev. 1:20); fishers of men (Matt. 4:19); and many more. All these have one thing in common, they are called to serve. The Master takes no pleasure in a disobedient servant. Oh, for a people to arise to soul winning, for it is rewarding!

> **Do you care less to see your loved ones lost forever in the unspeakable agony of hell?**

God is still calling busy men and women today. Saving sinners and building believers should be our lively pursuit. Whatever profession we are in, we can still be soul winners. The Bible is full of professional people who still served God: Adam, the gardener; Abraham, the rancher; David, the shepherd; Daniel, the government official; Gideon, the wheat farmer; Jacob, the herdsman; Joseph, the wise ruler; Moses, the legislator; Nehemiah, the statesman; Noah, the zoologist; Luke, the doctor; Peter, the fisherman; Paul, the lawyer and tent maker; Lydia, a great merchant; Esther, the queen; and Deborah, a prophetess, wife, and judge.

Therefore, being conscious of fearing the Lord with respect and reverence, we seek to win people over [to persuade them]. But what sort of persons we are, is plainly recognized and thoroughly understood by God, and I hope that it is plainly recognized and thoroughly understood also by your consciences (your inborn discernment).

—2 CORINTHIANS 5:11, AMP

Oh, that the zeal for the lost be kindled in our souls and our spirits. I challenge you with the words of Frances Jane Crosby, the blind hymnist:

Rescue the perishing, care for the dying,
Snatch them in pity from sin and grave;
Weep o'er the erring one, lift up the fallen,
Tell them of Jesus, the mighty to save
Rescue the perishing, care for the dying;
Jesus is merciful, Jesus will save.[2]

When all is done and our toiling is over, what would you present to the Savior of your soul? Do you care less to see your loved ones lost forever in the unspeakable agony of hell? No excuse would spare you for your inability to reach the lost. Never give up hope on anyone, considering that no price will be too great to save a soul. Charles C. Luther, a hymnist, prepared us for the meeting of our Lord and Savior with this song:

Must I go, and empty-handed,
Thus my dear Redeemer meet?
Not one day of service give Him,
Lay no trophy at His feet?
Must I go, and empty-handed?
Must I meet my Savior so?
Not one soul with which to greet Him:
Must I empty-handed go?[3]

Effective soul winning is proof that you are on the Lord's side, because you have tasted and partaken of His glory. Your earnest desire, therefore, would be to see others partake in the same. I quite understand how hard it may be because it is a war between light and darkness. But, "the king's business required haste" (1 Sam. 21:8). Let God use you as light so that those who are mightily oppressed can be mightily delivered.

Part Two

KINGDOM PROPHETIC PRAYERS

Chapter 12

FOUNDATIONAL DELIVERANCE PRAYERS

IT IS WRITTEN: "Shall the prey be taken from the mighty, Or the captives of the righteous be delivered? But thus says the LORD: 'Even the captives of the mighty shall be taken away, And the prey of the terrible be delivered; For I will contend with him who contends with you, And I will save your children. I will feed those who oppress you with their own flesh, And they shall be drunk with their own blood as with sweet wine. All flesh shall know That I, the LORD, am your Savior, And your Redeemer, the Mighty One of Jacob'" (Isa. 49:24–26).

"The hands of Zerubbabel Have laid the foundation of this temple; His hands shall also finish it. Then you will know That the LORD of hosts has sent Me to you" (Zech. 4:9).

"And even now the ax is laid to the root of the trees. Therefore every tree which does not bear good fruit is cut down and thrown into the fire" (Matt. 3:10).

"Therefore if the Son makes you free, you shall be free indeed" (John 8:36).

"A little while longer and the world will see Me no more, but you will see Me. Because I live, you will live also" (John 14:19).

"How God anointed Jesus of Nazareth with the Holy Spirit and with power, who went about doing good and healing all who were oppressed by the devil, for God was with Him" (Acts 10:38).

"Having wiped out the handwriting of requirements that was against us, which was contrary to us. And He has taken it out of the way, having nailed it to the cross. Having disarmed principalities and powers, He made a public spectacle of them, triumphing over them in it" (Col. 2:14–15).

"And they overcame him by the blood of the Lamb and by the word of their testimony, and they did not love their lives to the death" (Rev. 12:11).

"Then Death and Hades were cast into the lake of fire. This is the second death" (Rev. 20:14).

Prophetic declaration

It is written: "For no other foundation can anyone lay than that which is laid, which is Jesus Christ" (1 Cor. 3:11). Therefore, I declare that Jehovah God is my sure foundation. I am covenanted to Jesus Christ, "the root and the offspring of David" (Rev. 22:16), and so shall I spring forth in glory and blessings.

Prayer points

Through the blood of Jesus, I renounce all lust, perversion, immorality, uncleanness, impurity, and sexual sin, in the name of Jesus.

Through the blood of Jesus, I renounce all witchcraft, sorcery, divination, and occult involvement, in the name of Jesus.

Through the blood of Jesus, I renounce all ungodly soul ties and immoral relationships, in the name of Jesus.

Through the blood of Jesus, I renounce all hatred, anger, resentment, revenge, retaliation, unforgiveness, and bitterness, in the name of Jesus.

Through the blood of Jesus, I forgive any person who has ever hurt me, disappointed me, abandoned me, mistreated me, or rejected me, in the name of Jesus.

Through the blood of Jesus, I renounce all addiction to drugs, alcohol, or any legal or illegal substance that has bound me, in the name of Jesus.

Through the blood of Jesus, I renounce all pride, haughtiness, arrogance, vanity, ego, disobedience, and rebellion, in the name of Jesus.

Through the blood of Jesus, I renounce all envy, jealousy, and covetousness, in the name of Jesus.

Through the blood of Jesus, I renounce all fear, unbelief, and doubt, in the name of Jesus.

Through the blood of Jesus, I renounce all selfishness, self-will, self-pity, self-rejection, and self-hatred, in the name of Jesus.

Through the blood of Jesus, I renounce all ungodly thought patterns and belief systems, in the name of Jesus.

Through the blood of Jesus, I renounce all ungodly covenants, oaths, and vows made by myself or my ancestors, in the name of Jesus.

It is written: "Suddenly there was a great earthquake, so that the foundations of the prison were shaken; and immediately all the doors were opened and everyone's chains were loosed" (Acts 16:26). Therefore, by

Prophetic declaration

Thank You, my Lord and Messiah, Jesus Christ, because You are the Mediator of a better covenant, which was established upon better promises. I, therefore, lay claim on Your shed blood to break loose and break free from all ungodly covenants. I am forever established on the covenant blood of Jesus.

Prayer points

Through the blood of Jesus, I break and annul all ungodly covenants, oaths, and pledges I have made with my lips, in the name of Jesus.

Through the blood of Jesus, I renounce and break all ungodly oaths made by my ancestors to idols, demons, false religions, or ungodly organizations, in the name of Jesus.

Through the blood of Jesus, I break and annul all covenants with death and hell, made by my ancestors, in the name of Jesus.

Through the blood of Jesus, I break and annul all ungodly covenants made with idols or demons by my ancestors, in the name of Jesus.

Through the blood of Jesus, I break and annul all blood covenants made through sacrifice that would affect my life, in the name of Jesus.

Through the blood of Jesus, I command all demons that claim any legal right to my life through covenants to come out and never return, in the name of Jesus.

Through the blood of Jesus, I break and annul any covenant made with false gods and demons through the occult involvement and witchcraft, in the name of Jesus.

Through the blood of Jesus, I break and annul any conscious and/or unconscious marriage to any demon that would affect my life, in the name of Jesus.

I have a covenant with God, through the blood of Jesus Christ. I am joined to the Lord and I am one spirit with Him. I break all ungodly covenants and renew my covenant to God in Jesus' name.

Through the blood of Jesus, I bind and cast out any family demons that would follow my life through ancestral covenants, in the name of Jesus.

In the name of Jesus, I reject and annul the claims of witnesses attached to any evil vow and covenant.

Henceforth, Holy Spirit is my true witness, to establish me in God's covenants, in Jesus' name.

In the name of Jesus, I command executors of evil covenants over my life to give up and be desolate, in the name of Jesus.

It is written: "So Joshua let the people depart, each to his own inheritance" (Josh. 24:28). So am I established in my godly inheritance, in Jesus' name.

Chapter 14

BREAKING CURSES AND DESTROYING GENERATIONAL BONDAGE

IT IS WRITTEN: "Therefore know that the LORD your God, He is God, the faithful God who keeps covenant and mercy for a thousand generations with those who love Him and keep His commandments" (Deut. 7:9).

"And you shall remember the LORD your God, for it is He who gives you power to get wealth that He may establish His covenant which He swore to your fathers, as it is this day" (Deut. 8:18).

"'And if it seems evil to you to serve the LORD, choose for yourselves this day whom you will serve, whether the gods which your fathers served that were on the other side of the River, or the gods of the Amorites, in whose land you dwell. But as for me and my house, we will serve the LORD.' So the people answered and said: 'Far be it from us that we should forsake the LORD to serve other gods'" (Josh. 24:15–16).

"Yet the LORD would not destroy the house of David, because of the covenant that He had made with David, and since He had promised to give a lamp to him and to his sons forever" (2 Chron. 21:7).

"'For I will be merciful to their unrighteousness, and their sins and their lawless deeds I will remember no more.' In that He says, 'A new covenant,' He has made the first obsolete. Now what is becoming obsolete and growing old is ready to vanish away" (Heb. 8:12–13).

"Christ has redeemed us from the curse of the law, having become a curse for us (for it is written, "Cursed is everyone who hangs on a tree"), that the blessing of Abraham might come upon the Gentiles in Christ Jesus, that we might receive the promise of the Spirit through faith" (Gal. 3:13–14).

"And there shall be no more curse, but the throne of God and of the Lamb shall be in it, and His servants shall serve Him" (Rev. 22:3).

Prophetic declaration

"For whatever is born of God overcomes the world. And this is the victory that has overcome the world—our faith" (1 John 5:4). I am born of God, saved by grace alone through His mercies. And being redeemed by the blood of the Lamb, I prevail over curses and overcome generational bondages, in Jesus' name.

Prayer points

Through the blood of Jesus, I break all generational curses of pride, lust perversion, rebellion, witchcraft, idolatry, poverty, rejection, fear, confusion, addiction, death, and destruction, in the name of Jesus.

Through the blood of Jesus, I command all generational spirits that came into my life during conception, in the womb, in the birth canal, and through the umbilical cord to come out, in the name of Jesus.

Through the blood of Jesus, I break all spoken curses and negative words that I have spoken over my life, in the name of Jesus.

Through the blood of Jesus, I break all spoken curses and negative words spoken over my life by others, including those in authority, in the name of Jesus.

Through the blood of Jesus, I command all ancestral spirits of freemasonry, idolatry, witchcraft, false religion, polygamy, lust, and perversion, to come out of my life, in the name of Jesus.

Through the blood of Jesus, I command all hereditary spirits of lust, rejection, fear, sickness, infirmity, disease, anger, hatred, confusion, failure, and poverty, to come out of my life, in the name of Jesus.

Through the blood of Jesus, I break the legal rights of all generational spirits operating behind a curse, in the name of Jesus; you have no legal right to operate in my life.

Through the blood of Jesus, I bind and rebuke all familiar spirits and spirit guides that would try to operate in my life from my ancestors, in the name of Jesus.

Through the blood of Jesus, I renounce all false beliefs and philosophies inherited by my ancestors, in the name of Jesus.

Through the blood of Jesus, I break all curses on my finances from any ancestors that cheated or mishandled money, in the name of Jesus.

Through the blood of Jesus, I break all curses of sickness and disease and command all inherited sickness to leave my body now and never return, in the name of Jesus.

Through the blood of Jesus, I break all oaths and vows made with the devil by my ancestors, and I break loose and break free from their bondages, in the name of Jesus.

Through the blood of Jesus, I break all curses by agents of Satan, spoken against my life in secret or open, in the name of Jesus.

Through the blood of Jesus, I annul all written and unwritten curses that would affect my life, in the name of Jesus.

Through the blood of Jesus, I break and terminate every time-release curse that would activate in my life as I grow older, in the name of Jesus.

Through the blood of Jesus, I break and terminate all generational rebellion that would cause me to resist the Holy Spirit, in the name of Jesus.

Through the blood of Jesus, I break all curses of death spoken by people in authority over my life, in the name of Jesus.

The blood of Jesus rebukes and condemns all curses of sickness and infirmity in my life, in the name of Jesus.

Anointing of the Holy Spirit, destroy all curses of poverty, lack, and debt in my life, in the name of Jesus.

Every mind-attacking demon, the blood of Jesus rebukes you; let go of me now, in Jesus' name.

Through the blood of Jesus, I am delivered from all curses of confusion and mental illness, in the name of Jesus.

Holy Ghost Fire, consume all witchcraft, sorcery, and divination targeted at me, in the name of Jesus.

The blood of Jesus has rescued me from all curses causing accidents and premature death, in the name of Jesus.

I am redeemed from all curses, through the blood of Jesus, in the name of Jesus.

Through the blood of Jesus, I choose blessing instead of cursing and life instead of death, in the name of Jesus.

Through the blood of Jesus, I break loose and break free from all self-inflicted curses by negative words and thoughts, in the name of Jesus.

Through the blood of Jesus, I command every demon hiding and operating behind a curse to come out of my life and vanish unto desolation, in the name of Jesus.

It is written: "Now all things are of God, who has reconciled us to Himself through Jesus Christ, and has given us the ministry of reconciliation" (2 Cor. 5:18). Therefore, O blood of Jesus, reconcile me now to blessing due to me in Jesus' name.

It is written: "Who also has sealed us and given us the Spirit in our hearts as a guarantee" (2 Cor. 1:22). Therefore, the seal of the Holy Spirit is upon me as a guarantee of deliverance, in Jesus' name.

O Lord God, fill me now with your Holy Spirit and power, in Jesus' name.

Chapter 15

PRAYERS FOR SELF-DELIVERANCE

IT IS WRITTEN: "But the LORD your God will deliver them over to you, and will inflict defeat upon them until they are destroyed. And He will deliver their kings into your hand, and you will destroy their name from under heaven; no one shall be able to stand against you until you have destroyed them" (Deut. 7:23–24).

"He shall deliver you in six troubles, Yes, in seven no evil shall touch you" (Job 5:19).

"He will redeem his soul from going down to the Pit, And his life shall see the light" (Job 33:28).

"Return, O LORD, deliver me! Oh, save me for Your mercies' sake!" (Ps. 6:4).

"Keep my soul, and deliver me; Let me not be ashamed, for I put my trust in You" (Ps. 25:20).

"I sought the LORD, and He heard me, And delivered me from all my fears" (Ps. 34:4).

"Be pleased, O LORD, to deliver me; O LORD, make haste to help me!" (Ps. 40:13).

"He has delivered us from the power of darkness and conveyed us into the kingdom of the Son of His love" (Col. 1:13).

Prophetic declaration

"For I delight in the law of God according to the inward man. But I see another law in my members, warring against the law of my mind, and bringing me into captivity to the law of sin which is in my members" (Rom. 7:22–23). Therefore, I yield my body, soul and spirit to God Almighty; gaining strength by the Holy Spirit to "resist the devil" (James 4:7) and all unfruitful works of darkness. I henceforth walk "in the liberty by which Christ has made [me] free" (Gal. 5:1), in Jesus' name.

Prayer points

Through the blood of Jesus, I command all generational and hereditary spirits operating in my life through curses to be bound and cast out, in the name of Jesus.

Through the blood of Jesus, I command all spirits of lust, perversion, adultery, fornication, uncleanness, and immorality to come out of my sexual character, in the name of Jesus.

Through the blood of Jesus, I command all spirits of hurt, rejection, fear, anger, wrath, sadness, depression, discouragement, grief, bitterness, and unforgiveness to come out of my emotions now and never return, in the name of Jesus.

Through the blood of Jesus, I command all spirits of confusion, forgetfulness, mind control, mental illness, double mindedness, fantasy, pain, and pride to come out of my mind now, in the name of Jesus.

Through the blood of Jesus, I command all spirits of guilt, shame, and condemnation to come out of my conscience, in the name of Jesus.

Through the blood of Jesus, I command all spirits of destructive addiction to come out of my life now, in the name of Jesus.

Through the blood of Jesus, I command all spirits of witchcraft, sorcery, divination, and the occult to come out of my life, in the name of Jesus.

Through the blood of Jesus, I command all demons operating in my head, eyes, mouth, tongue, and throat to come out and become desolate, in the name of Jesus.

Through the blood of Jesus, I command all demons operating in my chest and lungs to come out, in the name of Jesus.

By the authority in the name of Jesus, I command all demons operating in my back and spine to come out now.

Through the blood of Jesus, I command all demons operating in my stomach, navel, and abdomen to come out, in the name of Jesus.

Through the blood of Jesus, I command all demons operating in my heart, spleen, kidneys, liver, and pancreas to come out, in the name of Jesus.

Through the blood of Jesus, I command all demons operating in my sexual organs to let go of me, flee, and never return, in the name of Jesus.

Through the blood of Jesus, I command all demons operating in my hands, arms, legs, and feet to let go of me, flee, and never return, in the name of Jesus.

Through the blood of Jesus, I command all demons operating in my skeletal system, including my bones, joints, knees, and elbows to let go of me, flee, and never return, in the name of Jesus.

Through the blood of Jesus, I command all demons operating in my glands and endocrine system to let go of me now, flee, and never return, in the name of Jesus.

Let the blood of Jesus prevail over demons operating in my blood and circulatory systems come out now, in the name of Jesus.

Holy Ghost fire, flush out all demons operating in my muscles and muscular system, in the name of Jesus.

Through the blood of Jesus, I command all religious spirits of doubt, unbelief, error, heresy, and tradition to come out of my life now, in the name of Jesus.

Through the blood of Jesus, I command all spirits from my past that are hindering my present and future to come out now and be desolate, in the name of Jesus.

It is written: "As soon as they hear of me they obey me; The foreigners submit to me. The foreigners fade away, And come frightened from their hideouts" (Ps. 18:44–45). Therefore, I command all wicked spirits hiding in any part of my life to come out now, in the name of Jesus.

The blood of Jesus is upon me to repel evil and attract blessings, in Jesus' name.

O Most high God, fill me now with your Holy Spirit and power, in Jesus' name.

It is written: "In Him you also trusted, after you heard the word of truth, the gospel of your salvation; in whom also, having believed, you were sealed with the Holy Spirit of promise" (Eph. 1:13). Therefore, the seal of the Holy Spirit is upon me to manifest the promises of God, in Jesus' name.

Chapter 16

OVERCOMING THE ASSAULT OF SPIRIT HUSBAND (INCUBUS) AND SPIRIT WIFE (SUCCUBUS)

Incubus: An oppressive nightmare,
sexual intercourse with women

Succubus: An oppressive nightmare,
sexual intercourse with men

IT IS WRITTEN: "For your Maker is your husband, The LORD of hosts is His name; And your Redeemer is the Holy One of Israel; He is called the God of the whole earth" (Isa. 54:5).

"Your fierceness has deceived you, The pride of your heart, O you who dwell in the clefts of the rock, Who hold the height of the hill! Though you make your nest as high as the eagle, I will bring you down from there," says the LORD" (Jer. 49:16).

"Their Redeemer is strong; The LORD of hosts is His name. He will thoroughly plead their case, That He may give rest to the land, And disquiet the inhabitants of Babylon" (Jer. 50:34).

"Do you not know that you are the temple of God and that the Spirit of God dwells in you? If anyone defiles the temple of God, God will destroy him. For the temple of God is holy, which temple you are" (1 Cor. 3:16–17).

"Your covenant with death will be annulled, And your agreement with Sheol will not stand; When the overflowing scourge passes through, Then you will be trampled down by it" (Isa. 28:18).

Prophetic declarations

I am a chaste bride of Christ, purchased and redeemed by the precious blood of Jesus.

I have been rescued from the dominion of darkness and translated to the kingdom of light, in Christ Jesus. I have been cleansed, purged, and accepted in the beloved. For in Christ I live and move and have my being. The blood of Jesus has justified me and given access into God's presence.

The power of the Holy Spirit is my comforter, lifting up the standard against all evil visitations and attacks against my life. I am completely set free from the union of spiritual spouse, in Jesus' name.

Prayer points

In the name of Jesus Christ, I break asunder every evil soul tie between me and anyone dead or alive.

Every soul tie covenant that has held me bound, I break asunder, in Jesus' name.

The demand of darkness on my life, be abolished by the blood of Jesus.

The claims of spiritual spouses on my life, be annulled by the blood of Jesus.

Any vow I have with spirit husband or spirit wife, by the blood of Jesus be shattered, in Jesus' name.

The visitations of spiritual spouses to defile my life, be arrested by the terror of God, in Jesus' name.

The deposits of spiritual spouses on my life, be flushed out by the blood of Jesus.

It is written, "For our God is a consuming fire" (Heb. 12:29); therefore, let the consuming fire of the Living God devour all spiritual spouses attached to my life, in Jesus' name.

In the name of Jesus, I command the stronghold of spirit husbands and wives tormenting me to perish.

Thou networking of spiritual spouses over my life, be set ablaze by the Holy Ghost fire, in Jesus' name.

In the name of Jesus, I command the weapons of spirit husbands and wives against my life to be desolate.

The summoning of spiritual spouses on my life shall not prosper, in Jesus' name.

I decree a wall of partition between me and my spiritual spouses, in Jesus' name.

Let God arise and defend me against the raging of spiritual spouses, in Jesus' name.

Every good thing about my life under the bondage of spiritual spouses, be released unto me now, in Jesus' name.

Angels of the Living God, terrify the hiding places of spiritual spouses assigned against me and desolate them, in Jesus' name.

The doors open to the invasion of spiritual spouses in my life, be sealed now by the blood of Jesus, in Jesus' name.

Redemptive blood of Jesus, repel the trafficking of spiritual spouses in my life, in Jesus' name.

Holy Spirit, overwhelm my life with joy and peace, in Jesus' name.

I decree total deliverance into my life, in Jesus' name.

Give thanks to God for answered prayers, in Jesus' name.

Prophetic declaration

It is written: "The next day John saw Jesus coming toward him, and said, "Behold! The Lamb of God who takes away the sin of the world!" (John 1:29). Therefore, I behold Jesus the Lamb of God who "takes away the sin of the world," especially mine. So I will declare His praise forever.

Prayer points

I cover my mind and thoughts with the blood of Jesus.

I cover my doorpost and possessions with the blood of Jesus.

My conscience is purged from dead works to serve the living God through the blood of Jesus.

The blood of Jesus bears witness to my deliverance and salvation, in the name of Jesus.

I break the power of sin and iniquity in my life through the blood of Jesus.

My heart is sprinkled with the blood of Jesus from evil conscience, in the name of Jesus.

O voice of the blood of Jesus, silence every accusation and condemnation against me, in Jesus' name.

I identify with Jesus as the only atonement for sin, and I receive remission for my sin through the power of His blood, in Jesus' name.

With Jesus as my atonement, the consequences of sin in my life are purged and terminated, in Jesus' name.

Thank You, my Lord and Savior Jesus, the Messiah, for willingly offering Yourself to restore me to God, in Jesus' name.

Thank You, my Lord and Savior Jesus, the Messiah, for becoming my sin offering that I might be forgiven and restored to hope, in Jesus' name.

I have access to the throne of grace through the atonement of my Lord and Savior, Jesus Christ, in Jesus' name.

My Lord Jesus, You were conceived, born, and baptized in the Holy Spirit that You may fill me with the same to comfort and guard me, in Jesus' name.

I am clothed with the righteousness of Jesus, my Lord, in Jesus' name.

Dear Lord Jesus, You are my peace offering and my eternal source of joy, in Jesus' name.

With Jesus as my peace offering, my relationship and fellowship with God is secured, in Jesus' name.

Jesus has become my substitute, hence I am free from condemnation and death, in Jesus' name.

With Jesus as my substitute, I am free from woes and destruction, in Jesus' name.

Jesus paid the wages of sin and proclaimed, "It is finished"; therefore, every claim to my life to destroy it be abolished by the blood of Jesus, in Jesus' name.

It is written: "But one of the soldiers pierced His side with a spear, and immediately blood and water came out" (John 19:34). Therefore, let the blood and water from the pierced side of my Lord Jesus wash me clean and make me whole, in Jesus' name.

It is written: "For where there is a testament, there must also of necessity be the death of the testator" (Heb. 9:16). Therefore, with Jesus as the Testator of the new covenant, I receive the promise of eternal inheritance, in Jesus' name.

It is written: "Then Aaron took it as Moses commanded, and ran into the midst of the assembly; and already the plague had begun among the people. So he put in the incense and made atonement for the people. And he stood between the dead and the living; so the plague was stopped" (Num. 16:47–48). Therefore, through the atonement of my Lord Jesus, I command plagues to cease in my life, in Jesus' name.

Jesus wore the crown of thorns that I may wear the crown of glory. Therefore, I am crowned with glory and honor, in Jesus' name.

Jesus wore the crown of thorns to break the curse on my head, so I command curses on my head to break asunder through the atoning blood of Jesus, in Jesus' name.

Jesus, as "nail in sure places" surrendered Himself to be nailed, hands and feet; as a "fastened sacrifice" for my eternal redemption. Therefore, I decree bondages and afflictions on my hands and feet be destroyed through the atonement of the blood of Jesus, in Jesus' name.

The atonement of my Lord and Savior, Jesus Christ, has made "reconciliation for iniquity, and to bring in everlasting righteousness" (Dan. 9:24) in my life, in Jesus' name.

It is written: "For Christ also suffered once for sins, the just for the unjust, that He might bring us to God, being put to death in the flesh but made alive by the Spirit, by whom also He went and preached to the spirits in prison" (1 Pet. 3:18–19). Therefore, my imprisoned spirit man, break free and break loose through the atonement of my Lord Jesus, in Jesus' name.

By the eternal sacrifice of my Lord Jesus, I receive grace to walk worthy of God, in Jesus' name.

Every evil aroma in my life, be quenched by the blood of Jesus, in Jesus' name.

The root of evil aroma in me, be rooted out now, in Jesus' name.

Because Jesus Christ is my "sweet savor" offering, therefore, my life, bring forth a satisfaction aroma before the throne of grace, in Jesus' name.

Give thanks to God for answered prayers, Jesus' name.

Chapter 19

DELIVERANCE PRAYERS BASED ON HIS BETRAYAL

I REPENT OF EVERY way I have denied God, and I plead for forgiveness through the blood of Jesus, in Jesus' name.

My dear Lord Jesus, forgive me for denying You and Your kingdom, in Jesus' name.

Holy Spirit, forgive me for denying You, in Jesus' name.

I receive grace to watch and pray that I may not enter into temptation, in Jesus' name.

It is written: "Then the chief priests, the scribes, and the elders of the people assembled at the palace of the high priest, who was called Caiaphas" (Matt. 26:3). Therefore, any assembly set against me, scatter now, in Jesus' name.

In any way my spirit is willing to attain good thing but the flesh is weak, Holy Spirit quicken me to attain and fulfill, in Jesus' name.

"But Peter followed him afar off" (Matt. 26:58). My Lord Jesus, I repent for following You afar off; please forgive me, in Jesus' name.

"But again he denied with an oath, 'I do not know the Man!'" (Matt. 26:72). I withdraw every oath of denial of my faith in Christ Jesus and plead for forgiveness, in Jesus' name.

I reaffirm my oath to serve Jesus as my Lord and Savior and proclaim Him as my King and Messiah, in Jesus' name.

"He sat with the servants, and warmed himself at the fire" (Mark 14:54). I shall not walk in the counsel of the ungodly; neither shall I stand in the way of sinners nor sit in the seat of the scornful, in Jesus' name.

"Then Satan entered Judas, surnamed Iscariot, who was numbered among the twelve" (Luke 22:3). I pray that Satan shall not enter into my life, in Jesus' name.

Any power, spirit, and personality whom Satan has entered into shall not have their ways in my life, in Jesus' name.

"The Son of Man indeed goeth, as it is written of him" (Mark 14:21). Therefore, I receive grace to walk after what is divinely written of me, in Jesus' name.

Holy Spirit fire, flush the hold of denial out of my life, in Jesus' name.

"Now His betrayer had given them a signal, saying, 'Whomever I kiss, He is the One; seize Him and lead Him away safely'" (Mark 14:44). I reject and overcome every kiss of betrayal, in Jesus' name.

The covenants I have with my foundational elders to betray me, be abolished now by the blood of Jesus, in Jesus' name.

Every betrayal by covenant against my life, be broken asunder by my covenant of the blood of Jesus, in Jesus' name.

I command the covenant of betrayal over my life be shattered, in Jesus' name.

It is written: "He answered and said, 'He who dipped his hand with Me in the dish will betray Me'" (Matt. 26:23). Therefore, Holy Ghost fire, expose any intimacy that may hand me over to the tormentors, in Jesus' name.

It is written: "So from that time he sought opportunity to betray Him" (Matt. 26:16). Any power, spirit, and personality seeking opportunity to betray me shall perish in their search, in Jesus' name.

O heavens, withdraw now the opportunities to betray and afflict me, in Jesus' name.

It is written: "'What are you willing to give me if I deliver Him to you?' And they counted out to him thirty pieces of silver" (Matt. 26:15). I command every evil transaction against my life be nullified by the blood of Jesus, in Jesus' name.

Any power, spirit, and personality set to deliver me up to the destroyer shall not prosper, in Jesus' name.

The priests and the records holder assembled against me, scatter by terror, in Jesus' name.

Any summoning of my life to palaces in order to afflict me, be abolished by the blood of Jesus, in Jesus' name.

O rulers of palaces against my life, be subdued by the blood of Jesus and be shattered asunder, in Jesus' name.

It is written: "[They] plotted to take Jesus by trickery and kill Him" (Matt. 26:4). Therefore, any evil consultation on my life shall not stand, neither shall it be established, in Jesus' name.

Every subtilty to arrest and kill me, shall not come to light, in Jesus' name.

"And the chief priests and the scribes sought how they might take him by craft and put him to death" (Mark 14:1). I command every search and craftiness to kill me, be nullified by the blood of Jesus, in Jesus' name.

It is written: "But they said, 'Not during the feast, lest there be an uproar among the people'" (Matt. 26:5). I decree the feast of my life be free from evil arrest, in Jesus' name.

"And when they heard it, they were glad, and promised to give him money. So he sought how he might conveniently betray Him" (Mark 14:11). Every convenient betrayal shall not be established in my life, in Jesus' name.

"Now the chief priests and all the council sought testimony against Jesus to put Him to death, but found none" (Mark 14:55). The searches for false witnesses against me shall come to nought, in Jesus' name.

"For many bore false witness against Him, but their testimonies did not agree" (Mark 14:56). All witnesses against me shall not agree together, in Jesus' name.

I say after the manner of my Lord Jesus, "Woe unto that person by whom I shall be betrayed" (Matt. 26:24), in Jesus' name.

"But they said, 'Not during the feast, lest there be an uproar of the people'" (Mark 14:2). The feast of my life shall be free from uproar, in Jesus' name.

I command uproar among the arresters of my destiny to destroy one another, in Jesus' name.

"Then he threw down the pieces of silver in the temple and departed, and went and hanged himself" (Matt. 27:5). I command the strongman of betrayal set against me to hang yourself now, in Jesus' name.

"And immediately, while He was still speaking, Judas, one of the twelve, with a great multitude with swords and clubs, came from the chief priests and the scribes and the elders" (Mark 14:43). I command the great multitude with swords, staves, and all forms of weapons against me to turn against one another to their destruction, in Jesus' name.

"Now when He said to them, 'I am He,' they drew back and fell to the ground" (John 18:6). Therefore, I command all my adversaries to go backward and fall to the ground, in Jesus' name.

"Then he will show you a large upper room, furnished and prepared; there make ready for us" (Mark 14:15). My large upper room, furnished, prepared, and made ready for my glory, manifest now, in Jesus' name.

Chapter 20

DELIVERANCE PRAYERS BASED ON HIS SUFFERING AND TRIALS

WHAT DO YOU think?' They answered and said, 'He is deserving of death'" (Matt. 26:66). Thank You, my Lord Jesus, for being guilty of death for my sake, that I may be free, in Jesus' name.

"Then they spat in His face and beat Him; and others struck Him with the palms of their hands" (Matt. 26:67). Thank You, my Lord Jesus, for bearing my shame that I may enjoy favor, in Jesus' name.

"And when they had bound Him, they led Him away and delivered Him to Pontius Pilate the governor" (Matt. 27:2). Thank You, my Lord Jesus, because You were bound that I may be set free. Therefore, I command every bondage in my life to break asunder, in Jesus' name.

"Then the governor said, 'Why, what evil has He done?' But they cried out all the more, saying, 'Let Him be crucified!'" (Matt. 27:23). Thank You, my Lord Jesus, for accepting to be crucified that I might be set free, in Jesus' name.

"Then they spat on Him, and took the reed and struck Him on the head. And when they had mocked Him, they took the robe off Him, put His own clothes on Him, and led Him away to be crucified" (Matt. 27:30–31). Thank You, my Lord and Savior Jesus, for yielding unto suffering for my eternal salvation, in Jesus' name.

"And as they were eating, Jesus took bread, blessed and broke it, and gave it to them and said, 'Take, eat; this is My body.' Then He took the cup, and when He had given thanks He gave it to them, and they all drank from it. And He said to them, 'This is My blood of the new covenant, which is shed for many'" (Mark 14:22–24). Thank You, my Lord Jesus, for breaking Your body to offer Your blood for my redemption, in Jesus' name.

"Now as they came out, they found a man of Cyrene, Simon by name. Him they compelled to bear His cross" (Matt. 27:32). I accept with gladness to bear the cross of Jesus and identify with Him, in Jesus' name.

"Then he released Barabbas to them; and when he had scourged Jesus, he delivered Him to be crucified" (Matt. 27:26). I, therefore, identify with Jesus' suffering that I might enjoy freedom and peace, in Jesus' name.

"And all the people answered and said, 'His blood be on us and on our children'" (Matt. 27:25). Truly, let His redemptive blood be upon me and my generations, to restore us to divine purpose, in Jesus' name.

"Then they all forsook Him and fled" (Mark 14:50). I forgive all those who forsook and abandoned me in my trials, in Jesus' name.

O Lord God, raise up for me those who would stand by me and encourage Your divine purpose for my life, in Jesus' name.

"Assuredly, I say to you, wherever this gospel is preached in the whole world, what this woman has done will also be told as a memorial to her" (Mark 14:9). So Lord, I remember the woman with the alabaster box of ointment, who broke the box and poured the oil on Your head. I identify with this action and reap the blessings thereof, in Jesus' name.

"And the Lord said, 'Simon, Simon! Indeed, Satan has asked for you, that he may sift you as wheat. But I have prayed for you, that your faith should not fail; and when you have returned to Me, strengthen your brethren'" (Luke 22:31–32). I pray every satanic desire for my life be abolished now by the blood of Jesus, in Jesus' name.

I decree by the unction of the Holy Spirit that evil shall not have me, neither shall I be sifted as wheat, in Jesus' name.

My faith in Christ Jesus shall not fail, in Jesus' name.

"Then an angel appeared to Him from heaven, strengthening Him" (Luke 22:43). Therefore, angels of the Living God, strengthen me to overcome my hours of temptations, in Jesus' name.

"And being in agony, He prayed more earnestly. Then His sweat became like great drops of blood falling down to the ground" (Luke 22:44). Let the sweat of great drops of blood through the agonizing earnest prayer of my Lord and Savior Jesus Christ, avail for me to enjoy testimonies of prayers, in Jesus' name.

"This is your hour, and the power of darkness" (Luke 22:53). I command the hour of the power of darkness in my life be terminated by the blood of Jesus, in Jesus' name.

Let it be known in the heaven, on earth, and beneath that the divine hour of light and miracles has begun in my life, in Jesus' name.

"Do you think that I cannot now pray to My Father, and He will provide Me with more than twelve legions of angels?" (Matt. 26:53). I receive an innumerable company of angels to war on my behalf, until victory be perfected, in Jesus' name.

"Then the soldiers of the governor took Jesus into the Praetorium and gathered the whole garrison around Him" (Matt. 27:27). I command every encompassing army against me to scatter by confusion, in Jesus' name.

"Then Herod, with his men of war, treated Him with contempt and mocked Him, arrayed Him in a gorgeous robe, and sent Him back to Pilate" (Luke 23:11). I command every king with his men of war that are set against me to scatter unto desolation, in Jesus' name.

"When morning came, all the chief priests and elders of the people plotted against Jesus to put Him to death" (Matt. 27:1). Those who have taken counsel against my life shall fall by their own counsel, in Jesus' name.

As the high priest rent his clothes before Jesus (Matt. 26:55) so that He may step into his high priesthood, so I command all enchanting agents against me to give up now, in Jesus' name.

"And those who passed by blasphemed Him, wagging their heads" (Matt. 27:39). I overcome ridicule by the power of the cross of Jesus, in Jesus' name.

"But the chief priests and elders persuaded the multitudes that they should ask for Barabbas and destroy Jesus" (Matt. 27:20). Every persuasion to destroy me shall not be established, neither shall it come to pass, in Jesus' name.

"And while He was being accused by the chief priests and elders, He answered nothing" (Matt. 27:12). Therefore, by the accusation of my Lord Jesus, I overcome all accusations and the accusers, in Jesus' name.

"You have brought this Man to me, as one who misleads the people. And indeed, having examined Him in your presence, I have found no fault in this Man concerning those things of which you accuse Him" (Luke 23:14). Unto every accusation against me, I shall be found without fault, in Jesus' name.

"But they were insistent, demanding with loud voices that He be crucified. And the voices of these men and of the chief priests prevailed" (Luke 23:23). I decree that the voices of my adversaries shall not prevail against me, in Jesus' name.

"That very day Pilate and Herod became friends with each other, for previously they had been at enmity with each other" (Luke 23:12). I command every evil unity against me to scatter by confusion, in Jesus' name.

"For he knew that they had handed Him over because of envy" (Matt. 27:18). I silence unto desolation every envious attack on my life, in Jesus' name.

"While he was sitting on the judgment seat, his wife sent to him, saying, 'Have nothing to do with that just Man, for I have suffered many things today in a dream because of Him'" (Matt. 27:19). O Lord God, establish now Your terror in the dream life of my adversaries to forbid them from attacking me, in Jesus' name.

O Lord God, arrest the dream life of power, spirit, and personality to favor my life, in Jesus' name.

"So Pilate gave sentence that it should be as they requested" (Luke 23:24). Jesus was sentenced that I may be free. Therefore, any sentence of destruction on my life shall not be established, in Jesus' name.

"The Jews answered him, 'We have a law, and according to our law He ought to die, because He made Himself the Son of God'" (John 19:7). I, therefore, pray that the divine laws of the Most High God shall overrule and abolish any law set against me, in Jesus' name.

"(For it was necessary for him to release one to them at the feast)" (Luke 23:17). Therefore, of necessity, I am free to celebrate the feast of my life, in Jesus' name.

"And having blindfolded Him, they struck Him on the face and asked Him, saying, 'Prophesy! Who is the one who struck You?'" (Luke 22:64). My Lord Jesus was blindfolded that I might behold God's glory. Therefore, I command every blindfold on my life be taken off now, that I might behold the glory of God, in Jesus' name.

"And they stripped Him and put a scarlet robe on Him. When they had twisted a crown of thorns, they put it on His head, and a reed in His right hand. And they bowed the knee before Him and mocked Him, saying, 'Hail, King of the Jews!'" (Matt. 27:28–29). Through the mockery of Jesus, I silence unto desolation every mockery against my life, in Jesus' name.

"Then Jesus came out, wearing the crown of thorns and the purple robe. And Pilate said to them, 'Behold the Man!'" (John 19:5). Therefore, by Jesus' crown of thorns, I wear a crown of glory, in Jesus' name.

"And when they had come to a place called Golgotha, that is to say, Place of a Skull" (Matt. 27:33). I break the skull of the strongman set against me by the cross of Jesus, in Jesus' name.

"And a great multitude of the people followed Him, and women who also mourned and lamented Him. But Jesus, turning to them, said, 'Daughters of Jerusalem, do not weep for Me, but weep for yourselves and for your children'" (Luke 23:27–28). I decree against the company of wailers, mourners, and those who lament, who were set up for me: "Weep not for me, but weep for yourselves and for your children," in Jesus' name.

O ye company of wailers, mourners, and those who lament, who were set against me, scatter unto desolation, in Jesus' name.

"Two robbers were crucified with Him, one on the right and another on the left" (Matt. 27:38). I claim victory over robbers and thieves and regain all my stolen blessings, in Jesus' name.

"Then they crucified Him and divided His garments, casting lots, that it might be fulfilled which was spoken by the prophet: 'They divided My garments among them, And for My clothing they cast lots'" (Matt. 27:35). Let the parting of Jesus' garments cover my nakedness, in Jesus' name.

"And they put up over His head the accusation written against Him: THIS IS JESUS THE KING OF THE JEWS" (Matt. 27: 37). By the accusation against my Lord Jesus, I triumph over every accusation, in Jesus' name.

"And I bestow upon you a kingdom, just as My Father bestowed one upon Me" (Luke 22:29). I possess with gladness the kingdom prepared for me by my Lord Jesus, in Jesus' name.

Chapter 21

DELIVERANCE PRAYERS BASED ON HIS DEATH, RESURRECTION, AND ASCENSION

NOW FROM THE sixth hour until the ninth hour there was darkness over all the land" (Matt. 27:45). As my Lord Jesus overcame darkness, so do I by the power of His cross, in Jesus' name.

"And Jesus cried out again with a loud voice, and yielded up His spirit" (Matt. 27:50). I boldly declare that death has no dominion over me, in Jesus' name.

"Then, behold, the veil of the temple was torn in two from top to bottom; and the earth quaked, and the rocks were split" (Matt. 27:51). I command every veil hindering the glory of God in my life to tear apart from the top to the bottom, in Jesus' name.

O earth and rocks as strongholds of my adversaries I command you to quake and rent, in Jesus' name.

"And the graves were opened; and many bodies of the saints who had fallen asleep were raised" (Matt. 27:52). O graves, hold no longer my blessings, open up and release them now unto to me, in Jesus' name.

"And coming out of the graves after His resurrection, they went into the holy city and appeared to many" (Matt. 27:53). I command my glory to resurrect now, in Jesus' name.

"So when the centurion and those with him, who were guarding Jesus, saw the earthquake and the things that had happened, they feared greatly, saying, 'Truly this was the Son of God!'" (Matt. 27:54). Those who are appointed to watch over my life shall see my greatness and my glory and submit, in Jesus' name.

"And many women who followed Jesus from Galilee, ministering to Him, were there looking on from afar" (Matt. 27:55). O Lord God, raise people from near and far to behold Your glory in my life, in Jesus' name.

"The last error shall be worse than the first" (Matt. 27:64). So shall my adversaries multiply in errors to their shame, in Jesus' name.

"So they went and made the tomb secure, sealing the stone and setting the guard" (Matt. 27:66). My dear Lord Jesus, with Your secured sepulcher, You have secured my eternal destiny, so I triumph over the spirit of hell and death, in Jesus' name.

"And behold, there was a great earthquake; for an angel of the Lord descended from heaven, and came and rolled back the stone from the door, and sat on it" (Matt. 28:2). Angels of the Living God, roll away every stone preventing me from arising to greatness, in Jesus' name.

"And the guards shook for fear of him, and became like dead men" (Matt. 28:4). Therefore, O ye keepers assigned against me, be shaken out of your stronghold and become as dead men and women, in Jesus' name.

"Then the eleven disciples went away into Galilee, to the mountain which Jesus had appointed for them" (Matt. 28:16). I receive grace to be established in my appointed place to manifest God's glory, in Jesus' name.

"And Jesus came and spoke to them, saying, 'All authority has been given to Me in heaven and on earth'" (Matt. 28:18). Therefore, I manifest the divine powers that heaven and earth will work for my favor, in Jesus' name.

"And, lo, I am with you always, even unto the end of the world. Amen" (Matt. 28:20). Truly, this is confirmed in me, in Jesus' name.

This day is this scripture fulfilled in my life: "And these signs will follow those who believe: In My name they will cast out demons; they will speak with new tongues; they will take up serpents; and if they drink anything deadly, it will by no means hurt them; they will lay hands on the sick, and they will recover" (Mark 16:17–18), in Jesus' name.

This day is this scripture confirmed in my life: "And they went out and preached everywhere, the Lord working with them and confirming the word through the accompanying signs. Amen" (Mark 16:20), in Jesus' name.

I proclaim this before heaven and the earth: "Why seek ye the living among the dead? He is not here, but is risen" (Luke 24:5–6). So I am established among the living and not the dead, in Jesus' name.

"And they remembered His words" (Luke 24:8). I receive grace to always remember the Words of Jesus as my true guide, in Jesus' name.

"Behold My hands and My feet, that it is I Myself. Handle Me and see, for a spirit does not have flesh and bones as you see I have" (Luke 24:39). Dear Lord Jesus, I behold Your pierced hands and feet with thanksgiving, thus establishing my victories through Your shed blood, in Jesus' name.

"And He opened their understanding, that they might comprehend the Scriptures" (Luke 24:45). My dear Lord Jesus, open now my understanding that I might understand the Holy Scriptures, in Jesus' name.

"And you are witnesses of these things" (Luke 24:48). Truly, I am a living witness of God's miraculous power, in Jesus' name.

"Behold, I send the Promise of My Father upon you; but tarry in the city of Jerusalem until you are endued with power from on high" (Luke 24:49). I am endued with the power from on high and the promise of the Father is fulfilled in me, in Jesus' name.

"[They] were continually in the temple praising and blessing God " (Luke 24:53). I shall forever abide in God's presence with shouts of praise, in Jesus' name.

"Now it was Caiaphas who advised the Jews that it was expedient that one man should die for the people" (John 18:14). So, it was expedient for Jesus to die that I might live—praise God, in Jesus' name!

I proclaim that "to this end was I born, and for this cause came I into the world, that I should bear witness unto the truth" (John 18:37), in Jesus' name.

"Pilate answered, 'What I have written, I have written'" (John 19:22). Every written counsel of God for my life shall not be altered, in Jesus' name.

"After this, Jesus, knowing that all things were now accomplished, that the Scripture might be fulfilled, said, 'I thirst!'" (John 19:28). So shall all things that God has for my life be accomplished and be fulfilled, in Jesus' name.

"But one of the soldiers pierced His side with a spear, and immediately blood and water came out" (John 19:34). So, let the blood and the water from the side of Jesus make me whole now, in Jesus' name.

"Jesus came and stood in the midst and said unto them, 'Peace be with you'" (John 20:19). So, I receive peace, in Jesus' name.

"And when He had said this, He breathed on them, and said to them, 'Receive the Holy Spirit'" (John 20:22). So, I receive the Holy Spirit to the fullest, in Jesus' name.

"If you forgive the sins of any, they are forgiven them; if you retain the sins of any, they are retained" (John 20:23). I pray my sins be remitted and not retained, in Jesus' name.

"But these are written that you may believe that Jesus is the Christ, the Son of God, and that believing you may have life in His name" (John 20:31). I truly believe that Jesus Christ is the Son of God; thus, I have eternal life through His name, in Jesus' name.

"Then Jesus said, 'Father, forgive them, for they do not know what they do'" (Luke 23:34). So do I forgive those who trespass against me, in Jesus' name.

"And Jesus said to him, 'Assuredly, I say to you, today you will be with Me in Paradise'" (Luke 23:43). May the grace to abide with You until eternity rest upon me, in Jesus' name.

"When Jesus therefore saw His mother, and the disciple whom He loved standing by, He said to His mother, 'Woman, behold your son!' Then He said to the disciple, 'Behold your mother!' And from that hour that disciple took her to his own home" (John 19:26–27). I receive grace to behold my risen Savior, Jesus the Messiah, in Jesus' name.

"And about the ninth hour Jesus cried out with a loud voice, saying, 'Eli, Eli, lama sabachthani?' that is, 'My God, My God, why have You forsaken Me?'" (Matt. 27:46). O Lord God, deliver me from being forsaken and rescue me from abandonment, in Jesus' name.

"After this, Jesus, knowing that all things were now accomplished, that the Scripture might be fulfilled, said, 'I thirst!'" (John 19:28). Thank You, Jesus, for becoming thirsty that I might be eternally satisfied. So, Lord, fill my thirsty and hungry soul with Your presence, in Jesus' name.

"When Jesus had received the sour wine, He said, 'It is finished!' And bowing His head, He gave up His spirit" (John 19:30). So, let it be known in heaven, the earth, and beneath that affliction and sorrow are finished in my life; I enter into newness of life, in Jesus' name.

"It is finished." So also do I declare that tragedy is finished in my life, and I am established in victory, in Jesus' name.

"And when Jesus had cried out with a loud voice, He said, 'Father, "into Your hands I commit My spirit."' Having said this, He breathed His last" (Luke 23:46). I also commend my spirit unto Jehovah God, the Father of Spirits, the God of all flesh, to preserve me from all evil, in Jesus' name.

Chapter 22

DECLARING OPEN HEAVENS

IT IS WRITTEN: "The LORD will open to you His good treasure, the heavens, to give the rain to your land in its season, and to bless all the work of your hand. You shall lend to many nations, but you shall not borrow" (Deut. 28:12).

"Lift up your heads, O you gates! And be lifted up, you everlasting doors! And the King of glory shall come in. Who is this King of glory? The LORD strong and mighty, The LORD mighty in battle. Lift up your heads, O you gates! Lift up, you everlasting doors! And the King of glory shall come in. Who is this King of glory? The LORD of hosts, He is the King of glory. Selah" (Ps. 24:7–10).

"The people asked, and He brought quail, And satisfied them with the bread of heaven. He opened the rock, and water gushed out; It ran in the dry places like a river. For He remembered His holy promise, And Abraham His servant" (Ps. 105:40–42).

"Open to me the gates of righteousness; I will go through them, And I will praise the LORD" (Ps. 118:19).

"In the year that King Uzziah died, I saw the Lord sitting on a throne, high and lifted up, and the train of His robe filled the temple" (Isa. 6:1).

"Now it came to pass in the thirtieth year, in the fourth month, on the fifth day of the month, as I was among the captives by the River Chebar, that the heavens were opened and I saw visions of God" (Ezek. 1:1).

"When He had been baptized, Jesus came up immediately from the water; and behold, the heavens were opened to Him, and He saw the Spirit of God descending like a dove and alighting upon Him. And suddenly a voice came from heaven, saying, 'This is My beloved Son, in whom I am well pleased'" (Matt. 3:16–17).

"And raised us up together, and made us sit together in the heavenly places in Christ Jesus, that in the ages to come He might show the exceeding riches of His grace in His kindness toward us in Christ Jesus" (Eph. 2:6–7).

"After these things I looked, and behold, a door standing open in heaven. And the first voice which I heard was like a trumpet speaking with me, saying, 'Come up here, and I will show you things which must take place after this'" (Rev. 4:1).

Prayer points

I consecrate my heaven unto the blood of Jesus that speaks better things, in Jesus' name.

Through the blood of Jesus, the sun shall not smite me by day nor the moon by night, in the name of Jesus.

Angels of the Living God, be empowered by the blood of Jesus to war in my heaven and declare victory on my behalf, in Jesus' name.

Holy Spirit fire, shatter asunder the prince of the air and root out of my open heaven, in Jesus' name.

O Lord God, thunder in the heavens against the enemies of my soul, in the name of Jesus.

Fire from heaven, shake the wicked and their wickedness out of my heaven and desolate them, in Jesus' name.

Blood of Jesus, break asunder, rebuke, and desolate every program in the heavens that would operate against me through the sun, the moon, the stars, and the constellations, in the name of Jesus.

Through the blood of Jesus, I pray for the floodgates of heaven to be opened over my life, in the name of Jesus.

Through the blood of Jesus, I receive the rain and blessing from heaven upon my life, in the name of Jesus.

Atonement power of the blood of Jesus, avail for me in the heavenlies for an outpouring of blessings, in the name of Jesus.

It is written: "After these things I looked, and behold, the temple of the tabernacle of the testimony in heaven was opened" (Rev. 15:5). Therefore, "tabernacle of the testimony in heaven," unleash blessings upon me now, in the name of Jesus.

It is written: "The heavens declare the glory of God; And the firmament shows His handiwork" (Ps. 19:1). Therefore, O heaven of heavens, declare God's glory in my life, in Jesus' name.

I am connected to the throne of grace and mercies to manifest God's Shekinah glory, in Jesus' name.

Thank You, my dear Lord Jesus, for You are enthroned as Lord and King over my heaven, in Jesus' name.

Jesus Christ reigns and rules over my heaven, in Jesus' name.

Chapter 23

SHARPEN YOUR VISION

I T IS WRITTEN: "The secret things belong to the LORD our God, but those things which are revealed belong to us and to our children forever, that we may do all the words of this law" (Deut. 29:29).

"Teach me Your way, O LORD, And lead me in a smooth path, because of my enemies" (Ps. 27:11).

"There are many plans in a man's heart, Nevertheless the LORD's counsel—that will stand" (Prov. 19:21).

"Then the secret was revealed to Daniel in a night vision. So Daniel blessed the God of heaven. Daniel answered and said: 'Blessed be the name of God forever and ever, For wisdom and might are His. And He changes the times and the seasons; He removes kings and raises up kings; He gives wisdom to the wise And knowledge to those who have understanding. He reveals deep and secret things; He knows what is in the darkness, And light dwells with Him. I thank You and praise You, O God of my fathers; You have given me wisdom and might, And have now made known to me what we asked of You, For You have made known to us the king's demand'" (Dan. 2:19–23).

"And He said to them, 'To you it has been given to know the mystery of the kingdom of God; but to those who are outside, all things come in parables'" (Mark 4:11).

"That the God of our Lord Jesus Christ, the Father of glory, may give to you the spirit of wisdom and revelation in the knowledge of Him, the eyes of your understanding being enlightened; that you may know what is the hope of His calling, what are the riches of the glory of His inheritance in the saints, and what is the exceeding greatness of His power toward us who believe, according to the working of His mighty power which He worked in Christ when He raised Him from the dead and seated Him at His right hand in the heavenly places, far above all principality and power and might and dominion, and every name that is named, not only in this age but also in that which is to come. And He put all things under His feet, and gave Him to be head over all things to the church, which is His body, the fullness of Him who fills all in all" (Eph. 1:17–23).

"And there is no creature hidden from His sight, but all things are naked and open to the eyes of Him to whom we must give account" (Heb. 4:13).

Prophetic declaration

"Son of man, prophesy and say, 'Thus says the LORD!' Say: 'A sword, a sword is sharpened And also polished! Sharpened to make a dreadful slaughter, Polished to flash like lightning! Should we then make mirth? It despises the scepter of My son, As it does all wood'" (Ezek. 21:9–10). Lord God Almighty, I lay my life before Your throne of grace and mercies that You may sharpen me with the power of Your presence and furbish me with the glory of Your name, and that I may walk worthy of You.

Prayer points

It is written: "If the ax is dull, And one does not sharpen the edge, Then he must use more strength; But wisdom brings success" (Eccles. 10:10). Therefore, I present my life to You, O Lord; heal my blunt life and sharpen me with Your presence, in Jesus Christ's name.

The light of my glory shall not go dim, neither shall it be quenched, in Jesus Christ's name.

Holy Spirit fire, purge my senses from filthiness, in Jesus' name.

My sight be enlightened to behold God's glory, in Jesus' name.

It is written: "So he answered, 'Do not fear, for those who are with us are more than those who are with them.' And Elisha prayed, and said, 'LORD, I pray, open his eyes that he may see.' Then the LORD opened the eyes of the young man, and he saw. And behold, the mountain was full of horses and chariots of fire all around Elisha" (2 Kings 6:16–17). O Lord God, open my eyes and my understanding to behold Your abiding presence, in Jesus' name.

O Lord God, heal my ignorance to perceive Your glory, in Jesus' name.

My heart cry to Thee, O God, is: "Speak, LORD, for Your servant hears" (1 Sam. 3:9), in Jesus' name.

My taste and my desire shall forever be of Thee, O Lord, in Jesus' name.

I surrender my willpower unto You, O God; breathe upon it and fashion it after Your will, in Jesus' name.

My spirit man, be transformed by the power in the blood of Jesus, in Jesus' name.

My inner man, come alive and radiate God's glory, in Jesus' name.

Give thanks to God for answered prayers, in Jesus' name.

Chapter 24

WHAT SHALL SEPARATE ME FROM THE LORD?

IT IS WRITTEN: "Who shall separate us from the love of Christ? Shall tribulation, or distress, or persecution, or famine, or nakedness, or peril, or sword? As it is written: 'For Your sake we are killed all day long; We are accounted as sheep for the slaughter'" (Rom. 8:35–36).

"Do you not know that you are the temple of God and that the Spirit of God dwells in you?" (1 Cor. 3:16).

"For it is the God who commanded light to shine out of darkness, who has shone in our hearts to give the light of the knowledge of the glory of God in the face of Jesus Christ" (2 Cor. 4:6).

"Do not be unequally yoked together with unbelievers. For what fellowship has righteousness with lawlessness? And what communion has light with darkness? And what accord has Christ with Belial? Or what part has a believer with an unbeliever? And what agreement has the temple of God with idols? For you are the temple of the living God. As God has said: 'I will dwell in them And walk among them. I will be their God, And they shall be My people' (2 Cor. 6:14–16).

"Therefore, having these promises, beloved, let us cleanse ourselves from all filthiness of the flesh and spirit, perfecting holiness in the fear of God" (2 Cor. 7:1).

"For He Himself is our peace, who has made both one, and has broken down the middle wall of separation" (Eph. 2:14).

"But you are a chosen generation, a royal priesthood, a holy nation, His own special people, that you may proclaim the praises of Him who called you out of darkness into His marvelous light; who once were not a people but are now the people of God, who had not obtained mercy but now have obtained mercy" (1 Pet. 2:9–10).

Prophetic declaration

"Sing, O heavens! Be joyful, O earth! And break out in singing, O mountains! For the LORD has comforted His people, And will have mercy on His afflicted" (Isa. 49:13–17). So, I take comfort in the presence of the Almighty God and strengthened by His might to walk in victory, in Jesus' name.

Prayer points

As the Lord lives and as His Spirit lives, neither tribulation nor distress shall be able to separate me from the love of God, in Jesus' name.

I proclaim before the Living God that neither persecution nor famine shall be able to separate me from the love of God, in Jesus' name.

Let it be known that nakedness or danger cannot separate me from the love of Christ my Lord, in Jesus' name.

No weapon, however devastating or deadly, can make me turn back from Christ Jesus my Lord, in Jesus' name.

I am persuaded that neither death nor life can make me forsake my loving Savior and Lord, Jesus Christ, in Jesus' name.

Principalities and powers are not worthy enough to steal my love and devotion to Jesus Christ, my Lord and Savior, in Jesus' name.

Things present or things to come cannot shift my focus toward my Lord and King, Jesus Christ, in Jesus' name.

Height and death are subdued before me, in Jesus' name.

No creation is strong enough to make me withdraw my commitment for my Lord and Savior, Jesus Christ.

My dear Lord Jesus, grant me grace to stand by my commitment in serving You, in Jesus' name.

Dear Lord God, pour Your mercies and compassion upon me that I may serve You forever, in Jesus' name.

Give thanks to God for answered prayers, in Jesus' name.

Chapter 25

THE BATTLE IS THE LORD'S

I T IS WRITTEN: "The LORD will fight for you, and you shall hold your peace" (Exod. 14:14).

"For You have armed me with strength for the battle; You have subdued under me those who rose up against me. You have also given me the necks of my enemies, So that I destroyed those who hated me" (Ps. 18:39–40).

"Who is this King of glory? The LORD strong and mighty, The LORD mighty in battle" (Ps. 24:8).

"He makes wars cease to the end of the earth; He breaks the bow and cuts the spear in two; He burns the chariot in the fire" (Ps. 46:9).

"He has redeemed my soul in peace from the battle that was against me, For there were many against me" (Ps. 55:18).

"Behold, all those who were incensed against you Shall be ashamed and disgraced; They shall be as nothing, And those who strive with you shall perish. You shall seek them and not find them—Those who contended with you. Those who war against you Shall be as nothing, As a nonexistent thing. For I, the LORD your God, will hold your right hand, Saying to you, 'Fear not, I will help you'" (Isa. 41:11–13).

"And war broke out in heaven: Michael and his angels fought with the dragon; and the dragon and his angels fought, but they did not prevail, nor was a place found for them in heaven any longer. So the great dragon was cast out, that serpent of old, called the Devil and Satan, who deceives the whole world; he was cast to the earth, and his angels were cast out with him" (Rev. 12:7–9).

Prophetic declaration

I am not afraid, neither am I dismayed nor confounded by the reason of troubles or afflictions because my battles are the Lord's battles. "Then all this assembly shall know that the LORD does not save with sword and spear; for the battle is the Lord's, and He will give you into our hands" (1 Sam. 17:47). Therefore, O Lord God, scatter those who delight in war against my life, in Jesus' name.

Prayer points

It is written: "The Lord is a man of war; The Lord is His name" (Exod. 15:3). Therefore, Jehovah, the Man of War, I hand over the battles of my life to You; fight for me and give me victory, in Jesus' name.

The battle of my past and my fear of tomorrow, I hand over to the God of Hosts to fight for me and give me victory, in Jesus' name.

My dear Lord Jesus, possess the battleground of my life and ride majestic in victory, in Jesus' name.

I render a victory proclamation against all my adversaries, "The adversaries of the Lord shall be broken in pieces; From heaven He will thunder against them. The Lord will judge the ends of the earth. 'He will give strength to His king, And exalt the horn of His anointed'" (1 Sam. 2:10), in Jesus' name.

Unto every battle of my life I pray: "If the Lord have stirred you up against me, let Him accept an offering, but if they be of the children of men, cursed be they before the Lord; for they have driven me out this day from abiding in the inheritance of the Lord, saying, Go, serve other gods" (1 Sam. 26:19), in Jesus' name.

Unto every attacker of my life, destroy me not; "for who can stretch forth his hand against the Lord's anointed and be guiltless?" (1 Sam. 26:9), in Jesus' name.

It is written: "For in very deed, as the Lord God of Israel lives, who has kept me back from hurting you" (1 Sam. 25:34). Therefore, O Lord God of Israel, keep back powers, spirits, and personalities from hurting me, in Jesus' name.

It is written: "O God the Lord, the strength of my salvation, You have covered my head in the day of battle" (Ps. 140:7). Therefore, protect and preserve my soul from tragedies and chaos, in Jesus' name.

I covenant my life to victory through the blood of Jesus, in Jesus' name.

Through the strength of the Holy Spirit, I possess the rewards of victories, in Jesus' name.

My rewards of glorious victories manifest now in all areas of my life, in Jesus' name.

Thank God for answered prayers, in Jesus' name.

Chapter 26

LIFT UP YOUR HEADS

I T IS WRITTEN: "Blessing I will bless you, and multiplying I will multiply your descendants as the stars of the heaven and as the sand which is on the seashore; and your descendants shall possess the gate of their enemies" (Gen. 22:17).

"Open the gates, That the righteous nation which keeps the truth may enter in" (Isa. 26:2).

"See, I have this day set you over the nations and over the kingdoms, To root out and to pull down, To destroy and to throw down, To build and to plant" (Jer. 1:10).

"And I also say to you that you are Peter, and on this rock I will build My church, and the gates of Hades shall not prevail against it" (Matt. 16:18).

"But Jesus looked at them and said to them, 'With men this is impossible, but with God all things are possible'" (Matt. 19:26).

"He did not waver at the promise of God through unbelief, but was strengthened in faith, giving glory to God, and being fully convinced that what He had promised He was also able to perform" (Rom. 4:20–21).

"Therefore, my beloved brethren, be steadfast, immovable, always abounding in the work of the Lord, knowing that your labor is not in vain in the Lord" (1 Cor. 15:58).

Prophetic declaration

"Lift up your heads, O you gates! And be lifted up, you everlasting doors! And the King of glory shall come in. Who is this King of glory? The LORD strong and mighty, The LORD mighty in battle. Lift up your heads, O you gates! Lift up, you everlasting doors! And the King of glory shall come in. Who is this King of glory? The LORD of hosts, He is the King of glory. Selah" (Ps. 24:7–10). Gates must shift, and heads and knees must bow for the King of Glory; Jesus the Messiah, be enthroned in me.

Prayer points

Gates and doors of my life, open now, that Jesus be enthroned as Lord and King, in Jesus' name.

No evil shall possess the gates of my life, I command it to flee and become desolate, in Jesus' name.

Warfare at the gates of my life, give up to the Lord of Hosts and rise up no more, in Jesus' name.

Watchmen at the gate of my life assigned for evil purposes, fail and waste away, in Jesus' name.

All heads bow and all knees worship Jesus, the Messiah who reigns in me, in Jesus' name.

Jehovah God that is higher than the highest has absolute authority over my life; therefore, I triumph at the authority of His name, in Jesus' name.

It is written: "You shall write them on the doorposts of your house and on your gates" (Deut. 6:9). Any evil written at the gates and doors of my life, be abolished by the blood of Jesus, in Jesus' name.

Blessings be written at the gates and doors of my life, in Jesus' name.

Peace be upon my door post, in Jesus' name.

It is written: "And now my head shall be lifted up above my enemies all around me; Therefore I will offer sacrifices of joy in His tabernacle; I will sing, yes, I will sing praises to the Lord" (Ps. 27:6). Therefore, my eternal Father, lift high my head in joy and in victory, in Jesus' name.

My head be crowned with glory and favor, in Jesus' name.

Thank God for answered prayer, in Jesus' name.

Chapter 27

LET MY PEOPLE GO

IT IS WRITTEN: "And you shall say to him, 'The LORD God of the Hebrews has sent me to you, saying, 'Let My people go, that they may serve Me in the wilderness'; but indeed, until now you would not hear!" (Exod. 7:16).

"And the LORD spoke to Moses, 'Go to Pharaoh and say to him, "Thus says the LORD: 'Let My people go, that they may serve Me.'"'...And the LORD said to Moses, 'Rise early in the morning and stand before Pharaoh as he comes out to the water. Then say to him, "Thus says the LORD: 'Let My people go, that they may serve Me'"'" (Exod. 8:1, 20).

"Then the LORD said to Moses, 'Go in to Pharaoh and tell him, "Thus says the LORD God of the Hebrews: 'Let My people go, that they may serve Me.'"'...Then the LORD said to Moses, 'Rise early in the morning and stand before Pharaoh, and say to him, "Thus says the LORD God of the Hebrews: 'Let My people go, that they may serve Me'"'" (Exod. 9:1, 13).

"So Moses and Aaron came in to Pharaoh and said to him, 'Thus says the LORD God of the Hebrews: "How long will you refuse to humble yourself before Me? Let My people go, that they may serve Me'"'" (Exod. 10:3).

"Then we cried out to the LORD God of our fathers, and the LORD heard our voice and looked on our affliction and our labor and our oppression. So the LORD brought us out of Egypt with a mighty hand and with an outstretched arm, with great terror and with signs and wonders. He has brought us to this place and has given us this land, 'a land flowing with milk and honey'" (Deut. 26:7–9).

Prophetic declaration

"Now the Lord is the Spirit; and where the Spirit of the Lord is, there is liberty" (2 Cor. 3:17). By the liberty of the resurrection power of my Lord Jesus, I henceforth walk in freedom and joy in the Holy Spirit. I proclaim that I am God's heritage and the Lord is my portion forever, in Jesus' name.

Prayer points

Unto depression and guilt, thus says the Lord, "Let my people go," so let go of me now, in Jesus' name.

Stronghold of fear in me, thus says the Lord, "Let my people go," so let go of me now, in Jesus' name.

Unto condemnation and confusion, thus says the Lord, "Let my people go," so let go of me now, in Jesus' name.

Unto disaster and tragedy, thus says the Lord, "Let my people go," so let go of me now, in Jesus' name.

Unto woes and misfortune, thus says the Lord, "Let my people go," so let go of me now, in Jesus' name.

Unto the spirit of heaviness and mourning, thus says the Lord, "Let my people go," so let go of me now, in Jesus' name.

Unto weariness and lack, thus says the Lord, "Let my people go," so let go of me now, in Jesus' name.

Thus says the Lord unto torment and affliction, "Let my people go," so let go of me now, in Jesus' name.

Thus says the Lord unto oppression and defeat, "Let my people go," so let go of me now, in Jesus' name.

Thus says the Lord unto shame and ridicule, "Let my people go," so let go of me now, in Jesus' name.

Thus says the Lord unto reproach and failure, "Let my people go," so let go of me now, in Jesus' name.

By the power that plagues Egypt, I command the strongman and the stronghold of captivity in my life be shattered, in Jesus' name.

By the rod that parted the Red Sea, I command oppositions to blessings in my life to part asunder, in Jesus' name.

It is written: "You blew with Your wind, The sea covered them; They sank like lead in the mighty waters" (Exod. 15:10). Therefore, by the power that drowned the Egyptian army, I decree all unrighteousness in me to drown, in Jesus' name.

It is written: "Now when they came to Marah, they could not drink the waters of Marah, for they were bitter. Therefore the name of it was called Marah" (Exod. 15:23). By the power that sweetened the bitter water, I decree my life be sweetened with joy, in Jesus' name.

By the power that made Joshua possess the Promised Land, I also possess all my divinely appointed blessings, in Jesus' name.

By the scepter of Joseph that ruled Egypt, I subdue all adversaries and their adversities in Jesus' name.

By the power that raised Lazarus from death, I command all my buried glory to come alive now, in Jesus' name.

By the stone that killed Goliath, I decree the giants attacking my life to be slain now, in Jesus' name.

It is written: "But if the Spirit of Him who raised Jesus from the dead dwells in you, He who raised Christ from the dead will also give life to your mortal bodies through His Spirit who dwells in you" (Rom. 8:11). Therefore, I am quickened by the power of the Holy Spirit out of captivity unto miraculous blessings, in Jesus' name.

Give thanks to God for answered prayers, in Jesus' name.

Chapter 28

SUPERNATURAL WEAPONS FOR SUPERNATURAL ENCOUNTERS

I T IS WRITTEN: "Have you entered the treasury of snow, Or have you seen the treasury of hail, Which I have reserved for the time of trouble, For the day of battle and war? By what way is light diffused, Or the east wind scattered over the earth? Who has divided a channel for the overflowing water, Or a path for the thunderbolt, To cause it to rain on a land where there is no one, A wilderness in which there is no man; To satisfy the desolate waste, And cause to spring forth the growth of tender grass? Has the rain a father? Or who has begotten the drops of dew? From whose womb comes the ice? And the frost of heaven, who gives it birth?" (Job 38:22–28).

"Some trust in chariots, and some in horses; But we will remember the name of the LORD our God. They have bowed down and fallen; But we have risen and stand upright. Save, LORD! May the King answer us when we call" (Ps. 20:7–9).

"He makes wars cease to the end of the earth; He breaks the bow and cuts the spear in two; He burns the chariot in the fire" (Ps. 46:9).

"'No weapon formed against you shall prosper, And every tongue which rises against you in judgment You shall condemn. This is the heritage of the servants of the LORD, And their righteousness is from Me,' Says the LORD" (Isa. 54:17).

"For behold, the LORD will come with fire And with His chariots, like a whirlwind, To render His anger with fury, And His rebuke with flames of fire. For by fire and by His sword The LORD will judge all flesh; And the slain of the LORD shall be many" (Isa. 66:15–16).

"You are My battle-ax and weapons of war: For with you I will break the nation in pieces; With you I will destroy kingdoms; With you I will break in pieces the horse and its rider; With you I will break in pieces the chariot and its rider; With you also I will break in pieces man and woman; With you I will break in pieces old and young; With you I will break in pieces the young man and the maiden; With you also I will break in pieces the shepherd and his flock; With you I will break in pieces the farmer and his yoke of oxen; And with you I will break in pieces governors and rulers" (Jer. 51:20–23).

"Now out of His mouth goes a sharp sword, that with it He should strike the nations. And He Himself will rule them with a rod of iron. He Himself treads the winepress of the fierceness and wrath of Almighty God. And He has on His robe and on His thigh a name written: KING OF KINGS AND LORD OF LORDS" (Rev. 19:15–16).

Prophetic declaration

I take this prophetic lamentation against the strongman assigned against me: "The beauty of Israel is slain on your high places! How the mighty have fallen! Tell it not in Gath, Proclaim it not in the streets of Ashkelon—Lest the daughters of the Philistines rejoice, Lest the daughters of the uncircumcised triumph. O mountains of Gilboa, Let there be no dew nor rain upon you, Nor fields of offerings. For the shield of the mighty is cast away there! The shield of Saul, not anointed with oil. From the blood of the slain, From the fat of the mighty, The bow of Jonathan did not turn back, And the sword of Saul did not return empty....How the mighty have fallen in the midst of the battle! Jonathan was slain in your high places....'How the mighty have fallen, And the weapons of war perished!'" (2 Sam. 1:19–22, 25, 27).

Prayer points

My loin is girded with the truth of God's Word, in Jesus' name.

With my breastplate of righteousness, my heart is protected from mind-destructive demons, in Jesus' name.

My feet are shod with the preparation of the gospel of peace to possess my generation to God Almighty and to the kingdom of Jesus, in Jesus' name.

I take up the shield of faith to quench all the fiery darts of the wicked, in Jesus' name.

I am arrayed with the helmet of salvation for the right mind-set to walk with God, in Jesus' name.

I command the defensive and offensive weapons of my adversaries to fail and perish, in Jesus' name.

With the sword of the Spirit, I cut off every evil link and network of bondage set to hold me in captivity, in Jesus' name.

As it is written: "And the angel of the Lord stood in the way for an adversary against him" (Num. 22:22). So, let the angel of the Lord with his sword drawn out stand in the way of my adversaries to slay them, in Jesus' name.

It is written: "Now out of His mouth goes a sharp sword, that with it He should strike the nations. And He Himself will rule them with a rod of iron. He Himself treads the winepress of the fierceness and wrath of Almighty God" (Rev. 19:15). Therefore, Jesus, the King of kings, and the Lord of lords, with the sharp sword from Your mouth, slay all adversaries and adversities targeted at me, in Jesus' name.

It is written: "The first angel sounded: And hail and fire followed, mingled with blood, and they were thrown to the earth. And a third of the trees were burned up, and all green grass was burned up" (Rev. 8:7). Therefore, let hail and fire mingled with the blood of Jesus shatter the palaces of my tormentors, in Jesus' name.

It is written: "Upon the wicked He will rain coals; Fire and brimstone and a burning wind Shall be the portion of their cup" (Ps. 11:6). This shall be the portion of the afflicters of my soul, in Jesus' name.

It is written: "They fought from the heavens; The stars from their courses fought against Sisera" (Judg. 5:20). So, heavenly weapons, desolate the hiding places of the tormentors of my soul, in Jesus' name.

Unto all I have petitioned God, "Fire and hail, snow and clouds; Stormy wind, fulfilling His word" (Ps. 148:8), in Jesus' name.

It is written: "For we do not wrestle against flesh and blood, but against principalities, against powers, against the rulers of the darkness of this age, against spiritual hosts of wickedness in the heavenly places" (Eph. 6:12). Every wrestling of principalities, powers, rulers of the darkness of this world, and spiritual wickedness in high places against my life, I overcome you by the blood of Jesus, in Jesus' name.

I boldly confess that I am complete in Jesus my Messiah, who is the head of all principalities and power, in Jesus' name.

I make this solemn proclamation about Jesus my Messiah: "He is the image of the invisible God, the firstborn over all creation. For by Him all things were created that are in heaven and that are on earth, visible and invisible, whether thrones or dominions or principalities or powers.

All things were created through Him and for Him. And He is before all things, and in Him all things consist" (Col. 1:15–17), in Jesus' name.

Give thanks to God for answered prayers, in Jesus' name.

Chapter 29

DELIVERANCE FROM THE DEEP AND THE WATERS

Deep
(See Genesis 1:2; Psalm 42:7; Romans 8:35.)

The deepest part of the sea

The deep is a chaotic spirit of disorder, darkness, destruction, and death.

Water
Symbol of life

Earth founded upon the seas (Ps. 24:2)

Human body largely made up of water

Gateway to cities (seaports) (Ps. 24:7)

Major role in creation of heaven and earth
Day One: "The Spirit of God moved upon the face of the waters" (Gen. 1:2)

Day Two: Firmament (sky) separating the waters below and above (Gen. 1:6–8)

Day Three: The sea, earth, and vegetation (Gen. 1:9–10)

Day Five: Living creatures of water and air (Gen. 1:20–23)

Prophetic declarations
"He drew a circular horizon on the face of the waters, At the boundary of light and darkness. The pillars of heaven tremble, And are astonished at His rebuke. He stirs up the sea with His power, And by His understanding He breaks up the storm. By His Spirit He adorned the heavens; His hand pierced the fleeing serpent" (Job 26:10–13).

"He sent out His arrows and scattered the foe, Lightnings in abundance, and He vanquished them. Then the channels of the sea were seen, The foundations of the world were uncovered At Your rebuke, O Lord, At the blast of the breath of Your nostrils. He sent from above, He took me; He drew me out of many waters. He delivered me from my strong enemy, From those who hated me, For they were too strong for me" (Ps. 18:14-17)

"Give unto the LORD, O you mighty ones, Give unto the LORD glory and strength. Give unto the LORD the glory due to His name; Worship the LORD in the beauty of holiness. The voice of the LORD is over the waters; The God of glory thunders; The LORD is over many waters. The voice of the LORD is powerful; The voice of the LORD is full of majesty. The voice of the LORD breaks the cedars, Yes, the LORD splinters the cedars of Lebanon. He makes them also skip like a calf, Lebanon and Sirion like a young wild ox. The voice of the LORD divides the flames of fire. The voice of the LORD shakes the wilderness; The LORD shakes the Wilderness of Kadesh. The voice of the LORD makes the deer give birth, And strips the forests bare; And in His temple everyone says, 'Glory!' The LORD sat enthroned at the Flood, And the LORD sits as King forever. The LORD will give strength to His people; The LORD will bless His people with peace" (Ps. 29:1–11).

"For God is my King from of old, Working salvation in the midst of the earth. You divided the sea by Your strength; You broke the heads of the sea serpents in the waters. You broke the heads of Leviathan in pieces, And gave him as food to the people inhabiting the wilderness. You broke open the fountain and the flood; You dried up mighty rivers" (Ps. 74:12–15).

"The LORD reigns, He is clothed with majesty; The LORD is clothed, He has girded Himself with strength. Surely the world is established, so that it cannot be moved. Your throne is established from of old; You are from everlasting. The floods have lifted up, O LORD, The floods have lifted up their voice; The floods lift up their waves. The LORD on high is mightier Than the noise of many waters, Than the mighty waves of the sea. Your testimonies are very sure; Holiness adorns Your house, O LORD, forever" (Ps. 93:1–5).

"In His hand are the deep places of the earth; The heights of the hills are His also. The sea is His, for He made it; And His hands formed the dry land" (Ps. 95:4–5).

"Let the sea roar, and all its fullness, The world and those who dwell in it; Let the rivers clap their hands; Let the hills be joyful together before the LORD, For He is coming to judge the earth. With righteousness He shall judge the world, And the peoples with equity" (Ps. 98:7–9).

"You who laid the foundations of the earth, So that it should not be moved forever, You covered it with the deep as with a garment; The waters stood above the mountains. At Your rebuke they fled; At the voice of Your thunder they hastened away" (Ps. 104:5–7).

"The mountains saw You and trembled; The overflowing of the water passed by. The deep uttered its voice, And lifted its hands on high. The sun and moon stood still in their habitation; At the light of Your arrows they went, At the shining of Your glittering spear. You marched through the land in indignation; You trampled the nations in anger. You went forth for the salvation of Your people, For salvation with Your Anointed. You struck the head from the house of the wicked, By laying bare from foundation to neck. Selah" (Hab. 3:10–13).

"God, who at various times and in various ways spoke in time past to the fathers by the prophets, has in these last days spoken to us by His Son, whom He has appointed heir of all things, through whom also He made the worlds; who being the brightness of His glory and the express image of His person, and upholding all things by the word of His power, when He had by Himself purged our sins, sat down at the right hand of the Majesty on high, having become so much better than the angels, as He has by inheritance obtained a more excellent name than they" (Heb. 1:1–4).

Prayer points

Jehovah, my eternal Creator, thank you for giving me dominion over all the works of your hands, in Jesus Christ's name.

Through the blood of Jesus, I reject and renounce covenants and dedication to the waters and the deep, in Jesus Christ's name.

My life is totally dedicated and covenanted to Jesus Christ, my Savior, and the power of His blood, in Jesus Christ's name.

Holy Spirit, arise as my true witness against witnesses of covenants of the water spirit and the deep, in Jesus Christ's name.

Rituals and sacrifices to the waters and the deep, be disconnected from my life and perish, in Jesus Christ's name.

Consultation to the waters and the deep over my life, prosper no more, in Jesus Christ's name.

Ancestral marine spirit, I reject and renounce you by the blood of Jesus; cease your operations in my life, in Jesus Christ's name.

My Lord Jesus Christ said, "It is finished" at the cross. Therefore, the water spirit covenant and its operations in my life is finished forever, in Jesus Christ's name.

It is written: "A drought is against her waters, and they will be dried up. For it is the land of carved images, And they are insane with their idols" (Jer. 50:38). Therefore, I decree drought upon the waters that have caged my destiny, in Jesus Christ's name.

It is written: "Therefore thus says the LORD: 'Behold, I will plead your case and take vengeance for you. I will dry up her sea and make her springs dry'" (Jer. 51:36). Therefore, O Lord God, arise, take vengeance for me and dry up the spring of affliction in my life, in Jesus Christ's name.

It is written: "And there is no creature hidden from His sight, but all things are naked and open to the eyes of Him to whom we must give account" (Heb. 4:13). Therefore, hidden powers of the waters and the deep, be muzzled before me, in Jesus Christ's name.

Transforming demons of the waters and the deep, hold your peace and come out of me, in Jesus Christ's name.

Marine witchcraft, the Lord God of Hosts rebuke you; depart from my life, in Jesus Christ's name.

Lust and perversion, hold your peace and come out of me, in Jesus Christ's name.

Murder and death, hold your peace and come out of me, in Jesus Christ's name.

Violence and destruction, hold your peace and come out of me, in Jesus Christ's name.

Addiction to evil, hold your peace and come out of me, in Jesus Christ's name.

This is the divine judgment of the principalities of the waters and the deep assigned against my life: "O you who dwell by many waters, abundant in treasures, your end has come, the measure of your covetousness" (Jer. 51:13), in Jesus Christ's name.

It is written: "I will show you the judgment of the great whore that sits upon many waters" (Rev. 17:1). Therefore, principalities of the waters and the deep, set against me, be dethroned and be slain by your waters, in Jesus Christ's name.

It is written: "And I heard the angel of the waters saying: 'You are righteous, O Lord, the One who is and who was and who is to be, because You have judged these things'" (Rev. 16:5). Therefore, the judgment of God is upon the waters and the deep hindering my prospect in life, in Jesus Christ's name.

Holy Spirit fire, devour the altars, shrine, groves, strongholds, tents, and caves of the waters and the deep against my life, in Jesus Christ's name.

It is written: "Behold, the Lord will cast her out; He will destroy her power in the sea, and she will be devoured by fire" (Zech. 9:4). Therefore, in the name of Jesus Christ, I bind and cast the marine spirit out of my life, in Jesus Christ's name.

Overflowing scourge targeted at me, turn back to desolation, in Jesus Christ's name.

It is written: "He makes the deep boil like a pot; He makes the sea like a pot of ointment" (Job 41:31). Therefore, you boiling of the depth against me, hold your peace and peace be still, in Jesus Christ's name.

It is written: "The waters saw You, O God; the waters saw You, they were afraid; the depths also trembled" (Ps. 77:16). Therefore, marine spirit, hold your peace and come out of me, in Jesus Christ's name.

It is written: "Are you better than No Amon that was situated by the River, that had the waters around her, whose rampart was the sea, whose wall was the sea?" (Nah. 3:8). Therefore, I command the defenses of the water spirit against me to perish, in Jesus Christ's name.

It is written: "You rule the raging of the sea; when its waves rise, You still them" (Ps. 89:9). Therefore, raging waters and the deep against my life, peace, be still, in Jesus Christ's name.

It is written: "Speak, and say, 'Thus says the Lord God: "Behold, I am against you, O Pharaoh king of Egypt, O great monster who lies in the midst of his rivers, Who has said, 'My River is my own; I have made it for myself.' But I will put hooks in your jaws, And cause the fish of your rivers to stick to your scales; I will bring you up out of the midst of your rivers, And all the fish in your rivers will stick to your scales'"" (Ezek. 29:3–4). Therefore, principalities of the waters, be subdued before me, in Jesus Christ's name.

Networking and trafficking through the heavens, firmament, air, land, and waters against my life, let God arise and scatter them to desolation, in Jesus Christ's name.

It is written: "For I know that the Lord is great, and our Lord is above all gods. Whatever the Lord pleases He does, in heaven and in earth, In the seas and in all deep places" (Ps. 135:5–6). Therefore, I prevail over the spirit of the waters and the deep, in Jesus Christ's name.

It is written: "He binds up the water in His thick clouds, yet the clouds are not broken under it" (Job 26:8). Therefore, water spirit and the deep, reinforce no more against my life, in Jesus Christ's name.

It is written: "Who says to the deep, 'Be dry! And I will dry up your rivers'" (Isa. 44:27). Therefore, O deep and the waters against me, thus says the Lord God of Hosts, dry up, in Jesus Christ's name.

It is written: "He dams up the streams from trickling; what is hidden he brings forth to light" (Job 28:11). Therefore, water spirit and the deep, be muzzled before me, in Jesus Christ's name.

It is written: "Behold, at my rebuke, I dry up the sea, I make the rivers a wilderness: their fish stinks, because there is no water, and dies for thirst" (Isa. 50:2). Therefore, water creatures summoned against me, perish, in Jesus Christ's name.

It is written: "The gates of the rivers are opened, and the palace is dissolved" (Nah. 2:6). Therefore, gates and palaces of the waters over my life, perish, in Jesus Christ's name.

The noise of water spouting against me, be silenced, in Jesus Christ's name.

As my Lord and Savior, Jesus Christ walked upon the sea, so also I triumph over the waters, in Jesus Christ's name.

As the Red Sea parted, so also the wickedness of the deep and of the waters is separated from my life, in Jesus Christ's name.

As the River Jordan parted, so also the wickedness of the water spirit and the deep is separated from my life, in Jesus Christ's name.

It is written: "Then He arose and rebuked the wind, and said to the sea, 'Peace, be still!' And the wind ceased and there was a great calm" (Mark 4:39). Therefore, I receive great calmness over the rage of waters and the deep, in Jesus Christ's name.

It is written: "They see the works of the LORD, and His wonders in the deep" (Ps. 107:24). Therefore, hear O deep, spring up joyful wonders into my life, in Jesus Christ's name.

It is written: "By the God of your father who will help you, and by the Almighty who will bless you with blessings of heaven above, Blessings of the deep that lies beneath, Blessings of the breasts and of the womb" (Gen. 49:25). Henceforth, blessings of the deep spring forth into my life, in Jesus Christ's name.

It is written: "Praise the LORD from the earth, you great sea creatures and all the depths" (Ps. 148:7). Therefore, praise of the Almighty God, spring forth from the waters and the deep, in Jesus Christ's name.

Give thanks to God for answered prayers, in Jesus Christ's name.

Chapter 30

WITCHCRAFT DEFEATED

I T IS WRITTEN: "The LORD shall go forth like a mighty man; He shall stir up His zeal like a man of war. He shall cry out, yes, shout aloud; He shall prevail against His enemies. I have held My peace a long time, I have been still and restrained Myself. Now I will cry like a woman in labor, I will pant and gasp at once" (Isa. 42:13–14).

"For our soul is bowed down to the dust; Our body clings to the ground" (Isa. 44:25).

"Oh, clap your hands, all you peoples! Shout to God with the voice of triumph! For the LORD Most High is awesome; He is a great King over all the earth. He will subdue the peoples under us, And the nations under our feet. He will choose our inheritance for us, The excellence of Jacob whom He loves. Selah. God has gone up with a shout, The LORD with the sound of a trumpet" (Isa. 47:1–5).

"For behold, I have made you this day A fortified city and an iron pillar, And bronze walls against the whole land—Against the kings of Judah, Against its princes, Against its priests, And against the people of the land" (Jer. 1:18).

"I will cut off sorceries from your hand, And you shall have no sooth-sayers. Your carved images I will also cut off, And your sacred pillars from your midst; You shall no more worship the work of your hands; I will pluck your wooden images from your midst; Thus I will destroy your cities. And I will execute vengeance in anger and fury On the nations that have not heard" (Mic. 5:12–15).

"For unclean spirits, crying with a loud voice, came out of many who were possessed; and many who were paralyzed and lame were healed. And there was great joy in that city" (Acts 8:7–8).

"And this she did for many days. But Paul, greatly annoyed, turned and said to the spirit, 'I command you in the name of Jesus Christ to come out of her.' And he came out that very hour'" (Acts 16:18).

"Also, many of those who had practiced magic brought their books together and burned them in the sight of all. And they counted up the value of them, and it totaled fifty thousand pieces of silver. So the word of the Lord grew mightily and prevailed." (Acts 19:19–20).

Prophetic declaration

Thank You, my Lord Jesus, because You bruised the head of Satan to restore me back to God. I, therefore, reign together with my Lord Jesus in victory and in praise, in Jesus' name. "Having wiped out the handwriting of requirements that was against us, which was contrary to us. And He has taken it out of the way, having nailed it to the cross. Having disarmed principalities and powers, He made a public spectacle of them, triumphing over them in it" (Col. 2:14–15).

Prayer points

Through the blood of Jesus, I reject and renounce every dedication I have with witchcraft, familiar spirits, and all evil works, in Jesus' name.

Any evil representative of my life in witchcraft coven, be withdrawn and be set free now, in Jesus' name.

It is written: "The enemy said, 'I will pursue, I will overtake, I will divide the spoil; My desire shall be satisfied on them. I will draw my sword, My hand shall destroy them.' You blew with Your wind, The sea covered them; They sank like lead in the mighty waters" (Exod. 15:9–10). Therefore, every witchcraft vow on my life, be terminated by the blood of Jesus, in Jesus' name.

Principalities over my family line empowered to destroy, the blood of Jesus rebukes you, be emptied unto desolation, in Jesus' name.

Dominion and power over my household connecting with wicked forces, the blood of Jesus rebuke you, hold your peace and become desolate, in Jesus' name.

Rulers and authorities under satanic mandate, I subdue you by the blood of Jesus and I triumph over you, in Jesus' name.

Witchcraft agenda for my life, be aborted by the blood of Jesus, in Jesus' name.

It is written: "'Come down and sit in the dust, O virgin daughter of Babylon; Sit on the ground without a throne, O daughter of the Chaldeans! For you shall no more be called Tender and delicate. Take the millstones and grind meal. Remove your veil, Take off the skirt, Uncover the thigh, Pass through the rivers. Your nakedness shall be uncovered, Yes, your shame will be seen; I will take vengeance, And I will not arbitrate with a man.' As for our Redeemer, the LORD of hosts is His name, The Holy One of Israel. 'Sit in silence, and go into darkness, O daughter of the Chaldeans; For you shall no longer be called The Lady of Kingdoms'" (Isa. 47:1–5). Therefore, witchcraft throne against my life, be cast down and perish with all your summoning, in Jesus' name.

Any part of me tied to a witchcraft coven and altar, thus says the Lord God of Hosts, "Let my people go." Therefore, I break loose and break free now, in Jesus' name.

It is written: "And if anyone says to you, 'Why are you doing this?' say, 'The Lord has need of it,' and immediately he will send it here'" (Mark 11:3). Therefore, I proclaim before heaven and earth that "the Lord has need of me," so I am unquestionably free to declare the glory of God, in Jesus' name.

It is written: "The heavens declare the glory of God; And the firmament shows His handiwork" (Ps. 19:1). Therefore, O heavens, hold not back God's glory, unfold to fullest in all areas of my life, in Jesus' name.

O ye witchcraft mandate over my life, let it be known to you that Jesus, my Messiah is the "head of all principalities and powers"; therefore, shatter unto desolation, in Jesus' name.

By the anointing of the Holy Spirit, I break loose and break free from witchcraft traps, in Jesus' name.

It is written: "It is in my power to do you harm, but the God of your father spoke to me last night, saying, 'Be careful that you speak to Jacob neither good nor bad'" (Gen. 31:29). Therefore, O God of Abraham, Isaac, and Jacob, restrain witchcraft attacks in my life, forbid them as you weary, confuse, and desolate them, in Jesus' name.

"As smoke is driven away" (Ps. 68:2), so let all witchcraft rage be driven away from me, in Jesus' name.

"As wax melts before the fire" (Ps. 68:2), so let every witchcraft stronghold against me perish, in Jesus' name.

It is written: "Your hand shall be lifted against your adversaries, And all your enemies shall be cut off" (Mic. 5:9). Therefore, witchcraft domination is cut off from my life, in Jesus' name.

Every witchcraft ritual assigned to harm me, let God arise and shatter them to desolation, in Jesus' name.

Damages done to my life by witches, wizards, sorcerers, and warlocks, be repaired by the blood of Jesus, in Jesus' name.

Every blessing due to me under witchcraft attacks, come forth unto me now and manifest, in Jesus' name.

Give thanks to God for answered prayer, in Jesus' name.

Chapter 31

TRIUMPHING OVER DREAM ATTACKS

IT IS WRITTEN: "But God came to Abimelech in a dream by night, and said to him, 'Indeed you are a dead man because of the woman whom you have taken, for she is a man's wife'" (Gen. 20:3).

"Then he dreamed, and behold, a ladder was set up on the earth, and its top reached to heaven; and there the angels of God were ascending and descending on it. And behold, the LORD stood above it and said: 'I am the LORD God of Abraham your father and the God of Isaac; the land on which you lie I will give to you and your descendants. Also your descendants shall be as the dust of the earth; you shall spread abroad to the west and the east, to the north and the south; and in you and in your seed all the families of the earth shall be blessed. Behold, I am with you and will keep you wherever you go, and will bring you back to this land; for I will not leave you until I have done what I have spoken to you.' Then Jacob awoke from his sleep and said, 'Surely the LORD is in this place, and I did not know it'" (Gen. 28:12–16).

"But God had come to Laban the Syrian in a dream by night, and said to him, 'Be careful that you speak to Jacob neither good nor bad'" (Gen. 31:24).

"Now Joseph had a dream, and he told it to his brothers; and they hated him even more... Then he dreamed still another dream and told it to his brothers, and said, 'Look, I have dreamed another dream. And this time, the sun, the moon, and the eleven stars bowed down to me'" (Gen. 37:5, 9).

"In a dream, in a vision of the night, When deep sleep falls upon men, While slumbering on their beds, Then He opens the ears of men, And seals their instruction. In order to turn man from his deed, And conceal pride from man" (Job 33:15–17).

"But while he thought about these things, behold, an angel of the Lord appeared to him in a dream, saying, 'Joseph, son of David, do not be afraid to take to you Mary your wife, for that which is conceived in her is of the Holy Spirit'" (Matt. 1:20).

"Now when they had departed, behold, an angel of the Lord appeared to Joseph in a dream, saying, 'Arise, take the young Child and His mother, flee to Egypt, and stay there until I bring you word; for Herod will seek the young Child to destroy Him.'…Now when Herod was dead, behold, an angel of the Lord appeared in a dream to Joseph in Egypt, saying, 'Arise, take the young Child and His mother, and go to the land of Israel, for those who sought the young Child's life are dead'" (Matt. 2:13, 19–20).

Prophetic declaration

"When you lie down, you will not be afraid; Yes, you will lie down and your sleep will be sweet" (Prov. 3:24). So, I thank You, Almighty Father, because You give Your "beloved sleep" (Ps. 127:2).

Prayer points

I dedicate and covenant my sleep life unto the blood of Jesus, in Jesus' name.

Every dream covenant stirring up attacks on my life, be abolished by the blood of Jesus, in Jesus' name.

I overcome sleeplessness by the blood of Jesus, and I receive sound sleep to the glory of God, in Jesus' name.

It is written, "Consider and hear me, O LORD my God; Enlighten my eyes, Lest I sleep the sleep of death" (Ps. 13:3). Therefore, as the Lord God of Israel lives and His Spirit lives, I shall not sleep the sleep of the dead, in Jesus' name.

Whatever switches off my dreams preventing remembrance, the Lord God of Hosts rebuke you, hold your peace, and let go of me now, in Jesus' name.

Nightmares, come under divine arrest, and your effects be abolished by the blood of Jesus, in Jesus' name.

Every evil dream that I have ever had, let it be to them that hate me, and the interpretation thereof to my enemies (Dan. 4:19), in Jesus' name.

Any evil dream anyone has had about me, as it is written: "Thus says the Lord GOD: 'It shall not stand, Nor shall it come to pass'" (Isa. 7:7), in Jesus' name.

Regarding evil dreams and their interpretations in my life, I demand "an answer of peace" (Gen. 41:16), in Jesus' name.

It is written: "For He shall give His angels charge over you, To keep you in all your ways. In their hands they shall bear you up, Lest you dash your foot against a stone" (Ps. 91:11–12). So, Lord, I pray that You release Your angels to defend and protect me in my dreams, in Jesus' name.

Evil projected into my thoughts and imaginations, be flushed out by the Holy Spirit fire, in Jesus' name.

Human spirit trafficking and networking against me, come under divine arrest and be silenced, in Jesus' name.

Executors of evil dreams against my life, be bound and be rendered useless, in Jesus' name.

Creatures of the heavens, waters, air, earth, and beneath attacking my dream life, the Lord God of Hosts rebuke you, so I prevail over you, in Jesus' name.

Dream polluters, be terminated and let go of me now, in Jesus' name.

It is written: "And no wonder! For Satan himself transforms himself into an angel of light. Therefore it is no great thing if his ministers also transform themselves into ministers of righteousness, whose end will be according to their works" (2 Cor. 11:14–15). Therefore, powers, spirits, and personalities transforming themselves to attack my life, let God arise and shatter them to desolation, in Jesus' name.

Through the blood of Jesus, I forbid evil transformation in my dreams, in Jesus' name.

It is written: "I, Daniel, was grieved in my spirit within my body, and the visions of my head troubled me" (Dan. 7:15). Therefore, any dream that has troubled me until this day, I turn you over to the throne of grace, and I obtain mercy and deliverance, in Jesus' name.

It is written: "And there is no creature hidden from His sight, but all things are naked and open to the eyes of Him to whom we must give account" (Heb. 4:13). Therefore, deep dreams beyond clarifications and interpretations, I decree the veil be taken off now and be subdued in the blood of Jesus, in Jesus' name.

As the Lord God of Hosts lives and His Spirit lives, no evil dream shall be fulfilled in my life, in Jesus' name.

Hereditary and territorial dream attacks, destroy me not and prosper not, in Jesus' name.

I decree the roots of evil dreams in my life to wither and perish, in Jesus' name.

Altars of summoning set against me, Holy Spirit fire smite them asunder, in Jesus' name.

The strongman behind dream attacks in my life, perish with your strongholds, in Jesus' name.

Dream manipulators assigned against me, be terminated by the blood of Jesus, in Jesus' name.

Familiar spirits in my dream life, be rooted out and be consumed by the Holy Ghost fire, in Jesus' name.

Pursuers and invaders of my sleep, perish, in Jesus' name.

Dreams rooted in soul-tie covenants to afflict my life, the sword of the Lord cut them off and desolate them, in Jesus' name.

Spirit husbands and spirit wives invading my sleep, I break ties and covenant with you through the blood of Jesus, so let go of me and be shattered asunder, in Jesus' name.

Jesus, the Rock, strike down every sleep tormentor assigned against me, in Jesus' name.

Evil expectations in my sleep shall not come to pass, in Jesus' name.

It is written: "Then, behold, the veil of the temple was torn in two from top to bottom; and the earth quaked, and the rocks were split" (Matt. 27:51). Therefore, blockages to divine revelations in my life, shatter, in Jesus' name.

Henceforth, there shall be no more evil visitations in my dreams, in Jesus' name.

Henceforth, I receive divine encounters in my sleep, in Jesus' name.

Every good dream about my life, receive grace and strength to come to pass, in Jesus' name.

Henceforth, my sleep is connected to the throne of grace for unceasing flow of divine revelations, in Jesus' name.

Give thanks to God for answered prayers, in Jesus' name.

Chapter 32

THE DARKNESS IS PAST

IT IS WRITTEN: "He leads princes away plundered, And overthrows the mighty. He pours contempt on princes, And disarms the mighty" (Job 12:19, 21).

"He swallows down riches And vomits them up again; God casts them out of his belly" (Job 20:15).

"I broke the fangs of the wicked, And plucked the victim from his teeth" (Job 29:17).

"He brought them out of darkness and the shadow of death, And broke their chains in pieces" (Ps. 107:14).

"Who comforts us in all our tribulation, that we may be able to comfort those who are in any trouble, with the comfort with which we ourselves are comforted by God" (2 Cor. 1:4).

"That is, that God was in Christ reconciling the world to Himself, not imputing their trespasses to them, and has committed to us the word of reconciliation" (2 Cor. 5:19–20).

"You are of God, little children, and have overcome them, because He who is in you is greater than he who is in the world" (1 John 4:4).

Prophetic declaration

"For behold, the darkness shall cover the earth, And deep darkness the people; But the LORD will arise over you, And His glory will be seen upon you" (Isa. 60:2). "But you are a chosen generation, a royal priesthood, a holy nation, His own special people, that you may proclaim the praises of Him who called you out of darkness into His marvelous light; who once were not a people but are now the people of God, who had not obtained mercy but now have obtained mercy" (1 Pet. 2:9–10). I, therefore, rejoice exceedingly, "because the darkness is past, and the true light now shines" (1 John 2:8).

Prayer points

It is written: "God is light, and in Him is no darkness at all" (1 John 1:5). So, as there is no darkness in Him at all, and I am in Him, so I command darkness to depart from me, in Jesus' name.

Hidden things of darkness in me, vanish unto desolation, in Jesus' name.

It is written: "Then I saw that wisdom excels folly As light excels darkness" (Eccles. 2:13). Therefore, the light of God in me excels above darkness, in Jesus' name.

It is written: "He has delivered us from the power of darkness and conveyed us into the kingdom of the Son of His love" (Col. 1:13). Therefore, I proclaim that I am totally delivered from the power of darkness and established in the light of Jesus my Savior, in Jesus' name.

It is written: "And the light shines in the darkness, and the darkness did not comprehend it" (John 1:5). Therefore, no darkness shall overcome me, in Jesus' name.

It is written: "He will guard the feet of His saints, But the wicked shall be silent in darkness. For by strength no man shall prevail" (1 Sam. 2:9). Therefore, the wicked and their wickedness against me, be silenced in darkness, in Jesus' name.

You rulers of darkness of this world, my Lord Jesus who shed His precious blood has bruised your head; therefore, I triumph over you, in Jesus' name.

It is written: "You shall not be afraid of the terror by night, Nor of the arrow that flies by day, Nor of the pestilence that walks in darkness, Nor of the destruction that lays waste at noonday" (Ps. 91:56). Therefore, I overpower and overcome the pestilences that walk in darkness, in Jesus' name. All agents of darkness on assignment against me, let it be known that "the darkness is past, and the true light now shines" (1 John 2:8), in Jesus' name.

It is written: "'to open their eyes, in order to turn them from darkness to light, and from the power of Satan to God, that they may receive forgiveness of sins and an inheritance among those who are sanctified by faith in Me'" (Acts 26:18). Therefore, I decree to all the blessings due to me to turn from darkness into light, in Jesus' name.

Let it be known in the heavens, the earth, and beneath, that concerning my life, "the darkness is past, and the true light now shines" (1 John 2:8), in Jesus' name.

Give thanks to God for answered prayers, in Jesus' name.

Chapter 33

NO MORE CURSES

IT IS WRITTEN: "You have delivered me from the strivings of the people; You have made me the head of the nations; A people I have not known shall serve me. As soon as they hear of me they obey me; The foreigners submit to me. The foreigners fade away, And come frightened from their hideouts. The LORD lives! Blessed be my Rock! Let the God of my salvation be exalted" (Ps. 18:43–46).

"Thus says the Lord GOD: 'It shall not stand, Nor shall it come to pass'" (Isa. 7:7).

"Arise, shine; For your light has come! And the glory of the LORD is risen upon you. For behold, the darkness shall cover the earth, And deep darkness the people; But the LORD will arise over you, And His glory will be seen upon you. The Gentiles shall come to your light, And kings to the brightness of your rising" (Isa. 60:1–3).

"Let them be ashamed who persecute me, But do not let me be put to shame; Let them be dismayed, But do not let me be dismayed. Bring on them the day of doom, And destroy them with double destruction!" (Jer. 17:18).

"But the LORD is with me as a mighty, awesome One. Therefore my persecutors will stumble, and will not prevail. They will be greatly ashamed, for they will not prosper. Their everlasting confusion will never be forgotten" (Jer. 20:11).

"Who is he who speaks and it comes to pass, When the Lord has not commanded it?" (Lam. 3:37).

"Christ has redeemed us from the curse of the law, having become a curse for us (for it is written, "Cursed is everyone who hangs on a tree"), that the blessing of Abraham might come upon the Gentiles in Christ Jesus, that we might receive the promise of the Spirit through faith" (Gal. 3:13–14).

Prophetic declaration

"Nevertheless the LORD your God would not listen to Balaam, but the LORD your God turned the curse into a blessing for you, because the LORD your God loves you" (Deut. 23:5). Thank You, my eternal Father, because You love me so much as not to permit curses or any evil to reign in my life. Blessings shall, therefore, reign in my life, in Jesus' name.

Prayer points

Covenants and yokes of curses in my life, break asunder and your consequences be nullified, in Jesus' name.

Strongman behind curses in my life, let go of me and perish with your strongholds, in Jesus' name.

Altars and thrones behind curses set against my life, shatter asunder, in Jesus' name.

Curses activators and executors in my life, be wasted, in Jesus' name.

O blood of Jesus, terminate the reign of evil in my life, in Jesus' name.

Any part of my life manifesting curses, by the liberty of the Holy Spirit, be set free now, in Jesus' name.

My blessings delayed, transferred or stolen, by the resurrection power of my Lord Jesus, come forth unto me now, in Jesus' name.

Anointing of performance of blessings, rest upon me now, in Jesus' name.

Through the blood of Jesus, my life is covenanted to blessings and favor, sealed with the power of the Holy Spirit, in Jesus' name.

The blood of Jesus is upon me to repel curses and attract blessings, in Jesus' name.

Let it be known in heaven, on earth, and beneath that the power of curses and spells are broken asunder forever in my life by the power of the cross of Jesus, in Jesus' name.

Thank God for answered prayers.

Chapter 34

CURED WOUNDEDNESS

IT IS WRITTEN: "For there is hope for a tree, If it is cut down, that it will sprout again, And that its tender shoots will not cease" (Job 14:7).

"Why are you cast down, O my soul? And why are you disquieted within me? Hope in God, for I shall yet praise Him For the help of His countenance....Why are you cast down, O my soul? And why are you disquieted within me? Hope in God; For I shall yet praise Him, The help of my countenance and my God" (Ps. 42:5, 11).

"They reel to and fro, and stagger like a drunken man, And are at their wits' end. Then they cry out to the LORD in their trouble, And He brings them out of their distresses" (Ps. 107:27–28).

"'For I will restore health to you And heal you of your wounds,' says the LORD, 'Because they called you an outcast saying: "This is Zion; No one seeks her"'" (Jer. 30:17).

"Woe to the world because of offenses! For offenses must come, but woe to that man by whom the offense comes!" (Matt. 18:7).

"We are hard-pressed on every side, yet not crushed; we are perplexed, but not in despair; persecuted, but not forsaken; struck down, but not destroyed—always carrying about in the body the dying of the Lord Jesus, that the life of Jesus also may be manifested in our body" (2 Cor. 4:8–10).

Prophetic declaration

"The spirit of a man will sustain him in sickness, But who can bear a broken spirit?" (Prov. 18:14). Therefore, dear Lord God, I truly confess that I am wounded, overwhelmed, and vexed. Please help me. Jesus Christ, my burden bearer, You were wounded, bruised, and chastised for my sake, that I might be healed. Let Your healing power rest upon me now as you restore me to wholeness.

Prayer points

Dear Lord God, I present before You offenses that have vexed my spirit, and I request that You grant me grace to forgive and let go, in Jesus' name.

My emotional distortions are in Your hand, O God. I ask that You cure to the root, in Jesus' name.

Root of bitterness in me, be cured by the blood of Jesus.

Unforgiveness, anger, and rage in me, I surrender you at the foot of the cross to be crucified and control me no more, in Jesus' name.

My woundedness of heart, mind, and spirit, be cured by the blood of Jesus, in Jesus' name.

Holy Spirit fire, purge out the poisons in my wounds now, in Jesus' name.

It is written: "Cast your burden on the Lord, And He shall sustain you; He shall never permit the righteous to be moved" (Ps. 55:22). I cast all my burdens to You, O God, and I bear them no more. Therefore, I am free to declare God's glory, in Jesus' name.

It is written: "When they are diminished and brought low Through oppression, affliction, and sorrow" (Ps. 107:39). Therefore, cycle of oppression, affliction, and sorrow over my life, break asunder, in Jesus' name.

As the Lord God Israel lives and His Spirit lives, I shall not diminish in any good thing in life, in Jesus' name.

Mind blankness, mind dullness, and confusion of mind in me, be cured by the blood of Jesus, in Jesus' name.

Fear and torment in me, be rooted out now, in Jesus' name.

Henceforth, I possess power, love, and sound mind, in Jesus' name.

Holy Spirit fire, fortify me against offenses, in Jesus' name.

Thank God for answered prayers, in Jesus' name.

Chapter 35

FROM SCARS TO STARS

I T IS WRITTEN: "Joseph called the name of the firstborn Manasseh: 'For God has made me forget all my toil and all my father's house.' And the name of the second he called Ephraim: 'For God has caused me to be fruitful in the land of my affliction'" (Gen. 41:51–52).

"But as for you, you meant evil against me; but God meant it for good, in order to bring it about as it is this day, to save many people alive" (Gen. 50:20).

"You shall increase my greatness, And comfort me on every side" (Ps. 71:21).

"Then they cried out to the LORD in their trouble, And He delivered them out of their distresses. And He led them forth by the right way, That they might go to a city for a dwelling place" (Ps. 107:6–7).

"'Before she was in labor, she gave birth; Before her pain came, She delivered a male child. Who has heard such a thing? Who has seen such things? Shall the earth be made to give birth in one day? Or shall a nation be born at once? For as soon as Zion was in labor, She gave birth to her children. Shall I bring to the time of birth, and not cause delivery?' says the LORD. 'Shall I who cause delivery shut up the womb?' says your God" (Isa. 66:7–9).

"And I will restore to you the years that the locust hath eaten, the cankerworm, and the caterpillar, and the palmerworm, my great army which I sent among you. And ye shall eat in plenty, and be satisfied, and praise the name of the LORD your God, that hath dealt wondrously with you: and my people shall never be ashamed" (Joel 2:25–26, KJV).

"For our light affliction, which is but for a moment, is working for us a far more exceeding and eternal weight of glory" (2 Cor. 4:17).

Prophetic declaration

"Who has wounds without cause?" (Prov. 23:29). Dear Lord, I present the cause of my wounds; heal and make me whole, in Jesus' name. "He heals the brokenhearted And binds up their wounds" (Ps. 147:3).

Prayer points

It is written: "And I will restore to you the years that the locust hath eaten, the cankerworm, and the caterpillar, and the palmerworm, my great army which I sent among you. And ye shall eat in plenty, and be satisfied, and praise the name of the LORD your God, that hath dealt wondrously with you: and my people shall never be ashamed" (Joel 2:25–26, KJV). Therefore, thank You, my Lord Jesus, for restoring to me the years the locust, the cankerworm, the caterpillar, and the palmerworm have eaten, in Jesus' name.

My wilderness, thus says the Lord, becomes rivers of joy and blessings, in Jesus' name.

The dry ground of my life, henceforth, springs up blessing, in Jesus' name.

Barrenness in me, be gone and become fruitful, in Jesus' name.

After the order of apostle Paul, I declare: "From now on let no one trouble me, for I bear in my body the marks of the Lord Jesus" (Gal. 6:17), in Jesus' name.

Every scar on me attracting more wounds, be transformed by the Holy Spirit and become an emblem of peace, in Jesus' name.

Holy Spirit fire, walk back on my past and root out unforgiveness, in Jesus' name.

The blood of Jesus that speaks better things, call forth my glory to arise, shine, and prosper, in Jesus' name.

The Lord who promoted Joseph from the pit and prison to the throne of honor, for Your own name sake and for Your mercy sake, promote me to honor now, in Jesus' name.

The power that made Jesus rise from the dead, ascend into heaven, and be seated at the throne of power, quicken me now, in Jesus' name.

Every evil label and mark on my life, be taken away and be replaced by a godly label and the mark of victory, in Jesus' name.

Give thanks to God for answered prayers, in Jesus' name.

Chapter 36

BREAKING FREE FROM THE CURSE OF INFIRMITIES

I T IS WRITTEN: "For we do not have a High Priest who cannot sympa-thize with our weaknesses, but was in all points tempted as we are, yet without sin" (Heb. 4:15).

"However, the report went around concerning Him all the more; and great multitudes came together to hear, and to be healed by Him of their infirmities" (Luke 5:15).

"That it might be fulfilled which was spoken by Isaiah the prophet, saying: 'He Himself took our infirmities and bore our sicknesses'" (Matt. 8:17).

"But when Jesus saw her, He called her to Him and said to her, 'Woman, you are loosed from your infirmity'" (Luke 13:12).

"For He has delivered me out of all trouble; and my eye has seen its desire upon my enemies" (Ps. 54:7).

"Christ has redeemed us from the curse of the law, having become a curse for us for it is written, 'Cursed is everyone who hangs on a tree' that the blessing of Abraham might come upon the Gentiles in Christ Jesus, that we might receive the promise of the Spirit through faith" (Gal. 3:13–14).

"From now on let no one trouble me, for I bear in my body the marks of the Lord Jesus" (Gal. 6:17).

Prophetic declaration

By faith I declare that I have "come to Mount Zion and to the city of the living God, the heavenly Jerusalem, to an innumerable company of angels, to the general assembly and church of the firstborn who are reg-istered in heaven, to God the Judge of all, to the spirits of just men made perfect, to Jesus the Mediator of the new covenant, and to the blood of sprinkling that speaks better things than that of Abel" (Heb. 12:22–24). So, let there be divine transformation on my bodily structure for good health. "Do you not know that you are the temple of God and that the Spirit of God dwells in you?" (1 Cor. 3:16). My body is blessed, so also my soul and spirit. So, I decree the thriving of sickness and disease in my life, be rooted out now, in Jesus Christ's name. "And that very hour He cured many of infirmities, afflictions, and evil spirits; and to many blind He gave sight" (Luke 7:21). Therefore, let the lordship of my Lord and Savior Jesus Christ break me free and make me whole from plagues and infirmities, in Jesus Christ's name.

Prayer points

I thank God for the eternal sacrifice Jesus Christ made for my redemption, in Jesus Christ's name.

I am thankful to God for Jesus Christ bearing my sin and curses to set me free, in Jesus Christ's name.

I praise God because Jesus Christ annulled my curses that I may be a blessing, in Jesus Christ's name.

It is written: "The blessing of the LORD makes one rich, and He adds no sorrow with it" (Prov. 10:22). Therefore, no sorrow shall be added to my health, in Jesus Christ's name.

It is written: "The righteous is delivered from trouble, and it comes to the wicked instead" (Prov. 11:8). Therefore, let divine law of substitution turn to my favor, in Jesus Christ's name.

It is written: "How shall I curse whom God has not cursed? And how shall I denounce whom the LORD has not denounced?" (Num. 23:8). Therefore, I break loose and break free from curses and spells of infirmities, in Jesus Christ's name.

It is written: "God is not a man, that He should lie, nor a son of man, that He should repent. Has He said, and will He not do? Or has He spoken, and will He not make it good?" (Num. 23:19). Therefore, I possess the promise of healing now, in Jesus Christ's name.

It is written: "But as for you, you meant evil against me; but God meant it for good, in order to bring it about as it is this day, to save many people alive" (Gen. 50:20). Therefore, every evil targeted at me, become good now, in Jesus Christ's name.

In the name of Jesus Christ, I command healing strength to every cell of my body.

Let the healing blood of Jesus Christ flow from the crown of my head to the sole of my feet now, in Jesus Christ's name.

My body, soul, and spirit reject and repel curses, in Jesus Christ's name.

Henceforth, blessings and healing flow unhindered in my life, in Jesus Christ's name.

I have a godly and eternal inheritance which cannot be destroyed, in Jesus Christ's name.

Through the blood of Jesus, I rededicate my paternal and maternal family line to God Almighty, the Holy One of Israel, to Jesus Christ and the power of the Holy Spirit, in Jesus Christ's name.

It is written: "He who puts his trust in Me shall possess the land, and shall inherit My holy mountain" (Isa. 57:13). I put my trust in You, O God, therefore, I possess healing and deliverance, in Jesus Christ's name.

It is written: "Before I was afflicted I went astray, but now I keep Your word" (Ps. 119:67). Therefore, I pray that my past shall not afflict both my present and future, in Jesus Christ's name.

Through the blood of Jesus, I reject and renounce paternal and maternal infirmities, in Jesus Christ's name.

In the name of Jesus Christ, I am disconnected from generational infirmities.

Precious Holy Spirit, restructure my foundation to enjoy good health, in Jesus Christ's name.

My life is connected to the throne of grace for healing flow, in Jesus Christ's name.

Jehovah, the Ancient of Days, deliver me now from the bondages of my past, in Jesus Christ name.

Blood of Jesus, flush generational sickness and diseases out of my life, in Jesus Christ's name.

No longer shall I bear generational reproach of infirmities, in Jesus Christ's name.

I thank God for setting me free from generational infirmities, in Jesus Christ's name.

Chapter 37

DECREE AGAINST EVIL
MEDICAL PROPHECIES

IT IS WRITTEN: "Do not deliver me to the will of my adversaries; for false witnesses have risen against me, and such as breathe out violence" (Ps. 27:12).

"Deliver my soul, O LORD, from lying lips and from a deceitful tongue" (Ps. 120:2).

"Now a woman, having a flow of blood for twelve years, who had spent all her livelihood on physicians and could not be healed by any, came from behind and touched the border of His garment. And immediately her flow of blood stopped" (Luke 8:43–44).

"When the Lord saw her, He had compassion on her and said to her, "Do not weep" (Luke 7:13).

"You have also delivered me from the strivings of my people; You have kept me as the head of the nations. A people I have not known shall serve me. The foreigners submit to me; as soon as they hear, they obey me. The foreigners fade away, and come frightened from their hideouts" (2 Sam. 22:44–46).

"'And I will make you to this people a fortified bronze wall; and they will fight against you, but they shall not prevail against you; for I am with you to save you and deliver you,' says the LORD" (Jer. 15:20).

"Because with lies you have made the heart of the righteous sad, whom I have not made sad; and you have strengthened the hands of the wicked, so that he does not turn from his wicked way to save his life. Therefore you shall no longer envision futility nor practice divination; for I will deliver My people out of your hand, and you shall know that I am the LORD" (Ezek. 13:22–23).

Prophetic declaration

"Give no opportunity to the adversary to speak reproachfully" (1 Tim. 5:14). So, I refuse to be bound by any evil word, thought, or imagination, in Jesus Christ's name. "But the mouth of the upright shall deliver them" (Prov. 12:6). I, therefore, decree a healing word to rescue me from all medical threats, in Jesus Christ's name.

Prayer points

Jehovah Most High is above all, watching over my life, in Jesus Christ's name.

I hold on to the unfailing power of the Almighty God to rescue me from health hazards, in Jesus Christ's name.

O Lord God, great and mighty is Your power to heal and make me whole, in Jesus Christ's name.

God's power to heal me is divine, eternal, and excellent; therefore, I am healed, in Jesus Christ's name.

It is written: "But whether there are prophecies, they shall fail" (1 Cor. 13:8); so, let evil prophecy on my life fail, in Jesus Christ's name.

It is written: "Who is he who speaks and it comes to pass, when the Lord has not commanded it?" (Lam. 3:37). Therefore, no evil medical prophecy shall come to pass in my life, in Jesus Christ's name.

It is written: "Thus says the Lord GOD: 'It shall not stand, nor shall it come to pass'" (Isa. 7:7); so, no evil medical prophecy shall come to pass in my life, in Jesus Christ's name.

O Lord God, divinely correct any diagnosis and treatment contradicting my health, in Jesus Christ's name.

It is written: "He reveals deep and secret things; He knows what is in the darkness, and light dwells with Him" (Dan. 2:22); so, let there be divine revelation to instruct, direct, and guide me to good health, in Jesus Christ's name.

I receive mercies of God Almighty concerning my health that I shall not perish with any medical prophecy, in Jesus Christ's name.

As "mercy triumphs over judgment" (James 2:13), so I triumph over evil medial prophecies, in Jesus Christ's name.

It is written: "'No weapon formed against you shall prosper, and every tongue which raises against you in judgment You shall condemn. This is the heritage of the servants of the LORD, and their righteousness is from Me,' Says the LORD" (Isa. 54:17); so, I command evil medical prophecies against my life, be condemned now, in Jesus Christ's name.

Chapter 38

FLUSHING OUT THE POISONS

IT IS WRITTEN: "Scarcely shall they be planted, scarcely shall they be sown, scarcely shall their stock take root in the earth, when He will also blow on them, and they will wither, and the whirlwind will take them away like stubble" (Isa. 40:24).

"Shall the prey be taken from the mighty, or the captives of the righteous be delivered? But thus says the LORD: 'Even the captives of the mighty shall be taken away, and the prey of the terrible be delivered; for I will contend with him who contends with you, and I will save your children'" (Isa. 49:24–25).

"'They will fight against you, but they shall not prevail against you. For I am with you,' says the LORD, 'to deliver you'" (Jer. 1:19).

"My times are in Your hand; deliver me from the hand of my enemies, and from those who persecute me" (Ps. 31:15).

"Deliver me from my enemies, O my God; defend me from those who rise up against me" (Ps. 59:1).

"And the Lord will deliver me from every evil work and preserve me for His heavenly kingdom. To Him be glory forever and ever" (2 Tim. 4:18).

"And it happened that the father of Publius lay sick of a fever and dysentery. Paul went in to him and prayed, and he laid his hands on him and healed him" (Acts 28:8).

Prophetic declaration

"And these signs will follow those who believe: In My name they will cast out demons; they will speak with new tongues; they will take up serpents; and if they drink anything deadly, it will by no means hurt them; they will lay hands on the sick, and they will recover" (Mark 16:17–18). Therefore, I decree to my body, soul, and spirit, reject and eject evil deposits and plantations. Therefore, no poison shall be retained in my system, but flushed out by the fire of the Holy Spirit, in Jesus Christ's name.

Prayer points

I am grateful to God for proper functioning of my body, soul, and spirit, in Jesus Christ's name.

I am grateful to God because my body is created to sustain my health, in Jesus Christ's name.

Life and life in abundance, I receive, in Jesus Christ's name.

My body, soul, and spirit retain no more poisons, but flush them out, in Jesus Christ's name.

Anointing of the Holy Spirit, destroy the yoke of poisons in my life now, in Jesus Christ's name.

Hidden venom in my system, be flushed out now, in Jesus Christ's name.

I speak against every inflicting poison to let go of me now, in Jesus Christ's name.

Holy Spirit fire, purge every organ of my body from sickness and disease, in Jesus Christ's name.

It is written: "Strengthen the weak hands, and make firm the feeble knees" (Isa. 35:3). Therefore, I receive strength from God Almighty for good health, in Jesus Christ's name.

Any part of my body afflicted by poisons, be healed now, in Jesus Christ's name.

Healing power of God, flow through my life now, in Jesus Christ's name.

I praise God for making me whole, in Jesus Christ's name.

Chapter 39

DECREE WHOLENESS

I T IS WRITTEN: "And He said to her, 'Daughter, be of good cheer; your faith has made you well. Go in peace'" (Luke 8:48).

"Jesus said to him, 'If you can believe, all things are possible to him who believes'" (Mark 9:23).

"Wherever He entered, into villages, cities, or the country, they laid the sick in the marketplaces, and begged Him that they might just touch the hem of His garment. And as many as touched Him were made well" (Mark 6:56).

"And He said to her, 'Daughter, your faith has made you well. Go in peace, and be healed of your affliction'" (Mark 5:34).

"Many are the afflictions of the righteous, but the LORD delivers him out of them all. He guards all his bones; not one of them is broken" (Ps. 34:19–20).

"All my bones shall say, 'LORD, who is like You, delivering the poor from him who is too strong for him, yes, the poor and the needy from him who plunders him?'" (Ps. 35:10).

"That Your beloved may be delivered, save with Your right hand, and hear me" (Ps. 60:5).

Prophetic declaration

Now may the God of peace Himself sanctify you completely; and may your whole spirit, soul, and body be preserved blameless at the coming of our Lord Jesus Christ" (1 Thess. 5:23). Therefore, I claim wholeness and wellness of health, in Jesus Christ's name. My health shall not fail me. I shall flourish in good health, in Jesus Christ's name.

Prayer points

I praise God Almighty, because it is His will to make me whole, so I will be whole, in Jesus Christ's name.

Jehovah my Lord is excellent and perfect, so I possess wholeness of health now, in Jesus Christ's name.

It is written: "This is my comfort in my affliction, for Your word has given me life" (Ps. 119:50); so comfort me Lord with Your healing power, in Jesus Christ's name.

Anti-wholeness forces shall not prosper in my life, in Jesus Christ's name.

In the name of Jesus Christ, I receive soundness of health and wellness of Spirit.

Whatever God has conquered in my life shall not rise up again, in Jesus Christ's name.

Unfailing health is my portion in the land of the living, in Jesus Christ's name.

I decree to everything God has made in my life to work favorably to my good health, in Jesus Christ's name.

I shall no more relapse to ill health, in Jesus Christ's name.

I thank You, my Heavenly Father, for favoring me with good health, in Jesus Christ's name.

I decree to every cell of my body to triumph in good health, in Jesus Christ's name.

Anointing of wholeness, rest upon me now, in Jesus Christ's name.

Jesus, my Healer, thank You for paying the price for my healing and deliverance, in Jesus' name.

I dedicate my health to the blood of Jesus and to the power of the Holy Spirit, in Jesus' name.

Any claim of sickness, disease, and death to my body, soul, and spirit, the blood of Jesus rebukes you; hold your peace and let go of me now, in Jesus' name.

Demon-infested diseases and sickness, the blood of Jesus condemns you; hold your peace and let go of me now, in Jesus' name.

Territorial and generational sicknesses, hear ye the Word of the Lord: "Wherefore God also hath highly exalted him, and given him a name which is above every name: that at the name of Jesus every knee should bow, of things in heaven, and things in earth, and things under the earth" (Phil. 2:9–10, KJV). Therefore, be subdued before me and become desolate now, in Jesus' name.

Any part of my life resisting divine healing, Holy Spirit fire, break forth the resistance and establish healing there, in Jesus' name.

Hidden sicknesses and diseases in my life awaiting manifestation, dry up now, in Jesus' name.

Jesus, my Great Physician, work deep into every area of my life; heal and make me whole now, in Jesus' name.

Anointing of the Holy Spirit, destroy the yoke of sickness, disease, and death in my life, in Jesus' name.

Holy Spirit, the power of the Highest, work deep into my life to heal and to make me whole, in Jesus' name.

I sincerely agree with God Almighty, Jesus my Redeemer, and the Holy Spirit, my Comforter, that I am delivered, healed, and made whole now, in Jesus' name.

Give thanks to God for answered prayers, in Jesus' name.

Chapter 40

THE HOLY SPIRIT AND MY HEALING

I T IS WRITTEN: "The Spirit of God has made me, and the breath of the Almighty gives me life" (Job 33:4).

"But if the Spirit of Him who raised Jesus from the dead dwells in you, He who raised Christ from the dead will also give life to your mortal bodies through His Spirit who dwells in you" (Rom. 8:11).

"So he answered and said to me: 'This is the word of the LORD to Zerubbabel: "Not by might nor by power, but by My Spirit," says the LORD of hosts'" (Zech. 4:6).

"Now the Lord is the Spirit; and where the Spirit of the Lord is, there is liberty" (2 Cor. 3:17).

"So shall they fear the name of the LORD from the west, and His glory from the rising of the sun; when the enemy comes in like a flood, the Spirit of the LORD will lift up a standard against him" (Isa. 59:19).

"But if I cast out demons by the Spirit of God, surely the kingdom of God has come upon you" (Matt. 12:28).

"On the last day, that great day of the feast, Jesus stood and cried out, saying, 'If anyone thirsts, let him come to Me and drink. He who believes in Me, as the Scripture has said, out of his heart will flow rivers of living water'" (John 7:37–38).

Prophetic declaration

"It is the Spirit Who gives life [He is the Life-giver]; the flesh conveys no benefit whatever [there is no profit in it]. The words (truths) that I have been speaking to you are spirit and life" (John 6:63, AMP). Therefore, my life is opened to the life-quickening power of the Holy Spirit as seal on my healing and deliverance, in Jesus Christ's name.

Prayer points

Thank You, my dear heavenly Father, for the gift of the Holy Spirit to perfect my health, in Jesus Christ's name.

O Lord God, let Your living water cleanse, wash, and refresh me, in Jesus Christ's name.

I receive the comforting power of the Holy Spirit to perfect my health, in Jesus Christ's name.

Precious Holy Spirit, I give you absolute permission to work freely on my health for healing and wholeness, in Jesus Christ's name.

Holy Spirit, reveal Jesus Christ to me that I may be healed, in Jesus Christ's name.

Holy Spirit, lift up the standard against sicknesses, diseases, and death in my life, in Jesus Christ's name.

Anointing of the Holy Spirit, destroy the yoke of infirmities in me, in Jesus Christ's name.

Holy Spirit, flow into my innermost being with your healing virtue, in Jesus Christ's name.

Holy Spirit, strengthen my inner man to enjoy good health, in Jesus Christ's name.

Oh, my body, soul, and spirit, quench not the operation of the Holy Spirit, in Jesus Christ's name.

Holy Spirit, prevail over contrary spirits affecting my health, in Jesus Christ's name.

I receive the seal of the Holy Spirit on my health, in Jesus Christ's name.

Chapter 41

GRACE TO BEAR CHILDREN

Prayers for the Fruit of the Womb

I T IS WRITTEN: "Then God blessed them, and God said to them, 'Be fruitful and multiply; fill the earth and subdue it; have dominion over the fish of the sea, over the birds of the air, and over every living thing that moves on the earth'" (Gen. 1:28).

"Is anything too hard for the LORD? At the appointed time I will return to you, according to the time of life, and Sarah shall have a son" (Gen. 18:14).

"And the LORD visited Sarah as He had said, and the LORD did for Sarah as He had spoken. For Sarah conceived and bore Abraham a son in his old age, at the set time of which God had spoken to him" (Gen. 21:1–2).

"May God Almighty bless you, And make you fruitful and multiply you, That you may be an assembly of peoples" (Gen. 28:3).

"Then God remembered Rachel, and God listened to her and opened her womb. And she conceived and bore a son, and said, 'God has taken away my reproach'" (Gen. 30:22–23).

"So you shall serve the LORD your God, and He will bless your bread and your water. And I will take sickness away from the midst of you. No one shall suffer miscarriage or be barren in your land; I will fulfill the number of your days" (Exod. 23:25–26).

"You shall be blessed above all peoples; there shall not be a male or female barren among you or among your livestock. And the LORD will take away from you all sickness, and will afflict you with none of the terrible diseases of Egypt which you have known, but will lay them on all those who hate you" (Deut. 7:14–15).

"And the Angel of the LORD appeared to the woman and said to her, 'Indeed now, you are barren and have borne no children, but you shall conceive and bear a son'" (Judg. 13:3).

"Then she made a vow and said, 'O LORD of hosts, if You will indeed look on the affliction of Your maidservant and remember me, and not forget Your maidservant, but will give Your maidservant a male child, then I will give him to the LORD all the days of his life, and no razor shall come upon his head'" (1 Sam. 1:11).

"And Hannah prayed and said: 'My heart rejoices in the LORD; My horn is exalted in the LORD. I smile at my enemies, Because I rejoice in Your salvation. No one is holy like the LORD, For there is none besides You, Nor is there any rock like our God. Talk no more so very proudly; Let no arrogance come from your mouth, For the LORD is the God of knowledge; And by Him actions are weighed. The bows of the mighty men are broken, And those who stumbled are girded with strength. Those who were full have hired themselves out for bread, And the hungry have ceased to hunger. Even the barren has borne seven, And she who has many children has become feeble. The LORD kills and makes alive; He brings down to the grave and brings up. The LORD makes poor and makes rich; He brings low and lifts up. He raises the poor from the dust And lifts the beggar from the ash heap, To set them among princes And make them inherit the throne of glory. For the pillars of the earth are the LORD's, And He has set the world upon them. He will guard the feet of His saints, But the wicked shall be silent in darkness. For by strength no man shall prevail. The adversaries of the LORD shall be broken in pieces; From heaven He will thunder against them. The LORD will judge the ends of the earth. He will give strength to His king, And exalt the horn of His anointed" (1 Sam. 2:1–10).

"He grants the barren woman a home, Like a joyful mother of children. Praise the LORD!" (Ps. 113:9).

"Great is the LORD, and greatly to be praised; And His greatness is unsearchable" (Ps. 127:3).

"As you do not know what is the way of the wind, Or how the bones grow in the womb of her who is with child, So you do not know the works of God who makes everything" (Eccles. 11:5).

"Thus says the LORD who made you And formed you from the womb, who will help you: 'Fear not, O Jacob My servant; And you, Jeshurun, whom I have chosen. For I will pour water on him who is thirsty, And floods on the dry ground; I will pour My Spirit on your descendants, And My blessing on your offspring'" (Isa. 44:2–3).

"But Zion said, 'The LORD has forsaken me, And my Lord has forgotten me.' 'Can a woman forget her nursing child, And not have compassion on the son of her womb? Surely they may forget, Yet I will not forget you. See, I have inscribed you on the palms of My hands; Your walls are continually before Me'" (Isa. 49:14–16).

"'Who has heard such a thing? Who has seen such things? Shall the earth be made to give birth in one day? Or shall a nation be born at once? For as soon as Zion was in labor, She gave birth to her children. Shall I bring to the time of birth, and not cause delivery?' says the LORD. 'Shall I who cause delivery shut up the womb?' says your God" (Isa. 66:8–9).

"And the angel answered and said to her, 'The Holy Spirit will come upon you, and the power of the Highest will overshadow you; therefore, also, that Holy One who is to be born will be called the Son of God'" (Luke 1:35).

"Then she spoke out with a loud voice and said, 'Blessed are you among women, and blessed is the fruit of your womb!'" (Luke 1:42).

Prophetic declaration

Thank You, my heavenly Father, for renewing my youth so that I can bear children and nurse them. As I was formed in my mother's womb, so also shall babies be formed in my womb, in Jesus' name. The blood of Jesus shall thoroughly plead my case and grant me grace to conceive and bear children, in Jesus' name. Therefore, by the ordinances that made the heaven and the earth, I decree by the unction of the Holy Spirit, my womb open now and bring forth children, in Jesus' name.

Prayer points

Thanks be to God Almighty, who has remembered me for good to bear children, in Jesus' name.

It is written: "And I will make you exceedingly fruitful" (Gen. 17:6); so shall this Abrahamic covenant be fulfilled in me, in Jesus' name.

I dedicate my body, soul, and spirit unto the blood of Jesus for childbearing, in Jesus' name.

Through the blood of Jesus, I reject and renounce any covenants with spirit husband and spirit wife, in Jesus' name.

I command fire of separation between me and spirit husband and spirit wife, in Jesus' name.

Through the blood of Jesus, I renounce any claim to my life forbidding childbearing, in Jesus' name.

Through the blood of Jesus, I renounce any consent given to any power, spirit, and personality to afflict me with barrenness and childlessness, in Jesus' name.

Any covenant, rituals, and dedication resisting childbearing in my life, the Lord God of Hosts rebukes you; hold your peace and let go of me now, in Jesus' name.

Witnesses of covenants and vows at war with childbearing, let it be known that the Holy Spirit is my true witness, so I prevail over you, in Jesus' name.

Principalities over my family line, paternal and maternal, assigned against my fruitful childbearing, be subdued by the blood of Jesus and let go of me now, in Jesus' name.

The strongmen and strongwomen of childlessness, barrenness, miscarriage, and fruitlessness, the blood of Jesus rebukes you; be disconnected from me and perish with your strongholds, in Jesus' name.

Altars, shrines, groves, high, and low places withholding my joy of childbearing, the blood of Jesus rebukes you; let go of me and my children, in Jesus' name.

Priests and priestesses mandated to attack my childbearing, by the high priesthood of my Lord and Savior Jesus Christ, I subdue, overpower, and overcome you, in Jesus' name.

Any part of my body, soul, and spirit summoned and afflicted, in the name of Jesus, be set free now to enjoy the peace and miracles of God, in Jesus' name.

Thus says the Lord to the principalities enthroned against my childbearing: "Come down and sit in the dust, O virgin daughter of Babylon; Sit on the ground without a throne, O daughter of the Chaldeans! For you shall no more be called Tender and delicate" (Isa. 47:1). Therefore, be cast down unto desolations now, in Jesus' name.

Infertility and malfunctioning of my bodily system, be cured now by the blood of Jesus, in Jesus' name.

The spirit behind miscarriage and abortion, the Lord God of Hosts rebuke you; be disconnected and let go of me now, in Jesus' name.

The vows of the wasters and those who empty against my childbearing, be silenced and be dismissed, in Jesus' name.

Soul tie covenants resisting my childbearing, the blood of Jesus rebuke you; break asunder, and perish, in Jesus' name.

Let God arise and desolate leviathan pursuit over my life and children, in Jesus' name.

Serpentine grip on my life, be disconnected and flee, in Jesus' name.

Serpentine attacks on my children, be consumed by the Holy Spirit fire, in Jesus' name.

Holy Ghost fire, flush serpentine poisons out of my life now, in Jesus' name.

Blood of Jesus, repair damages done to my life now, in Jesus' name.

The guilt of my past, the condemnation of the present, and the fear of the future, afflict me no more; be repaired by the blood of Jesus, in Jesus' name.

"And when the LORD saw that Leah was hated, he opened her womb" (Gen. 29:31). Therefore, O Lord God of Israel, I pray Thee, open now my womb to conceive and bring forth children, in Jesus' name.

It is written, "Behold, children are a heritage from the LORD, The fruit of the womb is a reward" (Ps. 127:3). Therefore, O Lord God Almighty, in Your mercies, commit Your heritage (children) unto me now, in Jesus' name.

It is written: "Then God blessed them, and God said to them, 'Be fruitful and multiply; fill the earth and subdue it; have dominion over the fish of the sea, over the birds of the air, and over every living thing that moves on the earth'" (Gen. 1:28). Therefore, I thank You, O Lord my God, for fulfilling these promises in me now, in Jesus' name.

The Lord who commanded light to shine out of darkness has commanded my children to come forth unto me now, in Jesus' name.

Childlessness, barrenness, and fruitlessness, let it be known that "the darkness is past, and the true light now shines" (1 John 2:8) in me, in Jesus' name.

Miscarriage and abortion, let it be known that "the darkness is past, and the true light now shines" in me, in Jesus' name.

It is written, "And the light shines in the darkness, and the darkness did not comprehend it" (John 1:5). Therefore, no darkness can overcome my childbearing, in Jesus' name.

The resurrection power of my Lord and Savior Jesus Christ, bring alive every part of my body, soul, and spirit to bring forth children, in Jesus' name.

Thank You, redemptive blood of Jesus, for restoring my children unto me now, in Jesus' name.

Angels of the Living God, bring forth my children unto me now, in Jesus' name.

Everything that God has created, work to my favor now, in Jesus' name.

Through the blood of Jesus, I petition the throne of grace to stir up my miracle children to manifest in me, in Jesus' name.

I covenant my God-given children into the blood of Jesus and the power of the Holy Spirit, in Jesus' name.

I have this day obtained mercies and favor from God to conceive and bring forth children, in Jesus' name.

Thank You, my eternal Father, for releasing the anointing of child-bearing upon me, in Jesus' name.

Through the blood of Jesus, I defy prophesies, dreams, visions, curses, spells, incantations, bewitchments, and medical diagnoses that are contrary to my childbearing and prevail over them, in Jesus' name.

Give thanks to God for answered prayers, in Jesus' name.

Chapter 42

BREAKTHROUGH PRAYERS FOR PREGNANT WOMEN

I T IS WRITTEN: "No one shall suffer miscarriage or be barren in your land; I will fulfill the number of your days" (Exod. 23:26).

"For You formed my inward parts; You covered me in my mother's womb. I will praise You, for I am fearfully and wonderfully made; marvelous are Your works, and that my soul knows very well" (Ps. 139:13–14).

"So you shall serve the LORD your God, and He will bless your bread and your water. And I will take sickness away from the midst of you. No one shall suffer miscarriage or be barren in your land; I will fulfill the number of your days" (Exod. 23:25–26).

"You shall not be afraid of the terror by night, Nor of the arrow that flies by day, Nor of the pestilence that walks in darkness, Nor of the destruction that lays waste at noonday. A thousand may fall at your side And ten thousand at your right hand; But it shall not come near you. Only with your eyes shall you look, And see the reward of the wicked. Because you have made the LORD, who is my refuge, Even the Most High, your dwelling place, No evil shall befall you, Nor shall any plague come near your dwelling; For He shall give His angels charge over you, To keep you in all your ways. In their hands they shall bear you up, Lest you dash your foot against a stone" (Ps. 91:5–12).

"In righteousness you shall be established; you shall be far from oppression, for you shall not fear; and from terror, for it shall not come near you. Indeed they shall surely assemble, but not because of Me. Whoever assembles against you shall fall for your sake. 'Behold, I have created the blacksmith who blows the coals in the fire, who brings forth an instrument for his work; and I have created the spoiler to destroy. No weapon formed against you shall prosper, and every tongue which rises against you in judgment you shall condemn. This is the heritage of the servants of the LORD, and their righteousness is from Me,' says the LORD" (Isa. 54:14–17).

"You shall not be afraid of the terror by night, nor of the arrow that flies by day" (Ps. 91:5).

"The floods have lifted up, O LORD, the floods have lifted up their voice; the floods lift up their waves. The LORD on high is mightier than the noise of many waters, than the mighty waves of the sea. Your testimonies are very sure; Holiness adorns Your house, O LORD, forever" (Ps. 93:3–5).

"And the angel answered and said to her, 'The Holy Spirit will come upon you, and the power of the Highest will overshadow you; therefore, also, that Holy One who is to be born will be called the Son of God'" (Luke 1:35).

"Nevertheless she will be saved in childbearing if they continue in faith, love, and holiness, with self-control" (1 Tim. 2:15).

"And the Lord will deliver me from every evil work and preserve me for His heavenly kingdom. To Him be glory forever and ever. Amen!" (2 Tim. 4:18).

Prophetic declaration

I am grateful to God for "an inheritance incorruptible and undefiled, and that does not fade away, reserved" (1 Pet. 1:4) for me through my Lord Jesus Christ. Therefore, I am "kept by the power of God through faith" (1 Pet. 1:5). I am persuaded that I shall joyfully and gracefully carry this pregnancy through to maturity and safe delivery, in Jesus Christ's name.

Prayer points

I thank God for entrusting this precious seed unto me to bring forth my children, in Jesus Christ's name.

O Lord God, watch over this precious baby in my womb, in Jesus Christ's name.

Any hidden vow or covenant that may affect this baby, be cancelled now by the blood of Jesus, in Jesus Christ's name.

I dedicate this precious baby to my Lord Jesus Christ and the power of His blood, in Jesus Christ's name.

Precious Holy Spirit, fill this baby in my womb with life, joy, and peace, in Jesus Christ's name.

O Lord God, assign Your holy angels to protect this baby in my womb, in Jesus Christ's name.

I decree strength by the Holy Spirit into my bodily system to receive grace to carry this pregnancy through, in Jesus Christ's name.

I decree that no evil shall befall me and this pregnancy, in Jesus Christ's name.

It is written: "Woe to those who decree unrighteous decrees, Who write misfortune, Which they have prescribed" (Isa. 10:1). No decree shall afflict me and my baby, in Jesus' name.

Blessed shall be the delivery of my baby, in Jesus Christ' name.

I decree this child to develop without deformity unto safety in delivery, in Jesus Christ's name.

Anointing to carry this pregnancy through unto safe delivery is upon me, in Jesus' name.

The bringing forth of this child shall bring honor to God Almighty, in Jesus Christ's name.

I thank God for blessing me with this child, in Jesus Christ's name.

Chapter 43

BREAKTHROUGH PRAYERS FOR JOB SEEKERS AND BUSINESS PROFESSIONALS

IT IS WRITTEN: "And Abraham said, 'My son, God will provide for Himself the lamb for a burnt offering.' So the two of them went together" (Gen. 22:8).

"And he said to them, 'Do not hinder me, since the LORD has prospered my way; send me away so that I may go to my master'" (Gen. 24:56).

"The LORD was with Joseph, and he was a successful man; and he was in the house of his master the Egyptian. And his master saw that the LORD was with him and that the LORD made all he did to prosper in his hand" (Gen. 39:2–3).

"The LORD will cause your enemies who rise against you to be defeated before your face; they shall come out against you one way and flee before you seven ways" (Deut. 28:7).

"So I answered them, and said to them, 'The God of heaven Himself will prosper us; therefore we His servants will arise and build, but you have no heritage or right or memorial in Jerusalem'" (Neh. 2:20).

"For His anger is but for a moment, His favor is for life; Weeping may endure for a night, But joy comes in the morning. Now in my prosperity I said, 'I shall never be moved.' LORD, by Your favor You have made my mountain stand strong; You hid Your face, and I was troubled" (Ps. 30:5–7).

"Let them shout for joy and be glad, Who favor my righteous cause; And let them say continually, 'Let the LORD be magnified, Who has pleasure in the prosperity of His servant'" (Ps. 35:27).

"Save now, I pray, O LORD; O LORD, I pray, send now prosperity" (Ps. 118:25).

"Beloved, I pray that you may prosper in all things and be in health, just as your soul prospers" (3 John 2).

Prophetic declaration

My eternal Father, the Holy One of Israel is the "possessor of heaven and earth" (Gen. 14:19), who owns "the cattle upon a thousand hills" (Ps. 50:10). As Your covenant child, I am confident that "my God shall supply all my need according to His riches, in glory by Christ Jesus" (Phil. 4:19).

Prayer points

It written: "Pray for the peace of Jerusalem: 'May they prosper who love you. Peace be within your walls, Prosperity within your palaces'" (Ps. 122:6–7). Therefore, I proclaim my love for Jerusalem and decree peace upon her and the inhabitants thereof, in Jesus' name.

I decree that my staff of bread shall not be broken nor destroyed, in Jesus' name.

O Lord God, restore unto me my staff of bread, in Jesus' name.

Blood of Jesus, take away the curses of drought and famine from my life, in Jesus' name.

By the anointing of the Holy Spirit, I command the yoke of generational poverty upon my life be shattered asunder, in Jesus' name.

In the name of Jesus, I break loose and break free from territorial poverty.

In the name of Jesus, I break loose and break free from the cycle of lack, failure, and defeat.

Principalities in the marketplace, I subdue and overcome you by the blood of Jesus, in Jesus' name.

Angels of the Living God, bring forth my blessings in desolate places unto me now, in Jesus' name.

In the name of Jesus, I command the twin demons of loser and misfit, to let go of me and become desolate.

It is written: "Slay us not: for we have treasures in the field" (Jer. 41:8, KJV). Therefore, nothing shall slay me nor destroy my glorious inheritance, in Jesus' name.

As the Lord God of Israel lives and His Spirit lives, my harvest ground shall not become a battleground, in Jesus' name.

It is written: "Do not lay up for yourselves treasures on earth, where moth and rust destroy and where thieves break in and steal; but lay up for yourselves treasures in heaven, where neither moth nor rust destroys and where thieves do not break in and steal" (Matt. 6:19–20). Therefore, neither moth nor rust shall corrupt my glorious inheritance, in Jesus' name.

Robbers and thieves shall not prosper in my life, in Jesus' name.

Angelic harvesters, be strengthened by the Holy Spirit to bring forth blessings due to me, in Jesus' name.

In the name of Jesus, I receive strength to possess gates and heavens of nations and prosper therein.

In the name of Jesus, I dedicate and covenant my career (please mention your career) unto God Almighty and unto the blood of Jesus.

It is written: "Wisdom is the principal thing; Therefore get wisdom. And in all your getting, get understanding" (Prov. 4:7). Therefore, O Lord God, endue me with wisdom, knowledge, and understanding to prosper my life, in Jesus' name.

It is written: "The steps of a good man are ordered by the LORD, And He delights in his way" (Ps. 37:23). Therefore, O Lord God Almighty, order my steps unto miraculous prosperity in my career, in Jesus' name.

It is written: "The king's heart is in the hand of the LORD, Like the rivers of water; He turns it wherever He wishes" (Prov. 21:1). Therefore, O Lord God, touch the hearts of people to bless and profit my career, in Jesus' name.

It is written: "And you shall remember the LORD your God, for it is He who gives you power to get wealth, that He may establish His covenant which He swore to your fathers, as it is this day" (Deut. 8:18). Therefore, I establish a covenant of wealth with the Almighty God by the blood of Jesus, sealed with the Holy Spirit, in Jesus' name.

It is written: "For exaltation comes neither from the east Nor from the west nor from the south. But God is the Judge: He puts down one, And exalts another" (Ps. 75:6–7). Therefore, O Lord God, promote me now to greatness, in Jesus' name.

It is written: "He raises the poor out of the dust, And lifts the needy out of the ash heap, That He may seat him with princes—With the princes of His people" (Ps. 113:7–8). Therefore, O Lord God, raise me up and lift me up to reign among the princes of my career, in Jesus' name.

It is written: "For You are the glory of their strength, And in Your favor our horn is exalted" (Ps. 89:17). Therefore, O Lord God Almighty, exalt me in my career by your favor, in Jesus' name.

It is written: "You will arise and have mercy on Zion; For the time to favor her, Yes, the set time, has come" (Ps. 102:13). Therefore, I affirm this eternal Word of God in my life, that my "set time" to be blessed has come, in Jesus' name.

It is written: "I entreated Your favor with my whole heart; Be merciful to me according to Your word" (Ps. 119:58). Therefore, I pray mercy and favor to overwhelm every area of my life, in Jesus' name.

Holy Spirit of God, empower me to prevail over competition in my career, in Jesus' name.

Through the blood of Jesus, I possess the throne of my career and reign gloriously, in Jesus' name.

In the name of Jesus, I am connected to the throne of grace and mercy for unceasing flow of blessings into my life.

I receive grace to always remember God in my prosperity, in Jesus' name.

In the name of Jesus, I receive help indeed that will prosper my career.

I pray the seal of the Holy Spirit upon these declarations, in Jesus' name.

Give thanks to God for answered prayers, in Jesus' name.

Chapter 44

EGYPT AGAINST EGYPT

I T IS WRITTEN: "'Come, let Us go down and there confuse their language, that they may not understand one another's speech.' So the
LORD scattered them abroad from there over the face of all the earth,
and they ceased building the city" (Gen. 11:7–8).

"When the three hundred blew the trumpets, the LORD set every
man's sword against his companion throughout the whole camp; and the
army fled to Beth Acacia, toward Zererah, as far as the border of Abel
Meholah, by Tabbath" (Judg. 7:22).

"So they hanged Haman on the gallows that he had prepared for
Mordecai. Then the king's wrath subsided" (Esther 7:10).

"The heavens will reveal his iniquity, And the earth will rise up against
him" (Job 20:27).

"He breaks in pieces mighty men without inquiry, And sets others in
their place" (Job 34:24).

"And the king gave the command, and they brought those men who
had accused Daniel, and they cast them into the den of lions—them,
their children, and their wives; and the lions overpowered them, and
broke all their bones in pieces before they ever came to the bottom of
the den" (Dan. 6:24).

"For many bore false witness against Him, but their testimonies did
not agree" (Mark 14:56).

Prophetic declaration

Thank You, my Jehovah, the "Man of War," for riding upon a swift
cloud to my rescue. Thank You also for causing thrones that have risen
against me to turn against one another. "I will set Egyptians against
Egyptians; Everyone will fight against his brother, And everyone against
his neighbor, City against city, kingdom against kingdom" (Isa. 19:2).

Prayer points

Those who have turned to idols and charmers to fight against me, be stricken by confusion and perish, in Jesus' name.

It is written: "The rivers will turn foul; The brooks of defense will be emptied and dried up; The reeds and rushes will wither" (Isa. 19:6). Therefore, I command the defenses of my adversaries to collapse to their own ruin, in Jesus' name.

It is written: "The horse and its rider He has thrown into the sea!" (Exod. 15:1). Therefore, I command the adversities targeted at me to turn back to my adversaries, in Jesus' name.

All my oppressors, I refuse your oppression; take back your oppression, in Jesus' name.

Oh ye my afflicters, I reject your afflictions; take back your afflictions, in Jesus' name.

Oh ye my tormentors, I reject your torments; take back your torments, in Jesus' name.

Destroyer of souls, my life is not your landing place, therefore, destroy me not, in Jesus' name.

Angelic invaders, strike down the hiding places of the wicked on assignment against me, in Jesus' name.

It is written: "It is in my power to do you harm, but the God of your father spoke to me last night, saying, 'Be careful that you speak to Jacob neither good nor bad'" (Gen. 31:29). Therefore, O God of Jacob, refrain and restrain my adversaries from harming me, in Jesus' name.

Executors of evil on assignment against me, turn back against your senders, in Jesus' name.

My uncelebrated victories spring for joy now, in Jesus' name.

Give thanks to God for answered prayers.

Chapter 45

THY KINGDOM COME

I T IS WRITTEN: "For the kingdom is the LORD's, And He rules over the nations" (Ps. 22:28).

"The LORD has established His throne in heaven, And His kingdom rules over all" (Ps. 103:19). "To make known to the sons of men His mighty acts, And the glorious majesty of His kingdom. Your kingdom is an everlasting kingdom, And Your dominion endures throughout all generations" (Ps. 145:12–13).

"How great are His signs, And how mighty His wonders! His kingdom is an everlasting kingdom, And His dominion is from generation to generation" (Dan. 4:3).

"He has delivered us from the power of darkness and conveyed us into the kingdom of the Son of His love" (Col. 4:13).

"And the Lord will deliver me from every evil work and preserve me for His heavenly kingdom. To Him be glory forever and ever" (2 Tim. 4:18).

"Then the seventh angel sounded: And there were loud voices in heaven, saying, 'The kingdom of this world have become the kingdoms of our Lord and of His Christ, and He shall reign forever and ever!'" (Rev. 11:15).

Prophetic declaration

"Then comes the end, when He delivers the kingdom to God the Father, when He puts an end to all rule and all authority and power. For He must reign till He has put all enemies under His feet" (1 Cor. 15:24–25). So, Lord Jesus, reign supreme in my life; and I pray, "Your kingdom come. Your will be done On earth as it is in heaven" (Matt. 6:10).

Prayer points

I sincerely proclaim that the rule of the sovereign God over all His creatures is established in my life, in Jesus' name.

I pledge absolute allegiance to Jehovah, the holy one of Israel through the lordship of Jesus, my Savior, in Jesus' name.

Jehovah God is higher than the highest, so let all that is within me worship and exalt Him, in Jesus' name.

I pledge total allegiance to Jesus and His kingdom, who rules over all, in Jesus' name.

It is written: "Your kingdom come. Your will be done On earth as it is in heaven" (Matt. 12:28). Therefore, O Most High God, let Your kingdom be established in my life, in Jesus' name.

I proclaim, "Blessed is he that comes in the name of the Lord"; so Lord Jesus let your kingdom come into my life, in Jesus' name.

It is written: "He answered and said to them, 'Because it has been given to you to know the mysteries of the kingdom of heaven, but to them it has not been given'" (Matt. 13:11). O Lord God, reveal the glorious majesty of Your kingdom to me, in Jesus' name.

It is written: "And without controversy great is the mystery of godliness: God was manifested in the flesh, Justified in the Spirit, Seen by angels, Preached among the Gentiles, Believed on in the world, Received up in glory" (1 Tim. 3:16). So, I pray that the mysteries of godliness be fulfilled in me, in Jesus' name.

Dear Lord Jesus, let the effectual working of Your power establish Your kingdom in me, in Jesus' name.

I am endued with the power from on high to do glorious exploits for God and His kingdom, in Jesus' name.

It is written: "He gives power to the weak, And to those who have no might He increases strength. Even the youths shall faint and be weary" (Isa. 40:29). Therefore, empower me, O God, to advance Your kingdom here on earth, in Jesus' name.

Give thanks to God for answered prayers, in Jesus' name.

Chapter 46

FULFILLING MY TIME DIVINE

I T IS WRITTEN: "Now these are the judgments which you shall set before them" (Gen. 21:1).

"Then the LORD appointed a set time, saying, 'Tomorrow the LORD will do this thing in the land'" (Exod. 9:5).

"Though your beginning was small, Yet your latter end would increase abundantly" (Job 8:7).

"Thus says the LORD: 'In an acceptable time I have heard You, And in the day of salvation I have helped You; I will preserve You and give You As a covenant to the people, To restore the earth, To cause them to inherit the desolate heritages'" (Isa. 49:8).

"Then the LORD said to me, 'You have seen well, for I am ready to perform My word'" (Jer. 1:12).

"And He changes the times and the seasons; He removes kings and raises up kings; He gives wisdom to the wise And knowledge to those who have understanding. He reveals deep and secret things; He knows what is in the darkness, And light dwells with Him" (Dan. 2:21–22).

"Redeeming the time, because the days are evil. Therefore do not be unwise, but understand what the will of the Lord is" (Eph. 5:16–17).

Prophetic declaration

The Spirit of God speaks expressly to evil moments in my life: "time up" and to glorious seasons, "time in," in Jesus' name. "He has made everything beautiful in its time. Also He has put eternity in their hearts, except that no one can find out the work that God does from beginning to end" (Eccles. 3:11). Therefore, the God who "changes the times and the seasons" (Dan. 2:21) has changed my times and seasons for good, in Jesus' name.

Prayer points

I dedicate my time unto God Almighty and consecrate my life to Him forever, in Jesus' name.

I repent of the time of my life that does not honor God, and I receive forgiveness through the blood of Jesus.

It is written: "There is an evil which I have seen under the sun, and it is common among men" (Eccles. 6:1). So, I pray that the evil under the sun, common among men, shall not be my portion, in Jesus' name.

Familiar spirit interwoven with my time, the Lord God of Hosts rebukes you; be disconnected and let go of me now, in Jesus' name.

The time of my life tied down to ancestral altars, through the redemptive blood of Jesus, let loose unto glory now, in Jesus' name.

The time of my life under the control of wicked forces, be divinely rescued to enjoy the peace of God, in Jesus' name.

Time wasters shall not ruin my life; I prevail over you through the blood of Jesus, in Jesus' name.

Redemptive blood of Jesus, restore my wasted years with blessings, in Jesus' name.

The time of my life, be invested in eternal peace and blessings, in Jesus' name.

My past, be redeemed by the blood of Jesus; my present, be sanctified with the blood of Jesus; and my future, be anointed with the Holy Spirit power, in Jesus' name.

Jesus Christ is enthroned as Lord and Savior over the time of my life.

Give thanks to God for answered prayers, in Jesus' name.

Chapter 47

REMEMBER ME, O LORD!

IT IS WRITTEN: "Then God remembered Noah, and every living thing, and all the animals that were with him in the ark. And God made a wind to pass over the earth, and the waters subsided" (Gen. 8:1).

"Remember me, O my God, concerning this, and do not wipe out my good deeds that I have done for the house of my God, and for its services" (Neh. 13:14).

"He remembers His covenant forever, The word which He commanded, for a thousand generations" (Ps. 105:8).

"Who remembered us in our lowly state, For His mercy endures forever" (Ps. 136:23).

"You who have escaped the sword, Get away! Do not stand still! Remember the LORD afar off, And let Jerusalem come to your mind" (Jer. 51:50).

"O LORD, I have heard Your speech and was afraid; O LORD, revive Your work in the midst of the years! In the midst of the years make it known; In wrath remember mercy" (Hab. 3:2).

Prophetic declaration
"Then those who feared the LORD spoke to one another, And the LORD listened and heard them; So a book of remembrance was written before Him For those who fear the LORD And who meditate on His name" (Mal. 3:16). So, Lord I pray that You open Your "book of remembrance" and have mercy upon me, in Jesus' name.

Prayer points
The Lord God who remembered Noah and his household that they escaped the flood, rescue me and my household from destruction, in Jesus' name.

The Most High who remembered Abraham and Sarah, for Your own name sake, remember me for good, in Jesus' name.

The Lord who remembered Isaac and Rebekah to fulfill His covenant promise, fulfill Your promises also in my life, in Jesus' name.

The God who delivered Jacob from Esau, deliver me from every deadly vow, in Jesus' name.

The Lord God of Hosts who rescued Joseph from the pit and prison, do the same for me and promote me to honor, in Jesus' name.

The God of Israel who restored Caleb to his inheritance after a long wait, empower me now to possess my due blessings, in Jesus' name.

Jehovah God who remembered Israel when under the oppression of Egypt, for Your mercy sake, deliver me from the hands of my oppressors, in Jesus' name.

The Mighty God who remembered Hannah from relentless provocations, I entreat You by Your throne of grace, have mercy upon me, in Jesus' name.

The Lord who remembered David, the shepherd boy, and gave him everlasting inheritance, lift me up and raise me out of waste places, in Jesus' name.

The Lord God that reversed the death prophecy over Hezekiah to satisfy him with long life, do same for me now, in Jesus' name.

The Almighty God who rescued Daniel from the lions' den and replaced him with his enemies, arise and deliver me out of the lions' den and put my enemies in their den of destruction, in Jesus' name.

Give thanks to God for answered prayers, in Jesus' name.

Chapter 48

POWER MANTLE

I T IS WRITTEN: "God is my strength and power, And He makes my way perfect" (2 Sam. 22:33).

"God has spoken once, Twice I have heard this: That power belongs to God" (Ps. 62:11).

"They shall speak of the glory of Your kingdom, And talk of Your power, To make known to the sons of men His mighty acts, And the glorious majesty of His kingdom. Your kingdom is an everlasting kingdom, And Your dominion endures throughout all generations" (Ps. 145:11–13).

"Where the word of a king is, there is power; And who may say to him, "What are you doing?"" (Eccles. 8:4).

"He gives power to the weak, And to those who have no might He increases strength" (Isa. 40:29).

"But if the Spirit of Him who raised Jesus from the dead dwells in you, He who raised Christ from the dead will also give life to your mortal bodies through His Spirit who dwells in you" (Rom. 8:11).

Prophetic declaration

My heart is fixed on the Lord God, and my spirit is prepared. So Lord, fulfill Your promise in me. Empower me for glorious exploits. "But you shall receive power when the Holy Spirit has come upon you; and you shall be witnesses to Me in Jerusalem, and in all Judea and Samaria, and to the end of the earth" (Acts 1:8).

Prayer points

It is written: "Who has come, not according to the law of a fleshly commandment, but according to the power of an endless life" (Heb. 7:16). Therefore, thank You, Lord Jesus, because only You possess the power of an endless life, in Jesus' name.

Thank You, my Lord Jesus, for laying down Your life to save me and restore me to power, in Jesus' name.

Holy Spirit, thank You for bringing Jesus alive in Him, in Jesus' name.

It is written: "That at the name of Jesus every knee should bow, of those in heaven, and of those on earth, and of those under the earth, and that every tongue should confess that Jesus Christ is Lord, to the glory of God the Father" (Phil. 2:10–11). Therefore, powers in the heavens, earth, and beneath, bow before the lordship of Jesus in me, in Jesus' name.

It is written: "And the angel answered and said to her, 'The Holy Spirit will come upon you, and the power of the Highest will overshadow you; therefore, also, that Holy One who is to be born will be called the Son of God'" (Luke 1:35). Therefore, Holy Spirit, fill me now unto overflowing, in Jesus' name.

Thou power of the Highest, overwhelm my life now, in Jesus' name.

I pray that the effectual working of God's power will bring alive every good thing that concerns me, in Jesus' name.

O Lord God, let the exceeding greatness of Your power manifest in my life now, in Jesus' name.

It is written: "For the kingdom of God is not in word but in power" (1 Cor. 4:20). Therefore, I break forth in the power of the Holy Spirit to enjoy the peace of God, in Jesus' name.

Mantle from the throne of grace, rest upon me now, in Jesus' name.

Resurrection power of my Lord and Savior, Jesus Christ, restore me to honor and favor, in Jesus' name.

I am connected to the unceasing flow of God's miraculous power even now and forever more, in Jesus' name.

Give thanks to God for answered prayers, in Jesus' name.

Chapter 49

POWER PRAISE

IT IS WRITTEN: "He does great things past finding out, Yes, wonders without number" (Job 9:10).

"And in that day you will say: 'O LORD, I will praise You; Though You were angry with me, Your anger is turned away, and You comfort me. Behold, God is my salvation, I will trust and not be afraid; "For YAH, the LORD, is my strength and song; He also has become my salvation."' Therefore with joy you will draw water From the wells of salvation. And in that day you will say: 'Praise the LORD, call upon His name; Declare His deeds among the peoples, Make mention that His name is exalted. Sing to the LORD, For He has done excellent things; This is known in all the earth. Cry out and shout, O inhabitant of Zion, For great is the Holy One of Israel in your midst!'" (Isa. 12:1–6).

"Violence shall no longer be heard in your land, Neither wasting nor destruction within your borders; But you shall call your walls Salvation, And your gates Praise" (Isa. 60:18).

"Then I said, 'I will not make mention of Him, Nor speak anymore in His name.' But His word was in my heart like a burning fire Shut up in my bones; I was weary of holding it back, And I could not" (Jer. 20:9).

"Though the fig tree may not blossom, Nor fruit be on the vines; Though the labor of the olive may fail, And the fields yield no food; Though the flock may be cut off from the fold, And there be no herd in the stalls—Yet I will rejoice in the LORD, I will joy in the God of my salvation. The LORD God is my strength; He will make my feet like deer's feet, And He will make me walk on my high hills" (Hab. 3:17–19),

"Blessed be the God and Father of our Lord Jesus Christ, the Father of mercies and God of all comfort" (2 Cor. 1:3).

"Blessed be the God and Father of our Lord Jesus Christ, who according to His abundant mercy has begotten us again to a living hope through the resurrection of Jesus Christ from the dead, to an inheritance incorruptible and undefiled and that does not fade away, reserved in heaven for you" (1 Pet. 1:3–4).

"Now to Him who is able to keep you from stumbling, And to present you faultless Before the presence of His glory with exceeding joy, To God our Savior, Who alone is wise, Be glory and majesty, Dominion and power, Both now and forever. Amen" (Jude 24–25).

Prophetic declaration

"Who is like You, O LORD, among the gods? Who is like You, glorious in holiness, Fearful in praises, doing wonders?" (Exod. 15:11). "No one is holy like the LORD, For there is none besides You, Nor is there any rock like our God" (1 Sam. 2:2). So, everything within me declares the greatness of the Holy One of Israel.

Prayer points

It is written: "You have turned for me my mourning into dancing; You have put off my sackcloth and clothed me with gladness" (Ps. 30:11). Therefore, I put off sackcloth and put on the mantle of praise to exalt the Living God, in Jesus' name.

Thank You, my Lord and my God, for making me a praise in the earth, in Jesus' name.

It is written: "God has spoken once, Twice I have heard this: That power belongs to God" (Ps. 62:11). Therefore, let the power of the Most High God amplify His greatness in my life, in Jesus' name.

It is written: "Let them praise the name of the LORD, For He commanded and they were created" (Ps. 148:5). So, Lord, command Your creative blessings in my life, in Jesus' name.

I exalt the throne of the Holy One of Israel with praise and gratitude of heart and spirit, in Jesus' name.

With the fruit of my lips, I declare that only You are worthy of my praise, O Lord, God Almighty, in Jesus' name.

I dedicate all that I have to Your praise and glory, O God Almighty, in Jesus' name.

I triumph in the praise of Him who loves me and gave Himself to redeem my soul, in Jesus' name.

I dedicate my praises, thanksgiving, worship, and adoration unto Him whose name alone is holy, the everlasting eternal Father, in Jesus' name.

I am connected with the heavenly praise for unceasing flow of power and glory, in Jesus' name.

O blood of Jesus that speaks better things, speak the praise of the Almighty God into my life that I may manifest His greatness, in Jesus' name.

Give thanks to God for answered prayers, in Jesus' name.

NOTES

Chapter 1
The Foundation

1. *Hitchcock's Bible Names Dictionary*, s.v. "Ephraim," www.biblegateway.com/resources/dictionaries/ (accessed September 4, 2011).

Chapter 2
Freedom from Curses

1. For further information, see www.answers.com/topic/sparrow (accessed September 5, 2011).

2. For further information, see www.answers.com/topic/swallow (accessed September 5, 2011).

Chapter 3
Knowing Your Enemies

1. Christian Nevell Bovee quote found at http://quotationsbook.com/quote/32657/ (accessed August 24, 2011).

2. David Komolafe, *Unquestionably Free: Empowering Prayers for Champions* (Lake Mary, FL: Creation House, 2009), 1.

3. Christian Nevell Bovee quote found at http://quotationsbook.com/quote/1370/ (accessed August 24, 2011).

4. Winston Churchill quote found at http://www.brainyquote.com/quotes/quotes/w/winstonchu138231.html (accessed August 24, 2011).

5. Sam Snead quote found at http://quotationsbook.com/quote/10399/ (accessed August 24, 2011).

Chapter 4
Cutting Off Witchcraft

1. Benjamin Franklin quote found at http://www.quotationspage.com/quote/36318.html (accessed August 24, 2011).

Chapter 6
Self-Deliverance

1. Peter the Great quote found at http://quotationsbook.com/quote/6029/ (accessed August 24, 2011).

2. Stephen R. Covey quote found at http://thinkexist.com/quotation/private_victories_precede_public_victories-you/298370.html (accessed August 24, 2011).

3. Plato quote found at http://quotationsbook.com/quote/40570/ (accessed August 24, 2011).

4. For further information, see www.answers.com/topic/self-pity (accessed September 4, 2011).

Chapter 7
Territorial Spiritual Warfare

1. For further information, see www.answers.com/topic/cauldron (accessed September 4, 2011).

2. For further information, see http://en.wikipedia.org/wiki/National emblem (accessed September 5, 2011).

3. Audre Lorde quote found at http://thinkexist.com/quotation/even_the_smallest_victory_is_never_to_be_taken/297050.html (accessed August 24, 2011).

4. Wayne Mack and Joshua Mack, *Fear Factor: What Satan Doesn't Want You to Know* (Tulsa, OK: Hensley, 2002), 15.

5. Charles H. Spurgeon quote found at http://www.christianity.com/devotionals/faiths-checkbook-ch-spurgeon/11540017/ (accessed August 24, 2011).

6. David Komolafe, *365 Days of Fear Not* (Enumclair, WA: Pleasant Word, 2008), xv.

7. Georgia O'Keeffe quote found at http://www.brainyquote.com/quotes/quotes/g/georgiaok389819.html (accessed August 24, 2011).

Chapter 8
Marketplace Warfare

1. For further information, see www.answers.com/market (accessed September 5, 2011).

2. Quote found at http://quotationsbook.com/quote/25294/ (accessed August 24, 2011).

3. For further information, see www.http://en.wikipedia.org/wiki/capitol_Hill_Washington_D.C. (accessed September 5, 2011).

4. Kenneth Boa and Gail Burnett, *Wisdom at Work: A Biblical Approach to the Workplace* (Colorado Springs, CO: Navpress, 2000), 83.

5. Ibid., 53.

6. Dorothea Brande quote found at http://quotationsbook.com/quote/40758/ (accessed August 24, 2011).

7. Frank Gaines quote found at http://quotationsbook.com/quote/40782/ (accessed August 24, 2011).

8. Les Brown quote found at http://www.brainyquote.com/quotes/quotes/l/lesbrown393631.html (accessed August 24, 2011).

<h2 style="text-align:center">Chapter 9
Not Worthy to Die</h2>

1. For further information, see www.answers.com/topic/health (accessed September 5, 2011).

2. Peace Pilgrim quote found at http://www.quotesl.com/Peace_Pilgrim (accessed August 24, 2011).

3. For further information, see www.answers.com/topic/vulture (accessed September 5, 2011).

<h2 style="text-align:center">Chapter 10
Strategies for the Overcomers</h2>

1. Napoleon quote found at http://www.quotationspage.com/quote/2191.html (accessed August 24, 2011).

2. Henry Ward Beecher quote found at http://quotationsbook.com/quote/40529/ (accessed August 24, 2011).

3. Winston Churchill quote found at http://www.brainyquote.com/quotes/quotes/w/winstonchu138231.html (accessed August 24, 2011).

4. For further information, see www.answers.com/topic.palace (accessed September 5, 2011).

5. For further information, see www.answers.com/topic/throne (accessed September 5, 2011).

6. For further information, see answers.com/topic/Egypt (accessed September 5, 2011).

7. For further information, see www.answers.com/topic/raze (accessed September 6, 2011).

Chapter 11
Who Is on the Lord's Side?

1. George Whitefield quote found at http://www.sfpulpit.com/2008/05/26/praying-for-the-lost/ (accessed August 24, 2011).

2. Frances J. Crosby, "Rescue the Perishing," 1869, public domain.

3. Charles C. Luther, "Must I Go, and Empty-Handed?" 1877, public domain.

ABOUT THE AUTHOR

PASTOR DAVID KOMOLAFE learned kingdom-strategic warfare through his daily and habitual walk with Christ Jesus, his Lord and Savior. He has been laboring in God's kingdom for more than three decades. He and his wife, Mercy, are founding pastors of a full gospel ministry, Above All Christian Gathering, headquartered in Toronto, Canada. He is a biochemist and holds a master's degree in practical ministry from Wagner Leadership Institute in Colorado Springs, Colorado. He is the author of *40 Days of Prophetic Miracles, 365 Days of Fear Not, Unquestionably Free, and Repair the Ruins: Arise and Build.* He has also released a gospel album titled *Let the Fire Fall.* Pastors David and Mercy are blessed with three children, Esther, Grace, and Shalom.

CONTACT THE AUTHOR

www.davidkomolafe.com